BENSON and HEDGES ®

RACING YEAR

SECOND EDITION

EDITOR HOWARD WRIGHT
ASSOCIATE EDITOR JOHN OAKSEY

● **MORNING GLORY:** Going out for exercise as the sun rises over The Curragh. Picture: GERRY CRANHAM

RACING YEAR

SECOND EDITION

EDITOR HOWARD WRIGHT
ASSOCIATE EDITOR JOHN OAKSEY

PELHAM BOOKS

PELHAM BOOKS
Published by the Penguin Group
27 Wrights Lane, London W8 5TZ, England
Viking Penguin Inc., 40 West 23rd Street, New York, New York 10010, USA
Penguin Books Australia Ltd, Ringwood, Victoria, Australia
Penguin Books Canada Ltd, 2801 John Street, Markham, Ontario, Canada L3R 1B4
Penguin Books (NZ) Ltd, 182–190 Wairau Road, Auckland 10, New Zealand

Penguin Books Ltd, Registered Offices: Harmondsworth, Middlesex, England

First published 1988

British Library Cataloguing in Publication Data
Benson & Hedges racing year.—2nd ed.
1. Great Britain. Racehorses. Racing. Serials
798.4′00941

ISBN 0-7207-1817-1

The following contributors write for the *Racing Post:*
Adrian Cook, Ron Cox, Simon Crisford, Melvyn Day,
Graham Dench, Jeremy Early, George Ennor, Dan Farley,
Ray Gilpin, Paul Hayward, Paul Johnson, Colin Mackenzie,
J A McGrath, Neil Morrice, Tony Morris, Will O'Hanlon,
Tony O'Hehir, Tim Richards, Colin Russell, Desmond
Stoneham, Lawrence Wadey, Emily Weber, Howard Wright.

John Oaksey is racing correspondent for the *Daily* and *Sunday
Telegraph,* and a member of the Channel 4 racing team.

Richard Pitman is racing correspondent of the *Sunday
Express* and a member of the BBC TV racing team.

The maps of British racecourses are
reproduced by permission of *Racing Post.*

Photoset in Times, Rockwell and Helvetica by Cambridge Photosetting Services, Cambridge
Printed and bound in Great Britain by Hazell, Watson & Viney Limited,
member of BPCC plc, Aylesbury Bucks.

Sponsor's Message

1987 was a surprising and eventful year for the world of racing. It will be remembered as a great year for British owner breeders when Jim Joel, now in his nineties, won the Grand National with Maori Venture and Louis Freedman completed the Derby – St Leger double with Reference Point.

It was also memorable for the globetrotting success of the French trained fillies Miesque and Triptych, the remarkable transformation of Ajdal from Classic failure to sprint champion and the enthralling jockeys' championship battle between Steve Cauthen and Pat Eddery.

The second edition of the *Racing Year* continues to offer an unequalled standard of racing photography and an extensive review of Flat racing, both at home and abroad. It also offers an increased level of National Hunt racing coverage.

We hope you will enjoy it.

JOHN SLADE
Benson and Hedges

Racing Year Champions

HORSE OF THE YEAR
Reference Point, owned Louis Freedman, trained Henry Cecil
  Nominated by Howard Wright

SPRINTER
Ajdal, owned Sheikh Mohammed, trained Michael Stoute
  Nominated by Emily Weber

MILER
Miesque, owned Stavros Niarchos, trained Francois Boutin
  Nominated by Graham Dench

MIDDLE-DISTANCE
Reference Point
  Nominated by Paul Johnson

STAYER
Paean, owned Lord Howard de Walden, trained Henry Cecil
  Nominated by Ron Cox

TWO-YEAR-OLD
Warning, owned Khalid Abdullah, trained Guy Harwood
  Nominated by Melvyn Day

HANDICAPPER
Waajib, owned Hamdan Al-Maktoum, trained Alec Stewart
  Nominated by Will O'Hanlon

IRELAND
Barrow Line, owned Michael Foley, trained Pat Hughes
  Nominated by Tony O'Hehir

FRANCE
Miesque
  Nominated by Desmond Stoneham

UNITED STATES
Manila, owned Bradley M Shannon, trained LeRoy Jolley
  Nominated by Dan Farley

HURDLER
See You Then, owned Stype Wood Stud, trained Nick Henderson
  Nominated by Colin Russell

STEEPLECHASER
Desert Orchid, owned Richard Burridge, trained David Elsworth
  Nominated by Colin Russell

Horse of the Year

● **THE CHAMPION: Reference Point, winner of the Derby, St Leger and King George VI and Queen Elizabeth Diamond Stakes.**
Picture: DAVID HASTINGS

Turfcall gives you the winners instantly over the phone.

(Unfortunately, you still have to pick them first.)

Turfcall brings you the action as it happens, all the way from the starting gate to the finishing post.

Just pick up the phone for live commentary from meetings across the country with previews, interviews and results from daytime and evening races.

Our team of professionals also give the latest form on the runners and riders, the going at each meeting plus likely favourites and Turfcall's nap of the day.

After the racing, you can catch up on the day's events with Turfcall's classified results service.

Take your card and phone today.

TURFCALL
0898 121 121

Contents

Picture: DAVID HASTINGS

Picture: A. JOHNSON

Picture: MARTIN LYNCH

●HIGH POINT: Reference Point in his finest hour as he beats Celestial Storm (noseband), Triptych and Moon Madness (quartered cap) in the King George VI and Queen Elizabeth Diamond Stakes.
Picture: JOHN CROFTS

Horse of the Year

by JEREMY EARLY

Reference Point

by JEREMY EARLY

THE 1987 Flat season had its share of pretenders but above them soared Reference Point, a monarch among thoroughbreds who laid down the law with the vigour of an absolute ruler.

He overcame illness; he showed exceptional merit in winning five of his seven starts; he earned more in a season in England than any horse before, £726,608; he dominated the news pages from May to October.

Reference Point was by any standard Horse of the Year, yet ironically he did not gain the universal admiration which had overflowed for Dancing Brave in 1986. And that, ultimately, was because of his racing style.

No-one could complain about the style the Mill Reef colt showed in coming through the early part of the year. Courage and resilience were the be-all and end-all as he faced up to the affliction of significant breathing difficulties.

The solution was drastic – an operation in March, in which a hole was drilled in the horse's head and tubes inserted to drain the sinuses, and a course of antobiotics lasting five weeks.

To compound the problem, after the operation, mucus kept coming down Reference Point's nose, resulting in a cyst which was still requiring treatment at the end of May.

It is not easy to ascertain how much pain or discomfort horses are suffering – lack of speech is a fundamental disadvantage in this respect – but most humans who endured what Reference Point endured would believe they had reason to feel sorry for themselves.

The illness could have ruined him as a racehorse, and he was a long way from being any old horse. He had topped the International Classification for two-year-olds after storming home in the William Hill Futurity; he had been spoken of as a Triple Crown candidate.

The Guineas swiftly went by the board and reportedly in the spring there were times when his connections came close to despair.

History relates, though, that Reference Point, the perfect patient, gamely won this particular battle outright, thanks in no small part to the devotion of trainer Henry Cecil and stable lass Alison Dean. They, along with rider Steve Cauthen, owner

Louis Freedman and the colt himself, made up the team of the season.

If this unpleasant experience established Reference Point's character, subsequent proof came on the racecourse again and again as he more than made up for lost time.

Proof came in the Mecca-Dante Stakes, won in the pillar-to-post fashion that was his hallmark. It came in the Ever Ready Derby, where he was always in command in defeating Most Welcome and Bellotto. It came in the Coral-Eclipse Stakes, in which he failed to beat Mtoto but ran a magnificent race over a trip short of his best.

It came in the Great Voltigeur Stakes and Holsten Pils St Leger, which resulted in predictable victories over Dry Dock and Mountain Kingdom respectively.

Above all it came in the King George VI and Queen Elizabeth Diamond Stakes at Ascot, the high point of the season for the colt and for middle-distance racing in Britain.

Races restricted to one age-group, including the Classic par excellence, are a valid and vital test. But they alone do not identify an overall champion. That is why the Ascot showpiece in July stands head and shoulders above all other British middle-distance events.

The 1987 edition lacked Mtoto but the nine runners included winners of 20 Group One races.

Besides Reference Point they were the best middle-distance horses in France, Triptych, successful in the Prix Ganay and Coronation Cup in the current season; the best in Italy, Tony Bin; the best in Germany, Acatenango; St Leger and Grand Prix de Saint-Cloud winner Moon Madness; Irish Derby winner Sir Harry Lewis; and Oaks and Irish Oaks winner Unite.

The field was completed by St Leger and Champion Stakes runner-up Celestial Storm, fresh from a record-breaking success in the Princess of Wales's Stakes, and Oaks and Irish Oaks second Bourbon Girl.

Reference Point's victory was crushing.

Driven straight into the lead by Cauthen, he set a tremendous pace from Acatenango which had Sir Harry Lewis, Tony Bin and Bourbon Girl flat to the boards by halfway.

Rounding the home turn, Reference Point led by a couple of lengths from Acatenango, Sir Harry Lewis and Unite, with Celestial Storm and Triptych poised to make runs on the rails.

Kicked on, Reference Point extended his lead to three lengths at the quarter-mile pole, where most of his rivals had cried enough, finding nothing under the whip.

Two who still had something in reserve were Celestial Storm and Triptych, both of whom were switched outside and began to make headway. One hundred and fifty yards out they were within two lengths of the leader, but that was as close as they got.

Galloping on relentlessly, Reference Point began to go away again, and at the line he was three lengths clear of Celestial Storm, who snatched second from Triptych by a neck. Moon Madness was five lengths further back in fourth, followed by Tony Bin and Acatenango.

Apart from Tony Bin, who had a nasty journey across to Ascot, and

Unite, who was found to be wrong, the beaten runners had no semblance of an excuse. It was, quite simply, a brilliant performance, the best by any horse in Europe all season.

The form looked cast-iron at the time and seems just as good in retrospect. The winner gave Celestial Storm a 7lb beating, Triptych a 10lb beating, Moon Madness a 15lb beating, Tony Bin a 15lb beating and Acatenango a 17lb beating.

Triptych subsequently won three Group One races; Tony Bin won one and ran second in the Prix de l'Arc de Triomphe; and Moon Madness won two Pattern races and finished second to Acatenango in a Group One.

Here, then, was a true champion at a mile and a half. His form in beating Triptych compared very favourably with Dancing Brave's in beating the mare in the same race and in the Arc the year before, but there was the rub.

Reference Point's method of winning did not cause such an upsurge of enthusiasm as Dancing Brave's; it did not capture the imagination of the public or Press. It was devastatingly effective, but not stylish; phlegmatic, not ebullient.

The fault lay not with the horse but with the attitude of those watching and interpreting him, who fell into an age-old trap.

Style counts for a lot in British racing, with horses as much as humans. Observers tend to identify superlative merit in a thoroughbred with versatility and blinding acceleration, both of which Dancing Brave possessed.

The theory maintains it looks much better for a horse to scythe down its opponents within the last furlong than to bludgeon them into submission before the last furlong.

It maintains that this method is more exciting, more likely to send shivers up the spine, than Reference Point's way of doing things.

The Americans would not make the same mistake. There, rightly, front-runners of raw, naked power are just as highly acclaimed as those who arrive late on the scene.

Possessing acceleration does not necessarily make a horse better than one who can keep up a ferocious

gallop from end to end, for substance on its own is just as praiseworthy as substance allied with elan.

While versatility and pace are admirable, what counts on the bottom line is merit, and if the merit is there over any distance, the fashion in which it receives expression should not be called into question. Racing needs horses of supreme ability and horses who race differently.

Clashes between resolute gallopers and speed merchants make for superb racing. They call for top jockeyship; they create majestic closing furlongs, as the battle commences and it becomes apparent whether the front runner has managed to blunt his rival's speed.

Such clashes happen all too infrequently, but they would not happen at all if excellence consisted purely in one style of racing.

If Reference Point is not remembered as one of the best horses trained in Britain in the past decade, it will be a travesty.

Perhaps his anti-climactic last appearance in the Trusthouse Forte Prix de l'Arc de Triomphe will not help in that respect, though Dancing Brave's defeat in the Breeders' Cup did nothing to blunt his appeal.

In the Arc, Reference Point trailed home eighth of 11 behind Trempolino, setting a scorching pace until dropping out quickly in the straight when an abcess on a leg blew up.

It was a sorry end to a glorious career – Reference Point begins life as a stallion at Dalham Hall Stud in Newmarket in 1988, but the race can be consigned to the back of the mind as far as he is concerned.

It cannot take away any of the colt's earlier achievements. Nothing can do that.

Reference Point was a byword for idleness on the gallops, and so imperturbable in race preliminaries as to look half asleep, but his combination of machine-like power and flesh-and-blood talent was formidable.

That combination made him a credit to himself, to his connections and to the racing public. One can ask no more of any thoroughbred.□

● **FLYING A KITE:** Britain took a few tentative steps towards Sunday racing in 1987, but for the moment Epsom on a Sunday afternoon is a place for other forms of leisure.

Picture: GERRY CRANHAM

— CHAPTER 2 —

Sunday Racing

A personal view by JOHN OAKSEY

GERRY CRANHAM

Sunday Racing

A personal view by JOHN OAKSEY

SPEAKING as a part-time member of British racing's 100,000 workforce, I have never much liked the idea of Sunday racing. It sounds uncomfortably like another working day, and no-one has yet persuaded me that it will leave the average racing correspondent either happier or appreciably better off.

That, I suspect, is the first reaction of the average stable lad, who is a far more vital part of the said workforce, without whose co-operation Sunday racing will never get off the ground.

Although lads (and girls) have at long last got a national mimimum wage, their pay has never even started to keep pace with the spiralling costs and values of the thoroughbreds whose health and welfare depend on their hard work.

It is all very well to tell lads they will be generously compensated for weekend work. They have heard that before and it will take a clear-cut, detailed and, above all enforceable agreement to convince them.

But this, I submit, is their greatest opportunity, perhaps the best chance they have ever had to stand firm and demand new improved conditions, including, if possible, the introduction of a recognisable career structure with graded levels of pay rising with service and experience.

In theory, it should be child's play to convince any reasonable thinking man that by keeping Britain the only major racing country in the world (besides the wavering New Zealand) where Sunday racing is not allowed, the law of our land is making an

immortal ass of itself.

The Sunday Observance Act which in 1870 made it illegal to charge admission for sporting events on a Sunday is ignored and/or publicly flouted by nearly all our major spectator sports, including football, cricket, rugger, golf, tennis, snooker and motor racing. As the Jockey's Working Party on the subject reported, with understandable resentment: "The general public can take their families to every other kind of sporting fixture but they are not able to go racing."

It is a comparable anomaly that, while the Betting, Gaming and Lotteries Act of 1963 prohibits "betting by way of bookmaking or by means of a Totalisator on any track on any Sunday", you and I can, quite legally, ring up Ladbrokes on Sunday morning to have our boots on some well-fancied loser at Longchamp or, if that way inclined, risk as much as we please at a Casino or in a slot machine.

As with all the other sports mentioned, racing is a branch of the entertainment industry. It happens to depend much more heavily on gambling than any of its rivals. A large part of the racecourse audience is attracted, in the first place, by the chance of having a bet and the Betting Levy contributes several million pounds a year towards the sport's running costs.

That is why the Jockey Club (which, at one time, loftily claimed to "take no cognisance whatever of matters concerned with wagering") now frankly admits that without betting racing would be "neither practicable nor viable".

It also takes the Home Office line that to hold racing on Sundays with the betting shops closed and bookmakers operating on course only, would be guaranteed to encourage widespread illegal betting and avoidance of the Betting Tax.

Maybe it is right, although the only convicted "illegal punter" I ever met is Jeffrey Bernard, the Spectator's bibulous but brilliant "Low-life" correspondent. His lunchtime wagers can hardly have beggared the Customs and Excise, but I suppose it is probably true that Sunday racing with no betting shops would provide a fairly irresistible temptation – and opportunities for villians rather less acceptable than Jeffrey.

That now seems to be the feeling in Ireland, where after two seasons of highly successful experimental Sunday racing with only on-course betting, Lord Killanin has called for off-course SP offices to be opened.

In any case, as the law stands here, holding race meetings with no betting shops open would discriminate unacceptably against the millions of would-be punters who do not have credit accounts with bookmakers.

Whatever the truth about illegal betting, the Government has made very clear from the start that no bill to legalise Sunday racing will be supported unless it includes a clause to allow the opening of betting shops on racing days.

It was, therefore, a monumental setback when that very clause was amended out of Lord Wyatt's Sunday Sports Bill in the House Of Lords. The debate on 5 November (which is not only Guy Fawkes' day but Lester Piggott's birthday!) had gone on longer than expected and too high á proportion of their racing Lordships had either sloped off to dinner or failed to turn up at all!

But Lord Wyatt's Bill was not, after all, fatally emasculated. The betting shops' clause was reinstated at the Report Stage (when a record number of sporting peers came out of the backwoods to vote) and it now remains to be seen whether enough Government time can be found to get through the Commons.

There, as the defeat of the Shops Bill demonstrated, it would still be no odds-on certainty to overcome the opposition of the Keep Sunday Special campaigners. But the Home Secretary Douglas Hurd is a declared supporter of Sunday racing and Mrs Thatcher once refused to go to the Derby on the grounds that "Wednesday is a working day!" On that line of reasoning she should surely favour freedom to choose your own amusement on the Day of Rest.

Then it will be up to racing to make sure that Sunday on the racecourse really can be "something special", a day out for the whole family.

Getting back to the workforce in general and stablelads in particular, the House of Lords' Committee stage debate on 5 November did do them one invaluable service. It inserted a "Schedule", the effect of which is that no-one employed in the industry when the Sunday Sports' Bill becomes law can be compelled to work on Sunday or disciplined for refusing to do so. Nor can they "have their conditions of employment altered for the worse in any way."

So, if only they stand together, stablelads, and for that matter betting shop employees and the rest of racing's esential labour-force, do seem to be in a powerful bargaining position. They cannot be forced to work on Sundays and if Sunday racing comes that could be their chance to negotiate a new framework for the job.

"If only they stand together", there's the rub, because less than a quarter of nearly 4,000 lads belong to the Stablelads' Association, of which, "declaring an interest", I am a Trustee.

Until the abortive and disastrous strike in 1965, the Transport and General Workers' Union had been the only organisation representing stable lads, and almost all its members worked at Newmarket.

Horrified by the strike, a group of Lambourn lads asked Jimmy Hill (then fresh from his triumphs with the Football Players' Association) to help build a body to represent them. It was at about that time the Levy Board Chairman Lord Plummer compelled racing to set up its first National Joint Wages Council, by threatening to withhold a million pounds or so of prize money until a minimum wage was fixed for stable lads.

The newly-formed SLA worked alongside the TGWU on that first Council, which means that the trainers found themselves facing the formidable team of Moss Evans and Jimmy Hill! But although a minimum wage was fixed and small increases have been laboriously negotiated each year since, it would still be a gross exaggeration to call the stable lads a united or "unionised" workforce.

The structure of the industry is all against that sort of organisation, the lads themselves are temperamentally ill-suited to it and the trainers, understandably, loathe the thought of it.

But sometimes, as we were painfully reminded in 1987, the happy, carefree world of racing comes face to face with real life. Sunday racing may sound a lovely dream but, like so many dreams, it will cost money. If the lads have any sense – and their employers any sense of justice – quite a bit of that money will go towards rewarding their hard work.□

● DERBY DELIGHT: Reference Point has been in front from the start of the Ever Ready Derby, and beats Most Welcome (noseband) and Bellotto. Sir Harry Lewis (green cap) was fourth.
Picture: GERRY CRANHAM

CHAPTER 3

The Classics

by GEORGE ENNOR

○ **CLASSIC HONOURS** were spread around in 1987, only Reference Point bringing off a double for owner-breeder Louis Freedman. Miesque, from France, was also home-bred, while Don't Forget Me and Unite came from oposite ends of the bloodstock market.

Above left – 1,000 GUINEAS: **Miesque beats Milligram (left) and Interval (centre).**
Picture: EDWARD WHITAKER

Above – 2,000 GUINEAS: **Don't Forget Me beats Bellotto (right) and disqualified Most Welcome (noseband, left).**
Picture: ALEC RUSSELL

Left – ST LEGER: **Reference Point beats Mountain Kingdom.**
Picture: JOHN CROFTS

Above right – OAKS: **Unite beats Bourbon Girl (almost hidden), Three Tails and Bint Pasha (left).**
Picture: GEORGE SELWYN

Right – DERBY: **Reference Point beats Most Welcome (noseband) and Bellotto.**   Picture: KICKSPORTS

○ **IN A FLASH: Miesque races past Milligram (spots) and Interval to take the General Accident 1,000 Guineas.**

Picture: GERRY CRANHAM

1,000 Guineas

by GEORGE ENNOR

England and France spent the better part of 1,000 years at war until the defeat of Napoleon at Waterloo ended the blood-letting. Even then the entente cordiale was not declared until 1904 and as far as racing was concerned bad feeling existed for a great deal longer.

The idea of calling the 1865 Triple Crown hero Gladiateur "the avenger of Waterloo" clearly did not satisfy everyone, and English runners and jockeys in France were for many years guaranteed a tough time. The sentiments were, no doubt, mutual and though things have become more

harmonious over the years, one could almost have been forgiven for thinking that something approaching war was back on the agenda in the General Accident 1,000 Guineas of 1987.

It had become clear in the weeks before the race that the Nureyev filly Miesque, trained by Francois Boutin for Stavros Niarchos and ridden by Freddie Head, was going to be very hard to beat.

She had won the Prix Marcel Boussac in the last of her four juvenile starts and put up a totally satisfactory performance to win the traditional Guineas prep race, the Prix

Imprudence at Saint-Cloud.

At Newmarket she started a hot favourite at 15-8, with the major English hopes being Interval, who had won Kempton Park's Masaka Stakes with great ease, and Milligram (one of three runners for Michael Stoute), who had been second to Miesque in the Boussac.

Milligram had not had a previous three-year-old venture, and nor had Minstrella, controversially awarded the Cheveley Park Stakes the previous autumn. None of the other ten runners started at less than 12-1.

The three chief fancies needed to be

○**MIGHTY MIESQUE:**The queen of European milers parades before one of her finest moments in the **1,000 Guineas** at **Newmarket.**
Picture: GERRY CRANHAM

held up to use their speed to best advantage, and so they stayed off the pace as Linda's Magic made the running ahead of the Irish challenger Polonia.

Invited Guest, who had let down her admirers in the Nell Gwyn Stakes, Minstrella, Amber Cookie and Raahia chased the leading two from the start and Polonia went for home with more than two furlongs to go. By now, though, the major contenders were beginning to make their mark and as Polonia failed to last out the mile, Milligram took command well below the distance.

Miesque was just behind Milligram, and as Interval came up on the French filly's outside one could imagine the possibility of the theatre of war being re-enacted. It was not quite "cannon to right of her" etc., as in the Light Brigade; instead it was very much a case of Miesque being all dressed up with nowhere to go, and for several strides it seemed the favourite would not get out of her trap in time. When Interval worked her way past Milligram inside the final furlong, Miesque at last had room in which to run. But was there enough race left for her to do so? The answer came as emphatically as Miesque's admirers had proclaimed it would, and once Head had extracted her, she flew.

Miesque faced a formidable task to catch the two fillies in front, but her powerful stride devoured the ground with the inevitability of night following day.

Interval probably found the mile just too far, but of Milligram's stamina there was no doubt. There was no doubt about Miesque, either. She surged past Milligram and Interval 75 yards from home, and was going so fast that she passed the post with a length and a half to spare.

Interval lost second place by a head to Milligram and the big three of the race had drawn three lengths clear of Polonia in fourth.

It was not so narrow a victory as that of Oh So Sharp two years before, but it was just as dramatic.□

○ **FLYING FINISH: Freddie Head brings Miesque with a powerful run on the outside in the 1,000 Guineas.**　　Picture: EDWARD WHITAKER

○ **JOB DONE: The post is in sight and Miesque has taken the measure of Milligram (spots) and Interval.**　　Picture: EDWARD WHITAKER

30 April – Newmarket
GOOD TO FIRM   1m

General Accident 1,000 Guineas Stakes

1st £83,907 **2nd** £31,470.60 **3rd** £15,172.80 **4th** £6,669.60

1		**MIESQUE** 3 9-0	F Head	**15-8F**
2	1½	**MILLIGRAM** 3 9-0	W R Swinburn	**13-2**
3	hd	**INTERVAL** 3 9-0	Pat Eddery	**11-2**
4	3	**POLONIA** 3 9-0	C Roche	**25-1**
5	shd	**MAMOUNA** 3 9-0	Y Saint-Martin	**16-1**
6	½	**MINSTRELLA** 3 9-0	J Reid	**15-2**
7	4	**INVITED GUEST** 3 9-0	S Cauthen	**12-1**
8	8	**AMBER COOKIE** 3 9-0	W Newnes	**28-1**
9	shd	**HIAAM** 3 9-0	G Starkey	**20-1**
10	½	**RAAHIA** 3 9-0	R Cochrane	**20-1**
11	2½	**LINDA'S MAGIC** 3 9-0	B Thomson	**25-1**
12	nk	**CACHONDINA** 3 9-0	C Asmussen	**25-1**
13	shd	**STAY LOW** 3 9-0	P Robinson	**200-1**
14		**TRY THE DUCHESS** 3 9-0	D McKay	**200-1**

14 ran
TIME 1m 38.48s
1st OWNER: S Niarchos TRAINER: F Boutin, France
2nd OWNER: Helena Springfield Ltd TRAINER: M Stoute
3rd OWNER: K Abdullah TRAINER: J Tree
4th OWNER: H de Kwiatkowski TRAINER: J Bolger, Ireland

○ **STAVROS NIARCHOS.**   Picture: TONY EDENDEN

Miesque
(b f, 14-3-84)

Nureyev (b 1977)	Northern Dancer	Nearctic
		Natalma
	Special	Forli
		Thong
Pasadoble (b 1979)	Prove Out	Graustark
		Equal Venture
	Santa Quilla	Sanctus
		Neriad

Bred by Flaxman Holdings Limited, in United States

Milligram
(ch f, 3-4-84)

Mill Reef (b 1968)	Never Bend	Nasrullah
		Lalun
	Milan Mill	Princequillo
		Virginia Water
One In A Million (b 1976)	Rarity	Hethersett
		Who Can Tell
	Singe	Tudor Music
		Trial By Fire

Bred by J Weinfeld

Interval
(ch f, 27-4-84)

Habitat (b 1966)	Sir Gaylord	Turn-to
		Somethingroyal
	Little Hut	Occupy
		Savage Beauty
Intermission (ch 1973)	Stage Door Johnny	Prince John
		Peroxide Blonde
	Peace	Klairon
		Sun Rose

Bred by Juddmonte Farms, in Ireland

Polonia
(b f, 18-5-84)

Danzig (b 1977)	Northern Dancer	Nearctic
		Natalma
	Pas De Nom	Admiral's Voyage
		Petitioner
Moss (b 1965)	Round Table	Princequillo
		Knight's Daughter
	Delta	Nasrullah
		Bourtai

Bred by P Brant, in United States: $600,000 yearling Keeneland July Sale

○ **SO BRAVE: Don't Forget Me shows his courage to win the General Accident 2,000 Guineas from Belloto (sash). Most Welcome (noseband) was disqualified and third place went to Midyan (No 8) ahead of Ajdal.** Picture: GERRY CRANHAM

2,000 Guineas

by GEORGE ENNOR

Fashion dictates a great deal in racing; many feel it dictates too much. But those who are prepared to back their judgement against fashionable opinions came up trumps in the General Accident 2,000 Guineas.

In the Craven Stakes just over a fortnight earlier, the previous year's Dewhurst Stakes victor Ajdal had won by threequarters of a length from Don't Forget Me. Connections of the runner-up were adamant he might have won if more vigorous use had been made of him, but only a few were

prepared to listen.

Ajdal, who cost an arm and a leg, and Don't Forget Me, bought for 19,000gns, had to be given much the same sort of chance on Craven form, yet Ajdal started at 6-5 while Don't Forget Me drifted to 9-1 as it became known the vet had treated him since early morning for an injured hoof. It was touch and go whether Richard Hannon's best horse ran, but he made it.

Don't Forget Me was not even second favourite. That position was

filled by Bellotto, who was thought likely to reverse Greenham Stakes form with Risk Me on Newmarket's much faster ground. Risk Me, whose best form had been on soft going, was third-best, and after Don't Forget Me came the Free Handicap runner-up Midyan and the Craven third Most Welcome.

Neither France nor Ireland could muster a runner between them.

With Pat Eddery claimed for Bellotto, Willie Carson took over on Don't Forget Me, and the plan to make more aggressive use of the colt was soon manifest.

Don't Forget Me bowled out of the stalls in front, chased in the early stages by Rich Charlie and Lockton, with Ajdal on their heels after a couple of furlongs.

Any number were still in with a chance two furlongs from home — including Most Welcome, Deputy Governor, Midyan and Ongoing Situation — but Don't Forget Me was still holding them. And, with one exception, none of them looked like getting past him.

The exception was not Adjal but Bellotto, whose attack entering the final furlong seemed sure to carry him into the lead. Eddery thought so too, but he said later that just as he felt Bellotto was poised to strike, Don't Forget Me pulled out a little more.

It might have been only a little, but it was enough to see Don't Forget Me home by a neck, and he returned to a Cheltenham-type reception from a horde of Horgans over from Ireland.

○ **IT'S OVER: Don't Forget Me is on his way back to a rousing welcome after landing the 2,000 Guineas.** Picture: GERRY CRANHAM

○ **ALL OUT: Willie Carson drives Don't Forget Me for the line to beat Bellotto.** Picture: KICKSPORTS

Most Welcome finished third, a length behind Bellotto, but he was rightly adjudged to have bumped Ajdal (fifth) about a furlong from home. Most Welcome was disqualified and placed last, with Midyan, uninvolved in the incident, moved up to third and Ajdal qualifying for fourth-place money.

It is easy to be wise after the event and make the point about fashion apropos Don't Forget Me and Ajdal. But few will argue that had the horses swopped teams etc., the betting would have been more realistic. To emphasise the point, Don't Forget Me went on to beat Ajdal again in the Irish 2,000 Guineas a fortnight later. On that occasion they started equal favourites. Sense had finally prevailed.□

○ **CLASSIC CLUE: Ajdal beats Don't Forget Me and Most Welcome in their 2,000 Guineas warm-up in the Craven Stakes.** Picture: GEORGE SELWYN

○ **WELCOMING PARTY: Public, Press and photographers are on hand as Don't Forget Me returns in triumph after the 2,000 Guineas.** Picture: TONY EDENDEN

2 May – Newmarket
GOOD   1m

General Accident 2,000 Guineas Stakes

1st £98,928 **2nd** £37,182.40 **3rd** £17,991.20 **4th** £7,978.40

1		**DON'T FORGET ME** 3 9-0	W Carson **9-1**
2	*nk*	**BELLOTTO** 3 9-0	Pat Eddery **7-1**
3		**MIDYAN** 3 9-0	S Cauthen **12-1**
4		**AJDAL** 3 9-0	W R Swinburn **6-5F**
6	1½	**DEPUTY GOVERNOR** 3 9-0	T Ives **20-1**
7	2½	**NAHEEZ** 3 9-0	B Rouse **60-1**
8	1	**RICH CHARLIE** 3 9-0	J Reid **33-1**
9	*nk*	**JOLIGENERATION** 3 9-0	G Starkey **22-1**
10	1	**HYDRAULIC POWER** 3 9-0	C Asmussen **50-1**
11	2½	**LOCKTON** 3 9-0	M Hills **22-1**
12	2½	**RISK ME** 3 9-0	R Cochrane **15-2**
13	4	**ONGOING SITUATION** 3 9-0	P Cook **200-1**
0	*(disq)*	**MOST WELCOME** 3 9-0	Paul Eddery **14-1**

Most Welcome finished 3rd, beaten 1l by Bellotto, a head in front of Midyan and a further sh hd to Ajdal. After a Stewards' inquiry, Most Welcome was disqualified.
13 ran
TIME 1m 36.74s
1st OWNER: J Horgan TRAINER: R Hannon
2nd OWNER: K Abdullah TRAINER: J Tree
3rd OWNER: Prince A Faisal TRAINER: H Cecil
4th OWNER: Sheikh Mohammed TRAINER: M Stoute

○ **RICHARD HANNON.**   Picture: DAVID HASTINGS

Don't Forget Me
(b c, 10-4-84)

		Klairon
Ahonoora (ch 1975)	Lorenzaccio	Phoenissa
	Helen Nichols	Martial
		Quaker Girl
African Doll (b 1978)	African Sky	Sing Sing
		Sweet Caroline
	Mithrill	Princely Gift
		Baraka

Bred by Mrs F Hutch: 19,000gns yearling Newmarket October Yearling Sale

Bellotto
(b c, 27-4-84)

		Native Dancer
Mr Prospector (b 1970)	Raise A Native	Raise You
	Gold Digger	Nashua
		Sequence
Shelf Talker (b 1968)	Tatan	The Yuvaraj
		Valkyrie
	Melody Mine	The Doge
		Magic Melody

Bred by Glen Hill Farm, in United States: $700,000 yearling Keeneland July Sale

Midyan
(b c, 27-4-84)

		Raise A Native
Miswaki (ch 1978)	Mr Prospector	Gold Digger
	Hopespringseternal	Buckpasser
		Rose Bower
Country Dream (b 1970)	Ribot	Tenerani
		Romanella
	Equal Venture	Bold Venture
		Igual

Bred by King Ranch Farm, in United States: $165,000 yearling Keeneland September Sale

Ajdal
(b c, 2-4-84)

		Nearco
Northern Dancer (b 1961)	Nearctic	Lady Angela
	Natalma	Native Dancer
		Almahmoud
Native Partner (b 1966)	Raise A Native	Native Dancer
		Raise You
	Dinner Partner	Tom Fool
		Bluehaze

Bred by R Wilson, in United States: sold privately as a yearling

○ **THAT'S MY BOY: Alison Dean leads Reference Point and Steve Cauthen back after their Ever Ready Derby triumph.**
Picture: JOHN CROFTS

○ **LEADING THE CHARGE: Reference Point takes the Derby field round Tattenham Corner. Chasing him are Ascot Knight and Most Welcome (noseband).**
Picture: ALAN JOHNSON

The Derby

by GEORGE ENNOR

There was nothing surprising about Reference Point winning the Ever Ready Derby on Wednesday, 3 June 1987; nor that he started 6-4 favourite to do so. What was surprising was that Reference Point was there at all.

As little as six weeks before the Derby there were plenty of people prepared to wager that he would not be in the field, and their reasoning seemed totally sound.

In the Spring the colt had developed a serious infection in his sinus, which had been cured only by major veterinary attention, involving the insertion of tubes in his nose. Thanks to the vets' expertise and the devotion of Alison Dean, the girl who looked after Reference Point at Henry Cecil's stables, he recovered fully.

The big question was whether there would be time to get him ready for the Derby with a proper preparation. Already the 2,000 Guineas had been ruled out and the Triple Crown dreams of owner-breeder Louis Freedman had gone.

Cecil decided that Reference Point's target should be the Mecca-Dante Stakes at York in May, but two weeks before the race he warned that the colt would not be at peak fitness.

However ill-prepared Reference Point might have been, he was more than strong enough to dispose of his seven rivals, all of whom had had a previous 1987 race. Those who had not been keen to lay big odds against him for Epsom were suddenly rather quiet.

Eighteen hopefuls lined up against Reference Point at Epsom, including his stablemate Legal Bid, winner of the Lingfield Derby Trial; Bellotto and Most Welcome, who had finished second and third in the Guineas; the Irish Guineas runner-up Entitled, and Groom Dancer and Sadjiyd from France.

It was Sadjiyd, the Aga Khan's colt and the last Derby ride for Yves Saint-Martin, who was widely thought to be the biggest threat and in a major raceday gamble he was backed down to 11-2. But Sadjiyd forgot his lines and after a furlong he was a remote and hard-ridden last as Reference Point, in what had become his customary way, went off in front.

Close behind Reference Point came the Dante runner-up Ascot Knight, that colt's stablemate Ajdal, Most Welcome, Ibn Bey and Legal Bid, but gradually many of them found the leader was too tough to crack.

Neither Ajdal nor Ascot Knight stayed the mile and a half, but even though he had seen them off, Reference Point still had two formidable challenges with a furlong to go.

Bellotto, coming from a long way

○ **ON THE LINE: Reference Point collects the Derby from Most Welcome and Bellotto (nearside).** Picture: ALAN JOHNSON

off the pace, joined Most Welcome in the attack but they, like many before and after, learned the hard way that getting to Reference Point is one thing, getting past is another. It is probably also true that a mile and a half is beyond the optimum for both colts.

In any event Reference Point had the legs of both of them in the final 100 yards. He galloped on to win by a length and a half from Most Welcome, with Bellotto a short head back in third, to give Henry Cecil and Steve Cauthen their second Derby in three years.

Reference Point probably ran the fastest Derby of all time. Officially his 2min. 33.9sec. was fractionally slower than the 2min. 33.8sec. taken by Mahmoud in 1936.

But the hand-taken times of that era cannot compare for accuracy with today's electrically-operated system. It has to take some time, surely more than 0.1sec. for the eyes, mind and hand of a clocker to start a stopwatch. He will never coincide with the actual moment the stalls open, and although the record books will presumably never say so, Reference Point ought to be credited with the fastest time. That's the least he deserves.□

○ **BACK IN STYLE: After a worrying spring for his connections, Reference Point reappears to win the Mecca-Dante Stakes from Ascot Knight and Persifleur.** Picture: GEORGE SELWYN

3 June – Epsom
GOOD

1m 4f

Ever Ready Derby Stakes

1st £282,024 **2nd** £106,629.20 **3rd** £52,114.60 **4th** £23,672.20

1		REFERENCE POINT 3 9-0	S Cauthen **6-4F**
2	1½	MOST WELCOME 3 9-0	Paul Eddery **33-1**
3	shd	BELLOTTO 3 9-0	Pat Eddery **11-1**
4	2	SIR HARRY LEWIS 3 9-0	J Reid **66-1**
5	½	ENTITLED 3 9-0	C Asmussen **11-1**
6	nk	MOUNTAIN KINGDOM 3 9-0	M Roberts **33-1**
7	1	GROOM DANCER 3 9-0	D Boeuf **16-1**
8	nk	SADJIYD 3 9-0	Y Saint-Martin **11-2**
9	1	AJDAL 3 9-0	R Cochrane **25-1**
10	1½	PERSIFLEUR 3 9-0	A Cruz **33-1**
11	¾	ASCOT KNIGHT 3 9-0	W R Swinburn **25-1**
12	3	LOVE THE GROOM 3 9-0	W Carson **33-1**
13	1	IBN BEY 3 9-0	T Quinn **40-1**
14	1	LEGAL BID 3 9-0	T Ives **8-1**
15	4	GULF KING 3 9-0	P Cook **100-1**
16	6	WATER BOATMAN 3 9-0	B Rouse **150-1**
17	2½	ANGARA ABYSS 3 9-0	G Starkey **100-1**
18	5	ALWASMI 3 9-0	R Hills **150-1**
19	8	ROMANTIC PRINCE 3 9-0	W Ryan **150-1**

19 ran
TIME 2m 33.90s
1st OWNER: L Freedman TRAINER: H Cecil
2nd OWNER: E Moller TRAINER: G Wragg
3rd OWNER: K Abdullah TRAINER: J Tree
4th OWNER: H Kaskel TRAINER: B Hills

○ **LOUIS FREEDMAN.**   Picture: W EVERITT

Reference Point
(b c, 26-2-84)

		Nasrullah
Mill Reef (b 1968)	Never Bend	Nasrullah
		Lalun
	Milan Mill	Princequillo
		Virginia Water
Home On The Range (br 1978)	Habitat	Sir Gaylord
		Little Hut
	Great Guns	Busted
		Byblis

Bred by Cliveden Stud

Most Welcome
(ch c, 15-4-84)

		Nearctic
Be My Guest (ch 1974)	Northern Dancer	Nearctic
		Natalma
	What A Treat	Tudor Minstrel
		Rare Treat
Topsy (ch 1976)	Habitat	Sir Gaylord
		Little Hut
	Furioso	Ballymoss
		Violetta

Bred by White Lodge Stud Limited

Bellotto
(b c, 27-4-84)

		Native Dancer
Mr Prospector (b 1970)	Raise A Native	Native Dancer
		Raise You
	Gold Digger	Nashua
		Sequence
Shelf Talker (b 1968)	Tatan	The Yuvaraj
		Valkyrie
	Melody Mine	The Doge
		Magic Melody

Bred by Glen Hill Farm, in United States: $700,000 yearling Keeneland July Sale

Sir Harry Lewis
(b c, 24-1-84)

		Tom Rolfe
Alleged (b 1974)	Hoist The Flag	Tom Rolfe
		Wavy Navy
	Princess Pout	Prince John
		Determined Lady
Sue Baby (b 1978)	Mr Prospector	Raise A Native
		Gold Digger
	Sleek Belle	Vaguely Noble
		Sleek Dancer

Bred by J Allen and Regent Farm, in United States

○ **THAT'S MY GIRL: Sheikh Mohammed greets his Gold Seal Oaks winner Unite after her six-length success at Epsom.**
Picture: GERRY CRANHAM

The Oaks

by GEORGE ENNOR

Few owners can have gone into a recent Classic with a stronger hand than Sheikh Mohammed in the Gold Seal Oaks at Epsom on 6 June. Three of the 11 fillies carried his maroon and white colours: Scimitarra, who was trained by Henry Cecil; Three Tails, from John Dunlop's yard; and Unite, who was with Michael Stoute.

Scimitarra, whom the Sheikh bought at the previous year's December sales for 620,000gns, went off as favourite at 5-2 after her stylish success in the Lupe Stakes at

Goodwood the previous month.

It is interesting to look back at that race from this distance and to recall the thought that she had not beaten a lot, as the runner-up was a 33-1 chance called Bint Pasha. In view of what Bint Pasha achieved later in the year (admittedly she was only a well-beaten fourth in the Oaks), the form has a different look.

Three Tails, who had been narrowly beaten on unfavourable terms in the Sir Charles Clore Memorial Stakes at Newbury, started second favourite at

3-1. Unite, was an 11-1 shot, and as two of the three filled two of the first three places it might be easy to think their owner must have enjoyed the race.

For much of the contest no doubt he did, but it is equally certain that if the final quarter of a mile had not taken place he would have been much happier. And this despite Unite's easy victory by five lengths and three from Bourbon Girl and Three Tails.

As Unite swept past the post to give Walter Swinburn his first Oaks triumph, the Epsom crowd gazed a furlong down the course, where Steve Cauthen had dismounted from Scimitarra. The filly clearly had a serious injury to her off foreleg. She had cracked her cannon bone, and though she was saved for stud, her racing days were over.

Scimitarra's misfortune inevitably detracted from the style of Unite's win. Swinburn said that he had Scimitarra covered before she broke down. In any event once Unite hit the front she was never in the slightest danger.

Bourbon Girl stayed on at the same pace in the last quarter-mile to be second, while Three Tails was off the bit so far from home it was amazing

○ **THREE INTO TWO: A warm day at Epsom and a trio of racegoers contemplate the Oaks.**
Picture: TONY EDENDEN

○ **MIXED FORTUNES: Sheikh Mohammed's Unite romps away with the Oaks, beating Bourbon Girl and his second runner Three Tails, but the Sheikh's Scimitarra, who started favourite, can be seen on the other side of the course being pulled up with a leg injury.**
Picture: GEORGE HERRINGSHAW

○ **MOMENT OF GLORY: Unite and Walter Swinburn pass the winning post five lengths ahead of the rest in the Oaks.**

Picture: TONY EDENDEN

that she got as close as she did.

The decision to run Unite appeared to presume a considerable degree of optimism. On her only previous three-year-old venture Unite, who had cost 310,000gns as a yearling, had won an ordinary graduation race, admittedly at Ascot, in what looked ordinary style. And the race did not look any better when In the Habit, who also belonged to Sheikh Mohammed, failed at odds on in a Leicester maiden race three weeks later.

But that Ascot race had been only the second of Unite's career, and though trainer Stoute had for some time been cautious about running her in the Oaks, a gallop some 12 days before opened his eyes to how much she was improving. Unite made a few things plain to the rest of us at Epsom.

She later won the Irish Oaks at The Curragh, beating Bourbon Girl again, before running badly in the King George VI. Injury denied her the chance of trying to retrieve whatever of her reputation that Ascot display may have lost, and she is booked for the paddocks this spring.□

6 June – Epsom
GOOD TO SOFT   1m 4f

Gold Seal Oaks Stakes

1st £148,650 **2nd** £56,150 **3rd** £27,400 **4th** £12,400

1		UNITE 3 9-0	W R Swinburn	**11-1**
2	*5*	BOURBON GIRL 3 9-0	C Asmussen	**12-1**
3	*3*	THREE TAILS 3 9-0	W Carson	**3-1**
4	*hd*	BINT PASHA 3 9-0	T Quinn	**66-1**
5	*7*	ON THE STAFF 3 9-0	W Newnes	**25-1**
6	*2½*	SAKURA REIKO 3 9-0	A Cruz	**6-1**
7	*3*	MOUNTAIN MEMORY 3 9-0	B Rouse	**40-1**
8	*20*	BRACORINA 3 9-0	T Ives	**200-1**
9	*7*	BALABINA 3 9-0	Pat Eddery	**4-1**
10	*4*	HONEY LINE 3 9-0	R Cochrane	**25-1**
PUp		SCIMITARRA 3 9-0	S Cauthen	**5-2F**

11 ran
TIME 2m 38.17s
1st OWNER: Sheikh Mohammed TRAINER: M Stoute
2nd OWNER: K Abdullah TRAINER: B Hills
3rd OWNER: Sheikh Mohammed TRAINER: J Dunlop
4th OWNER: F Salman TRAINER: P Cole

○ **SHEIKH MOHAMMED.**   Picture: ALEC RUSSELL

Unite
(ch f, 3–4-84)

		Atan
Kris (ch 1976)	Sharpen Up	Atan
		Rocchetta
	Doubly Sure	Reliance
		Soft Angels
Pro Patria (b 1976)	Petingo	Petition
		Alcazar
	Joyful	Princely Gift
		My Game

Bred by E Loder, in Ireland: 310,000gns yearling Newmarket Highflyer Sale

Bourbon Girl
(b f, 9-2-84)

Ile De Bourbon (b 1975)	Nijinsky	Northern Dancer
		Flaming Page
	Roseliere	Misti
		Peace Rose
Fleet Girl (ch 1975)	Habitat	Sir Gaylord
		Little Hut
	Fleet Noble	Vaguely Noble
		Limey's Moppet

Bred by Juddmonte Farms

Three Tails
(b f, 3-3-84)

Blakeney (b 1966)	Hethersett	Hugh Lupus
		Bride Elect
	Windmill Girl	Hornbeam
		Chorus Beauty
Triple First (b 1974)	High Top	Derry-Do
		Camenae
	Field Mouse	Grey Sovereign
		Meadow Song

Bred by Hesmond Stud Limited: 290,000gns yearling Newmarket Highflyer Sale

Bint Pasha
(ch f, 7-3-84)

Affirmed (ch 1975)	Exclusive Native	Raise A Native
		Exclusive
	Won't Tell You	Crafty Admiral
		Scarlet Ribbon
Icely Polite (b or br 1979)	Graustark	Ribot
		Flower Bowl
	Royal Kin	Sir Gaylord
		Myth

Bred by Spendthrift Thoroughbred Breeding No 1, in United States: $220,000 yearling Fasig-Tipton Saratoga Sale

○ **DOUBLE DASH:** Reference Point follows up his Derby win by landing the Holsten Pils St Leger from Mountain Kingdom.
Picture: ALAN JOHNSON

The St Leger

by GEORGE ENNOR

In the last 20 years or so there has been a vociferous, if misguided, campaign to denigrate the St Leger, the oldest and last of our five Classics. Even some elements of the Doncaster management have been heard to suggest that the race should be opened to horses of all ages and that it should be reduced in distance to a mile and a half.

This is nothing better than a pathetic attempt to emulate the Prix de l'Arc de Triomphe, which the St Leger — now sponsored by Holsten — was never intended to do, and a further example of how slavish devotion to apparent fashion can lead to unjustifiable conclusions.

The argument that the St Leger is sometimes won by a horse of limited

ability, and therefore must be altered, holds less water than a bottomless bucket. Plenty of moderate horses have won the Derby but there have not been many cries for that race to be changed.

The theory that the Leger is a graveyard for Arc horses started in earnest when Nijinsky was beaten at Longchamp after his Doncaster win. Its advocates conveniently forget that Alleged won the Arc after being beaten in the St Leger, and to claim that Leger winners such as Oh So Sharp, Commanche Run, Moon Madness and Bustino are moderate horses is simply risible. Not that Reference Point's owner-breeder Louis Freedman had any doubts about where he wanted to go.

As soon as his colt had won the King George VI he made it plain that the St Leger was his objective. The Arc was almost an afterthought.

There may be, depending on where you are sitting, mixed feelings about races such as the 1987 St Leger. On all available form Reference Point so outclassed his six opponents that he started at 11-4 on, and at one time in the run-up to the race he looked like being even shorter odds.

From the betting point of view, therefore, there is probably little attraction, but the belief that people put betting before the chance of seeing a good horse was hardly upheld by the spectators who turned up at Town Moor.

By the time of the race there was no

○ **THEY'RE OFF: Dry Dock, Reference Point and Love The Groom (hooped cap) are first away in the St Leger, followed by Waterfield (left) and Mountain Kingdom.**   Picture: ALAN JOHNSON

doubt that setting off in front was Reference Point's ideal tactic, but as the Arc had become a firm objective, all being well, Steve Cauthen could not set out to grind his rivals into the dust with no thought to the future.

Cauthen, whose move to this country from the United States nine years ago has been such a success, has shown time after time that his judgement of pace is second to none.

Reference Point set off in front, pursued from the start by the Chester Vase winner Dry Dock, who had been well backed at long odds (20-1 to 11-1) and whose team were hopeful of a better show on the firmer ground than in the Voltigeur at York, where he had been a well-beaten second.

King of Mercia chased these two, ahead of Mountain Kingdom, but the other three runners never even got close enough to look a temporary threat.

Dry Dock was struggling with a

○ **SITTING PRETTY: There's time to reflect for these St Leger day racegoers.**
Picture: TONY EDENDEN

○ **BACKWARD GLANCE: Pat Eddery looks round for those following Mountain Kingdom in the St Leger, but Reference Point has already got the race in the bag.**
Picture: TONY EDENDEN

quarter-mile to go and from thereon Reference Point had only one horse to beat, Mountain Kingdom, who was not going to submit simply by bowing the knee.

With just over a furlong to run, Mountain Kingdom had every chance of upsetting the favourite, but Cauthen had kept enough left for Reference Point to retain his lead without having to dig too deep into his resources.

At the line Reference Point was a length and a half to the good, with Mountain Kingdom, eight lengths clear of Dry Dock in third, beaten, but having acquitted himself with distinction.

Owner, Freedman said that Reference Point's St Leger victory had given him at least as much pleasure as all the others. Since these included the King George VI as well as the Derby, those words were a major compliment.

Sadly Reference Point's bid for Longchamp glory ended in defeat. But to the best of my recollection no-one claimed that he had left the Arc behind at Doncaster. Perhaps the critics are learning.□

12 September – Doncaster
GOOD   1m 6f 127y

Holsten Pils St Leger Stakes

1st £106,077 **2nd** £39,506.90 **3rd** £18,815.80 **4th** £8,020.60

1		REFERENCE POINT 3 9-0	S Cauthen **4-11F**
2	1½	MOUNTAIN KINGDOM 3 9-0	Pat Eddery **9-1**
3	8	DRY DOCK 3 9-0	W Carson **11-1**
4	1	WATERFIELD 3 9-0	B Thomson **60-1**
5	8	KING OF MERCIA 3 9-0	R Cochrane **28-1**
6	10	LOVE THE GROOM 3 9-0	T Ives **8-1**
7	5	GULF KING 3 9-0	A Cruz **66-1**

7 ran
TIME 3m 5.91s
1st OWNER: L Freedman TRAINER: H Cecil
2nd OWNER: Pin Oak Stable TRAINER: C Brittain
3rd OWNER: R Hollingsworth TRAINER: W Hern
4th OWNER: A D Oldrey TRAINER: P Walwyn

○ **STEVE CAUTHEN.**   Picture: GEORGE SELWYN

Reference Point
(b c, 26-2-84)

Mill Reef (b 1968)	Never Bend	Nasrullah
		Lalun
	Milan Mill	Princequillo
		Virginia Water
Home On The Range (br 1978)	Habitat	Sir Gaylord
		Little Hut
	Great Guns	Busted
		Byblis

Bred by Cliveden Stud

Mountain Kingdom
(b c, 30-5-84)

Exceller (b 1973)	Vaguely Noble	Vienna
		Noble Lassie
	Too Bald	Bald Eagle
		Hidden Talent
Star In The North (b 1971)	Northern Dancer	Nearctic
		Natalma
	Lighted Lamp	Sir Gaylord
		Chandelier

Bred by Pin Oak Farm, in United States

Dry Dock
(b c, 17-3-84)

High Line (ch 1966)	High Hat	Hyperion
		Madonna
	Time Call	Chanteur
		Aleria
Boathouse (b 1978)	Habitat	Sir Gaylord
		Little Hut
	Ripeck	Ribot
		Kyak

Bred by R D Hollingsworth

Waterfield
(ch c, 21-5-84)

Le Moss (ch 1975)	Le Levenstell	Le Lavandou
		Stella's Sister
	Feemoss	Ballymoss
		Feevagh
Shannon Princess (b 1972)	Connaught	St Paddy
		Nagaika
	Bluecourt	Court Martial
		Alcyone

Bred by Seend Stud

— CHAPTER 4 —

Sprinters

by LAWRENCE WADEY

● **POWER AND GLORY: Ajdal proved the leading sprinter in a season which took him from the Guineas to the Derby and back to five furlongs.**

Picture: JOHN CROFTS

○ **RAIL BIRD: Polonia (right) lands the Prix de l'Abbaye from La Grande Epoque and Tenue de Soiree, while Hallgate (hoops) has traffic problems.**

Picture: JOHN CROFTS

Sprinters

by LAWRENCE WADEY

RARELY have we had it so good.

In other areas, with one competitor measureably better than the rest, it would suffice to chronicle him or her (in this case Michael Stoute's Ajdal) and be done with.

But sprinting is Flat Racing's enigma, where the form book often bears close approximation to a Grimm Brothers anthology. Rather it is a microcosm of the sport, where elusive dreams really do come true; where a season can open humbly with a 33-1 success in an Ayr seller and culminate six months, 13 races and £38,818 later in one cavalry-charge of a grand finale with glorious victory in the Ayr Gold Cup.

That was Not So Silly, and this is sprinting, where reputations can be made, redeemed or shattered, with scant regard to pedigree or price-tag.

When Ajdal, highly impressive winner of his three starts as a juvenile including the Dewhurst Stakes, stepped out for the Norcos July Cup his reputation was in tatters.

For many he had not trained on; for others, he was not wholly enthusiastic.

It was thought superior fitness had helped him scramble home from Don't Forget Me in the Craven Stakes. He was not good enough to win the 2,000 Guineas, a view confirmed by his third-past-the-post in the Irish equivalent. And he tamely

dropped away round Tattenham Corner to finish ninth in the Derby.

It took Ajdal 1 min 11.02 sec to re-establish himself.

In the fastest six-furlong race seen on the July Course, Ajdal broke smartly and was always travelling smoothly for Walter Swinburn. Accelerating to the front over a furlong out, he stuck on tenaciously to hold long-time leader Gayane by a head, with Bluebird a length back in third, the rest nowhere.

Sadly Gayane, a lightly-framed filly, did not reproduce that level of form. Bluebird, too, was on the wane.

And after Bluebird's mulish display behind Ajdal in the William Hill

Sprint Championship at York, it was difficult to believe he had led the mud-splattered field a merry dance from the furlong pole in the King's Stand Stakes at Royal Ascot.

It was even harder to imagine he was the colt whom trainer Vincent O'Brien, stoic in his dealings with the Press and certainly not given to hyperbole, had compared to Thatching, his star sprinter of the late Seventies.

Ajdal, though, stamped himself a worthy champion at York and sauntered through the Vernons Sprint Cup at Haydock Park to confirm his superiority over the sprinting class of '87.

Admittedly opposition in the William Hill Sprint was not what it might have been. But on rain-softened ground, he made all, cruising home three lengths clear of Sizzling Melody.

Without being asked a serious question at any stage, Ajdal covered the five furlongs, rated good to soft, in 58.48 sec, 0.12 sec below standard and the fastest speed figure recorded at the two-day meeting.

That, coupled with his scintillating performance in the July Cup, suggests he could have matched strides with the best.

○ **FLYING FINISH: Polonia (Stephen Craine) on her way to winning the Phoenix Flying Five.**   Picture: CAROLINE NORRIS

But more, Ajdal reached the pinnacle by way of a smart about-turn effected by trainer Michael Stoute. He did something similar with the aspiring milers Green Desert and Marwell but this was in a different league — the same Racing Calendar containing Ajdal's July Cup entry held an alternative engagement, the King George VI and Queen Elizabeth II Diamond Stakes.

On the go since mid-April, Ajdal proved nothing more in his trailing seventh of nine to Polonia in the Prix de L'Abbaye de Longchamp than that he had trained off one race before he was retired to stand at owner Sheikh Mohammed's Dalham Hall Stud.

Polonia's Abbaye success was emphatic, if belated, confirmation of the huge reputation she had brought from Ireland to Royal Ascot the year before, when she was an expensive failure for the Irish behind Cutting Blade in the Coventry Stakes.

Polonia also started the season tackling longer distances, but after dropping away tamely in the English and Irish 1,000 Guineas, and Pacemaker International at Phoenix Park, Jim Bolger brought her back in distance to win her last three races.

To his and the owner's credit, Polonia stays in training and looks set to prove a potent threat to Barry Hills' Gallic League this summer.

Like Polonia, Gallic League failed to justify favouritism at Royal Ascot. Troubled by sore shins, he was beaten two and a half lengths by Colmore Row. Subsequent victory in the Flying Childers Stakes, followed by a blistering turn of speed in the Middle Park, established him as No 1

○ **GOOD START: Hallgate opens the season with a Palace House Stakes win from Clantime (right) and Carol's Treasure (left).**   Picture: JOHN CROFTS

○ **CHAMPION STYLE: Ajdal begins to draw clear of Sizzling Melody and Perion (centre) in the William Hill Sprint Championship.** Picture: ALAN JOHNSON

contender for the vacant sprint crown. But first he will have to train on, let alone stay sound.

With soundness in mind, there was much to admire about Lord John FitzGerald's handling of Sizzling Melody, an intermittent sufferer from back trouble, bruised feet, joint problems, and lameness during the summer.

The second-season Newmarket trainer nursed him back to full fitness for a gainful autumn campaign, and following a listed race win at Doncaster, he survived a 20-minute Stewards' inquiry to keep the Prix du Petit Couvert at Longchamp.

Sizzling Melody's was the story of success from modest beginnings, the sort for which sprinting is noted, especially in handicaps.

The point could not have been more heavily underscored than by Dawn's Delight, Ken Ivory's perennial gelding who at nine became the oldest winner of Doncaster's Portland Handicap this side of 1900. Victory reduced Ivory to tears, and no wonder, for he bought Dawn's Delight as a yearling for 500gns and was placing him to win for the 16th time, collecting £100,000

(give or take £39) in win money on the way.

Madraco's bolt from the blue in another top sprint handicap, Goodwood's Stewards' Cup, was also stirring stuff.

Virtually unknown, and more-or-less unbacked, Madraco and his young apprentice rider Peter Hill, hurtled from the No 12 stall, scooted up the stands' rail and that, as they say, was that.

Yet trainer Peter Calver had wanted

to sidestep the £40,000-added race, preferring a tilt at less-fashionable Thirsk three days later. But owner Bernard Hampson insisted, had his tenner each-way on the Tote to pick up £2,849.00, and the rest is part of the sprint fairytales.

Dowsing, under 9st 10lb, ran into fourth at Goodwood and later took the Diadem Stakes at Ascot. What a certainty he must have been carrying 7st 10lb in the William Hill Golden Spurs Handicap at York!

And what a good thing Perion, successful seven times from 13 races for Geoff Lewis in 1987, should have been in the lowly Newmarket seller which concluded his 1985 season. In keeping with the romance of this helter-skelter distance, he was beaten, but he's hardly looked back since. In 1986 he gained four victories, and the seven in '87 included two listed races, and the Channel 4 Trophy for the season's winningmost horse.

Perion pipped the Alan Bailey-trained Not So Silly, who also won seven times but had fewer placings than Perion.

Terry Ramsden, who has since sold Not So Silly to race in Saudi Arabia, had mixed fortunes with Hallgate, who came up against a wall of horses when brought to challenge in the Prix de l'Abbaye de Longchamp in his last race. Forced to miss three months with a pulled muscle in his off-hip, Hallgate was unable to add to his success in the Palace House Stakes. Still, Not So Silly kept the flag flying and the dreams alive.□

○ **NO DANGER: Ajdal seals the speedsters' title in the Vernons Sprint Cup.**
Picture: ALEC RUSSELL

19 June – Royal Ascot
HEAVY   5f

King's Stand Stakes

1st £57,724.20 **2nd** £21,526.36 **3rd** £10,275.68 **4th** £4,405.76

1		BLUEBIRD 3 8-9	C Asmussen **7-2**
2	4	PERION 5 9-3	R Quinton **25-1**
3	1½	ORIENT 4 9-0	D McKeown **33-1**
4	1½	SHARP ROMANCE 5 9-3	P Cook **50-1**
5	1½	CLANTIME 6 9-3	W Carson **20-1**
6	nk	GAYANE 3 8-7	S Cauthen **15-8F**
7	nk	FLAWLESS IMAGE 3 8-6	C Roche **14-1**
8	2	SINGING STEVEN 3 8-9	B Rouse **33-1**
9	nk	GOVERNOR GENERAL 4 9-3	R Cochrane **14-1**
10	3	WHIPPER IN 3 8-9	K Darley **20-1**
11	hd	CAROL'S TREASURE 3 8-9	M Hills **33-1**
12		HALLGATE 4 9-3	G Starkey **100-30**

12 ran
TIME 65.25s
1st OWNER: R Sangster TRAINER: M V O'Brien, Ireland
2nd OWNER: E&B Productions (Theatre) Ltd TRAINER: G Lewis
3rd OWNER: Mrs R Watson TRAINER: R Whitaker
4th OWNER: Sheikh Mohamed Al Sabah TRAINER: J Bethell

○ **ROBERT SANGSTER**   Picture: TONY EDENDEN

Bluebird
(b c, 2-4-84)

		Nearctic
	Northern Dancer	Natalma
Storm Bird (b 1978)		New Providence
	South Ocean	Shining Sun
		Sir Gaylord
	Sir Ivor	Attica
Ivory Dawn (b 1978)		Tim Tam
	Dusky Evening	Home By Dark

Bred by F Seitz, in United States: $1,100,000 yearling Keeneland July Sale

Perion
(ch g, 30-3-82)

		Nearctic
	Northern Dancer	Natalma
Northfields (ch 1968)		Occupy
	Little Hut	Savage Beauty
		War Relic
	Relic	Bridal Colours
Relanca (ch 1968)		Prince Taj
	Garrucha	Gibellina

Bred by James Egan, in Ireland, 2,100gns 3yo 1985 Newmarket Horses in Training Autumn Sale

Orient
(b f, 5-6-83)

		Polic
	Polyfoto	Brabantia
Bay Express (b 1971)		Palestine
	Pal Sinna	Sinna
		Sing Sing
	Mummy's Pet	Money for Nothing
Gundi (b 1976)		Only for Life
	Little Bird	Cuckoo

Bred by Mr and Mrs R Watson

Sharp Romance
(b h, 15-4-82)

		Native Dancer
	Atan	Mixed Marriage
Sharpen Up (ch 1977)		Rockefella
	Rocchetta	Chambiges
		Sir Gaylord
	Sir Ivor	Attica
Sir Ivor's Favour (b 1973)		Irish Lancer
	Choke Point	Esoteric

Bred by W Little, in United States

9 July – Newmarket
GOOD TO FIRM 6f

Norcros July Cup

1st £48,900 **2nd** £18,375 **3rd** £8,887.50 **4th** £3,937.50

1		**AJDAL** 3 8-11	W R Swinburn **9-2**
2	_hd_	**GAYANE** 3 8-8	S Cauthen **7-2**
3	_1_	**BLUEBIRD** 3 8-11	C Asmussen **4-5F**
4	_3_	**RICH CHARLIE** 3 8-11	J Reid **66-1**
5	_shd_	**CRICKET BALL** 4 9-6	G W Moore **66-1**
6	_1½_	**A PRAYER FOR WINGS** 3 8-11	Pat Eddery **20-1**
7		**MISTER MAJESTIC** 3 8-11	R Cochrane **25-1**
8		**POLYKRATIS** 5 9-6	C Rutter **66-1**
9		**SHARP ROMANCE** 5 9-6	G Starkey **66-1**
10		**ORIENT** 4 9-3	D McKeown **20-1**
11		**GINNY BINNY** 4 9-3	W Carson **50-1**

11 ran
TIME 1m 11.02s
1st OWNER: Sheikh Mohammed TRAINER: M Stoute
2nd OWNER: N Phillips TRAINER: H Cecil
3rd OWNER: R Sangster TRAINER: M V O'Brien, Ireland
4th OWNER: R Sangster TRAINER: C Nelson

○ **WALTER SWINBURN** Picture: PRESS ASSOCIATION

Ajdal
(b c, 2-4-84)

		Nearco
	Nearctic	Lady Angela
Northern Dancer (b 1961)		Native Dancer
	Natalma	Almahmoud
		Native Dancer
	Raise A Dancer	Raise You
Native Partner (b 1966)		Tom Fool
	Dinner Partner	Bluehaze

Bred by R Wilson, in United States: sold privately as a yearling

Gayane
(b f, 24-1-84)

		Nearactic
	Northern Dancer	Natalma
Nureyev (b 1977)		Forli
	Special	Thong
		Sir Gaylord
	Habitat	Little Hut
Roussalka (b 1972)		Graustark
	Oh So Fair	Chandelle

Bred by Somerhall Bloodstock Limited

Bluebird
(b c, 2-4-84)

		Nearctic
	Northern Dancer	Natalma
Storm Bird (b 1978)		New Providence
	South Ocean	Shining Sun
		Sir Gaylord
	Sir Ivor	Attica
Ivory Dawn (b 1978)		Tim Tam
	Dusky Evening	Home By Dark

Bred by F Seitz, in United States: $1,100,000 yearling Keeneland July Sale

Rich Charlie
(ch c, 11-2-84)

		Will Somers
	Balidar	Violent Bank
Young Generation (b 1976)		Shantung
	Brig O'Doon	Tom O'Shanter
		Atan
	Sharpen Up	Rocchetta
Maiden Pool (ch 1976)		Reform
	Valiant Heart	Valdesta

Bred by Miss V Hermon-Hodge: 18,000gns yearling Doncaster St Leger Sale

20 August – York
GOOD TO SOFT   5f

William Hill
Sprint Championship

1st £55,467 **2nd** £20,661.10 **3rd** £9,843.05 **4th** £4,198.85

1		**AJDAL** 3 9-2	W R Swinburn **2-1**
2	*3*	**SIZZLING MELODY** 3 9-2	R Hills **33-1**
3	*nk*	**PERION** 5 9-6	S Cauthen **16-1**
4	*3*	**BLUEBIRD** 3 9-2	C Asmussen **5-4F**
5	*shd*	**COME ON CHASE ME** 3 9-2	K Darley **50-1**
6	*1*	**LA GRANDE EPOQUE** 3 8-13	B Thomson **100-1**
7		**TENUE DE SOIREE** 3 8-13	G W Moore **12-1**
8		**CLANTIME** 6 9-6	W Carson **50-1**
9		**RICH CHARLIE** 3 9-2	J Reid **20-1**
10		**TREASURE KAY** 4 9-6	Pat Eddery **9-1**
11		**ARAMOR** 3 9-2	T Ives **200-1**

11 ran
TIME 58.48s
1st OWNER: Sheikh Mohammed TRAINER: M Stoute
2nd OWNER: Mrs M Watt TRAINER: Lord John FitzGerald
3rd OWNER: E&B Productions (Theatre) Ltd TRAINER: G Lewis
4th OWNER: R Sangster TRAINER: M V O'Brien, Ireland

○ **AJDAL**   Picture: EDWARD WHITAKER

Ajdal   (b c, 2-4-84)

		Nearco
	Nearctic	Lady Angela
Northern Dancer (b 1961)		Native Dancer
	Natalma	Almahmoud
		Native Dancer
	Raise A Dancer	Raise You
Native Partner (b 1966)		Tom Fool
	Dinner Partner	Bluehaze

Bred by R Wilson, in United States: sold privately as a yearling

Sizzling Melody   (b c, 3-3-84)

		Tudor Minstrel
	Sing Sing	Agin The Law
Song (b 1966)		Vilmorin
	Intent	Under Canvas
		Will Somers
	Balliol	Violent Bank
Mrs Bacon (b 1975)		Major Portion
	Miss Dorothy	Tarara

Bred by Mrs B Skinner: 14,000gns Newmarket October Yearling Sale

Perion   (ch g, 30-3-82)

		Nearctic
	Northern Dancer	Natalma
Northfields (ch 1968)		Occupy
	Little Hut	Savage Beauty
		War Relic
	Relic	Bridal Colours
Relanca (ch 1968)		Prince Taj
	Garrucha	Gibellina

Bred by J Egan, in Ireland: 2,100gns 3yo 1985 Newmarket Autumn Horses in Training Sale

Bluebird   (b c, 2-4-84)

		Nearctic
	Northern Dancer	Natalma
Storm Bird (b 1978)		New Providence
	South Ocean	Shining Sun
		Sir Gaylord
	Sir Ivor	Attica
Ivory Dawn (b 1978)		Tim Tam
	Dusky Evening	Home By Dark

Bred by F Seitz, in United States: $1,100,000 yearling Keeneland July Sale

— CHAPTER 5 —

Milers

by GRAHAM DENCH

○ **WELL DONE:** Freddie Head salutes the victory of Miesque in the Breeders' Cup Mile at Hollywood Park.

Picture: STEVE STIDHAM

Milers

by GRAHAM DENCH

MIESQUE was crowned the season's undisputed champion miler at Hollywood Park in November with a performance as spectacular as any in her 12-race career.

She was simply magnificent, powering away in the straight for an impressive three-and-a-half length win from pacemaking Show Dancer in the Breeders' Cup Mile, in track record time.

Remarkably, her claim to the title was in doubt until that day, and had either Sonic Lady or Milligram come up with a similar performance, the honour could equally have been theirs.

But although Sonic Lady, the top specialist miler of 1986, stepped up considerably on her effort in the corresponding race a year earlier, she could finish only third.

And stablemate Milligram, whose participation was still in doubt hours before the event because of a bruised near-fore, ran no sort of race and finished last but one.

It was a brilliant performance from trainer Francois Boutin to get Miesque back in such outstanding condition after a season lasting nearly eight months, and it showed beyond much doubt that she simply had an 'off day' when beaten so decisively by

Milligram in the Queen Elizabeth II Stakes at Ascot in September.

Miesque had a superb season, winning six of her eight starts and establishing herself one of the outstanding milers of the decade and one of the very best miling fillies of post-war years.

There may have been one or two better individual performances at the trip since 1980 (a vintage year for milers with Miesque's sire Nureyev, Known Fact, Kris and Posse around), such as El Gran Senor's defeat of Chief Singer in the 1984 2,000 Guineas and Northjet's win from To-Agori-Mou and King's Lake in the 1981

Jacques le Marois. But no individual has repeatedly dealt so decisively with the best that could be mustered of both sexes and all ages.

Those who saw Miesque beat Milligram in the Prix Marcel Boussac at Longchamp on Arc day 1986 knew she would take some beating in the 1,000 Guineas, but her performance at Newmarket in the spring had to be seen to be believed. The breathtaking acceleration she showed to get out of difficulties and beat Milligram a length and a half became the hallmark of her subsequent successes.

Miesque went on to beat Sakura Reiko in the French Guineas at Longchamp, to account for Nashmeel in fast time in the Haras de Fresnay le Buffard Jacques le Marois at Deauville, and to beat Soviet Star in the Prix du Moulin at Longchamp, the sequence broken only by her second to Indian Skimmer in the Prix de Diane Hermes, where the combination of the longer trip and soft ground proved her undoing.

Her two-and-a-half length win over the French 2,000 Guineas winner Soviet Star in the Moulin was a tremendous effort, and not surprisingly she was a very warm order at 4-1 on for the Queen Elizabeth II Stakes, despite the opposition of Milligram and Sonic Lady and the absence of her regular partner Freddie Head, who was suspended and was replaced by Steve Cauthen.

Milligram, who had trotted up in the Coronation Stakes over the course and distance at the Royal meeting and had beaten Waajib and Star Cutter in the Waterford Crystal Mile at Goodwood, beat Miesque comprehensively by two and a half lengths, the result being in little doubt from the moment she took it up around two furlongs from home.

It could have been a truly exceptional performance from Milligram, and had there been no Breeders' Cup she would have had good claims to the milers' crown, particularly since Sonic Lady was well beaten in third, for she had clearly improved considerably since being beaten in the English and Irish 1,000 Guineas.

But with Miesque's turn of foot

○ **THAT'S THAT: Miesque, after winning the General Accident 1,000 Guineas at Newmarket.**
Picture: JOHN CROFTS

missing she surely was not herself, and the Breeders' Cup gave her the perfect opportunity of redeeming her reputation.

For Sonic Lady, winner of six of her eight starts as a three-year-old, the decision to stay in training was barely justified by her sole success in the Child Stakes at Newmarket's July meeting (sadly the last racecourse appearance of Ian Balding's Irish 1,000 Guineas winner Forest Flower), although her third in Hollywood Park, where Pincay took over from Swinburn and, like Milligram, she ran on medication, was a considerable step-up on her previous effort in the race.

With no worthwhile prizes to go for

until the second half of the season, Sonic Lady did not make her reappearance until Royal Ascot, when third to Then Again in the Queen Anne Stakes, and she had only four outings in all, her schedule being geared very much to the Breeders' Cup.

There was no single outstanding colt in the miling division, but Don't Forget Me's feat of winning both the English and Irish 2,000 Guineas (Right Tack was the last to achieve the double in 1969) deserved better than to be all but forgotten by Breeders' Cup day, by which time he was already standing alongside his sire Ahonoora at Coolmore stud.

A tremendously tough and resolute

galloper, and a great credit to his trainer Richard Hannon, Don't Forget Me was an unexceptional Guineas winner and had his limitations exposed when he was only fourth in both the St James's Palace Stakes at Royal Ascot and Prix Jacques le Marois at Deauville.

Luca Cumani's Half A Year, winner of the former, has better claims to being regarded the top male miler, for at Royal Ascot he beat almost the best field that could have been assembled at the time.

A winner merely of a maiden race and a minor event at Newmarket, Half A Year was taking on the Guineas winners Don't Forget Me and Soviet Star, as well as Risk Me, who had

○ **NO PEERS: Miesque is too good for the best French-trained milers. Top – she beats Soviet Star and Grecian Urn in the Prix du Moulin. Bottom – she races away from Nashmeel in the Prix du Haras de Fresnay-le-Buffard Jacques le Marois.**

Pictures: JOHN CROFTS

recently beaten Soviet Star in soft ground in the Prix Jean Prat Ecurie Fustok at Longchamp and went on to land the Grand Prix de Paris on the same course.

Half A Year won convincingly, if only narrowly, quickening well from a rails position under Ray Cochrane to win by a length from Soviet Star, with the other pair another neck and a short head away.

Soviet Star's jockey Starkey, who produced his mount on the wide outside, possibly underestimated the winner's turn of foot and concentrated too much on beating Don't Forget Me and Risk Me, but Half A Year still put up a marvellous performance for a colt having only his third race.

Unfortunately Half A Year fractured his off-fore cannon bone and was unable to race again, but he was reportedly recovering well during the winter and looks sure to be a force to reckon with when he returns to the fray.

Soviet Star confirmed the merit of the St James's Palace with wins in the Swettenham Stud Sussex Stakes at Goodwood and Prix de la Foret at Longchamp.

The Sussex Stakes, Europe's most valuable race over a mile, was at one time on the agenda for Sonic Lady, but she is owned by Sheikh Mohammed, who found himself with an embarassment of riches in the miling department. It made greater commercial sense to try and win such a prestigous race with one of his colts, Soviet Star, Star Cutter or Fair Judgment (winner of both his starts in Ireland including the Pacemaker International at Phoenix Park).

Despite his strong entry, Luca Cumani's Then Again, who had shown such a turn of foot to win the Lockinge and the Queen Anne, started odds on, but he finished only fifth, returning lame after losing the footing of his hind legs on the home turn, and he was not seen again.

Only five-year-old Hadeer prevented a clean sweep for the Sheikh, as Soviet Star got the better of Star Cutter by half a length, with Hadeer third and Fair Judgment fourth.

Hadeer, so successful in 1986, went

○ **BETTER THAN NONE: Half A Year gets through on the rails to win the St James's Palace Stakes from Soviet Star (right), Risk Me (yellow sleeves) and Don't Forget Me.**
Picture: JOHN CROFTS

through the season without a win, as did Bill Watts' tremendously popular old gelding Teleprompter.

Teleprompter ran well enough when runner-up to French challenger Vertige in the Trusthouse Forte Mile in the spring, when he lost out only in the dying strides, but his three subsequent efforts lacked sparkle and he was retired after finishing only fourth to Fair Judgment in the Pacemaker International at Phoenix Park in July, a race he had won twice before.

Alec Stewart's four-year-old Waajib, a close third there, won the newly-instituted Schweppes Golden Mile at Goodwood later that month (a handicap worth over £50,000 to the winner) and by the end of the season had grounds for being regarded the best domestically-trained older miler.

At Longchamp on Arc day he staged a tremendous late run to pip Shaikiya and a rejuvenated Shady Heights (who went on to gain two minor late-season successes) in the Prix du Rond-Point, and his trainer would have sent him to join Miesque and company at Hollywood Park had he been guaranteed a run.

But, realising Waajib would get a run only if one of the other European challengers dropped out, Stewart decided not to send him, wisely as things turned out.

Sonic Lady and Milligram remained in the States after the Breeders' Cup,

to visit Blushing Groom and Alleged respectively, but it is excellent news that Miesque stays in training.

She will not be out until the summer, since there are no worthwhile prizes for her, and her programme will be geared principally towards another crack at the Breeders' Cup, which will be held this time at Churchill Downs.

If all goes well with her, she should dominate the top mile races, but the likes of Half A Year, Soviet Star and Waajib, not to mention the up-and-coming-brigade of three-year-olds, will be doing their best to make sure she does not have things all her own way.□

○ **SONIC LADY wins the Child Stakes from Shaikiya.**   Picture: JOHN CROFTS

29 July – Goodwood
GOOD TO FIRM   1m

Swettenham Stud
Sussex Stakes

1st £152,800 **2nd** £56,970 **3rd** £27,185 **4th** £11,645

1		SOVIET STAR 3 8-10	G Starkey **3-1**
2	½	STAR CUTTER 4 9-7	S Cauthen **6-1**
3	1½	HADEER 5 9-7	Pat Eddery **33-1**
4	¾	FAIR JUDGMENT 3 8-10	C Asmussen **9-1**
5	1½	THEN AGAIN 4 9-7	R Cochrane **4-5F**
6	3	EFISIO 5 9-7	W Carson **33-1**
7	1½	LAURIES WARRIOR 3 8-10	M Roberts **66-1**

7 ran
TIME 1m 38.83s
1st OWNER: Sheikh Mohammed TRAINER: A Fabre, France
2nd OWNER: Sheikh Mohammed TRAINER: H Cecil
3rd OWNER: W Gredley TRAINER: C Brittain
4th OWNER: Sheikh Mohammed TRAINER: M V O'Brien, Ireland

○ **GREVILLE STARKEY**   Picture: TONY EDENDEN

Soviet Star
(b c, 20-4-84)

Nureyev (b 1977)	Northern Dancer	Nearctic
		Natalma
	Special	Forli
		Thong
Veruschka (b 1967)	Venture	Relic
		Rose O'Lynn
	Marie D'Anjou	Vandale
		Marigold

Bred by Kinderhill/Aron Association and Kinderhill Farm, in United States: $310,000 foal Keeneland Fall Sale

Star Cutter
(gr c, 8-3-83)

Star de Naskra (b or br 1975)	Naskra	Nasram
		Iskra
	Candle Star	Clandestine
		Star Minstrel
Axed (gr 1978)	Al Hattab	The Axe
		Abyssinia
	Ludham	Pampered King
		Sunward

Bred by Pillar Stud Inc, in United States: $190,000 yearling Keeneland Fall Sale

Hadeer
(ch h, 5-3-82)

General Assembly (ch 1976)	Secretariat	Bold Ruler
		Somethingroyal
	Exclusive Native	Raise A Native
		Exclusive
Glinting (ch 1975)	Crepello	Donatello
		Crepuscule
	Pelting	Vilmorin
		Firmament

Bred by Mr and Mrs D Wigan: 13,000gns 3yo Newmarket Autumn Horses in Training Sale

Fair Judgment
(b or br c, 26-3-84)

Alleged (b 1973)	Hoist The Flag	Tom Rolfe
		Wavy Navy
	Princess Pout	Prince John
		Determined Lady
Mystical Mood (b 1979)	Roberto	Hail To Reason
		Bramalea
	Mystery Mood	Night Invader
		Moaning Low

Bred by W S Farish, E Hodson and E Hodson Jr, in United States: $625,000 yearling Keeneland July Sale

26 September – Ascot
GOOD 1m

Queen Elizabeth II Stakes

1st £135,320.40 **2nd** £50,300.32 **3rd** £23,875.16 **4th** £10,088.12

1		**MILLIGRAM** 3 8-8	Pat Eddery **6-1**
2	2½	**MIESQUE** 3 8-8	S Cauthen **1-4F**
3	5	**SONIC LADY** 4 9-1	W R Swinburn **6-1**
4	4	**HOMO SAPIEN** 5 9-4	W Ryan **40-1**
5	25	**VERDANT BOY** 4 9-4	R Cochrane **250-1**

5 ran
TIME 1m 40.04s
1st OWNER: Helena Springfield Ltd TRAINER: M Stoute
2nd OWNER: S Niarchos TRAINER: F Boutin, France
3rd OWNER: Sheikh Mohammed TRAINER: M Stoute
4th OWNER: Mme M Niarchos TRAINER: H Cecil

⊙ **PAT EDDERY** Picture: TONY EDENDEN

Milligram (ch f, 3-4-84)

Mill Reef (b 1968)	Never Bend	Nasrullah
		Lalun
	Milan Mill	Princequillo
		Virginia Water
One In A Million (b 1976)	Rarity	Hethersett
		Who Can Tell
	Singe	Tudor Music
		Trial by Fire

Bred by J Weinfeld

Miesque (b f, 14–3-84)

Nureyev (b 1977)	Northern Dancer	Nearctic
		Natalma
	Special	Forli
		Thong
Pasadoble (b 1979)	Prove Out	Graustark
		Equal Venture
	Santa Quilla	Sanctus
		Neriad

Bred by Flaxman Holdings Limited, in the United States

Sonic Lady (b f, 15-2-83)

Nureyev (b 1977)	Northern Dancer	Nearctic
		Natalma
	Special	Forli
		Thong
Stumped (b 1977)	Owen Anthony	Proud Chieftain
		Oweninny
	Luckhurst	Busted
		Lucasland

Bred by J Allan Mactier: $500,000 yearling Fasig-Tipton Kentucky Summer Sale

Homo Sapien (b h, 24-3-82)

Lord Gayle (b 1965)	Sir Gaylord	Turn-to
		Somethingroyal
	Sticky Case	Court Martial
		Run Honey
Bold Caress (b 1975)	Bold Lad	Bold Ruler
		Barn Pride
	Time To Leave	Khalkis
		Dawn Chorus

Bred by Mrs R Marra: IR150,000gns Goffs October Yearling Sale

CHAPTER 6

Middle Distance

by PAUL JOHNSON

○ **PRETTY PICTURE: Indian Skimmer gives an early indication of her class by slamming Percy's Lass and 13 others in the Pretty Polly Stakes.**
Picture: EDWARD WHITAKER

Middle Distance

by PAUL JOHNSON

THERE CANNOT have been many harder acts to follow than Dancing Brave. Yet, despite the retirement of Guy Harwood's brilliant champion, racing's audience never yawned once. True, the limelight was shared a little more evenly but the show as a whole hardly suffered.

The previous year's top two-year-old, Reference Point, overcame adversity and did most to fill the void. But, in these times of commercial expediency, when a top-class middle-distance horse's career invariably terminates at the end of his or her three-year-old campaign, there was almost as much pleasure to be derived from the older horses Triptych, Moon Madness and Mtoto.

Mtoto, winner of a Haydock Park maiden race as a three-year-old and a five-length fourth to Sure Blade in the Queen Elizabeth II Stakes, had nothing to lose by racing as a four-year-old. His trainer Alec Stewart always believed him to be a class horse and his opinion was vindicated.

Moon Madness was a rather different proposition. Had he failed to train on, he could have been branded as a moderate St Leger winner and been shunned accordingly by breeders. He succeeded as a four-year-old, showing the speed to win the Grand Prix de Saint-Cloud from subsequent Arc runner-up Tony Bin as well as two other Pattern races. On fast ground he was a rattling good horse.

Contempt was the last thing bred by familiarity with the five-year-old Triptych, who seems to have contested most Pattern races in the last three years. The ubiquitous French-trained mare, a legend for her

○ **STANDING OUT: Indian Skimmer, who stamped her authority before injury put her on the sidelines until 1988.**

Picture: STEWART KENDALL

○ **EASY PICKINGS: Indian Skimmer strolls home from Bourbon Girl (right) and Mountain Memory in the Tattersalls Musidora Stakes.**
Picture: JOHN CROFTS

○ **INTERNATIONAL ASSIGNMENT: Triptych, from France, wins the Hanson Trust Coronation Cup from England's Rakaposhi King and Germany's Acatenango (left).**
Picture: JOHN CROFTS

durability, added five more Group One races to her stockpile.

If there were more like Triptych around, bookmakers might quickly become an endangered species. Japan Cup apart, whenever the opposition just missed being top of the top class, in she whizzed, like clockwork. And her honourabe thirds in the big ones, the Coral-Eclipse, the King George VI and the Arc de Triomphe, provided a feast of form-lines for hungry handicappers.

The Coral-Eclipse, at Sandown Park in July, brought together Reference Point and Triptych for the first time. Reference Point, hors de combat after a serious sinus operation until York's Mecca-Dante in May, won his trial when only three-parts fit and then gave a heart-warming display of courageous front-running to beat

Most Welcome in the Ever-Ready Derby at Epsom.

Triptych had trotted up in the Prix Ganay at Longchamp before blinding Rakaposhi King and Acatenango for speed over a mile and a half in the Hanson Trust Coronation Cup at the Derby meeting.

At Sandown the ground was faster than ideal for the Triptych and the trip shorter than optimal for the Derby winner, who had won going away at Epsom after looking in trouble two furlongs out. Neither could surmount those obstacles on guts alone.

Reference Point blazed his customary trail, dogged by Triptych's pacemaker Media Starguest, in an attempt to draw the sting out of

Triptych's finish. But his efforts were not enough to knock the stuffing out of the improving Mtoto, who had shown such a fine turn of speed to beat Allez Milord in the Brigadier Gerard Stakes at Sandown and Amerigo Vespucci in the Prince of Wales's Stakes at Royal Ascot.

Finding an extra gear for jockey Michael Roberts, Mtoto quickened to win his race inside the last furlong and then showed he had courage to match by holding Reference Point's renewed challenge by three-parts of a length, with Triptych a length and a half farther back in third.

It was Mtoto's finest hour. His performance at face value put him within two lengths of Dancing Brave

using Triptych as a yardstick.

Defeat caused Reference Point no loss of public esteem and he was sent off a hot favourite for the King George VI and Queen Elizabeth Diamond Stakes at Ascot later in the month. Triptych, inevitably, took him on again, joined by the St Leger runner-up Celestial Storm, who had been bedevilled by training setbacks but who had won the Princess of Wales's Stakes at Newmarket earlier in the month on his belated reappearance.

Unite and Bourbon Girl, first and second in both the Gold Seal Oaks and Gilltown Stud Irish Oaks represented the fillies' Classic form, while Budweiser Irish Derby winner

○ **JUST CHAMPION: Triptych continues her surge through the best races by beating Most Welcome (noseband) in the Dubai Champion Stakes.** Picture: DAVID HASTINGS

○ **MUD IN YOUR EYE: Triptych and Steve Cauthen had to overcome atrocious conditions in the Matchmaker International.**
Picture: GEORGE HERRINGSHAW

○ **POINTED REPLY: Mtoto foils Reference Point (left) in the Coral-Eclipse Stakes.** · Picture: JOHN CROFTS

Sir Harry Lewis attempted to make up the three and a half lengths he had been beaten by Reference Point at Epsom.

Moon Madness took his chance, even though his performance in the Hardwicke at the Royal meeting suggested the ground would be too soft for him; and Acatenango and Tony Bin came along despite form-book evidence that their prospects of even a place were slim.

On much softer ground than at Sandown, Reference Point took the race by the scruff of the neck from the off and ran his rivals ragged, extending his superiority over Triptych, who lost second place by a neck to Celestial Storm. The remainder, headed by Moon Madness, did not get a look in.

By any criterion, this was the day when Reference Point was seen at his best, and through Triptych, third to Dancing Brave a year earlier, he emerged a length and a half inferior to the 1986 champion.

By the time Reference Point and Triptych met again in the Trusthouse Forte Prix de l'Arc de Triomphe at Longchamp at the beginning of October they had picked up two more races apiece. Reference Point had gone through the virtual formalities of the Great Voltigeur at York and St Leger at Doncaster; Triptych, invigorated by a spell at Deauville, had clinically disposed of Ascot Knight in the Matchmaker

○ **NAP HAND: Infamy (right) makes it five wins in a row by beating On The Staff in the Cheveley Park Stud Sun Chariot Stakes.** Picture: JOHN CROFTS

International at York and Entitled in the Phoenix Champion Stakes.

Mtoto, out of action since Sandown, rejoined the fray, trying to prove himself as good at a mile and a half as he had been over two furlongs shorter in the Eclipse. But there was a new star waiting in the wings.

Reference Point attempted to dominate as usual but was a beaten horse early in the straight, surrendering as the French Derby runner-up Trempolino scorched to victory in course-record time.

Under a masterly ride from Pat Eddery, Trempolino won by two lengths from Tony Bin, with Triptych three lengths farther back in third, just in front of Mtoto. Reference Point hobbled home in eighth, ten lengths behind stablemate Orban, who had run away with the Hardwicke Stakes and who was to beat Tony Bin half a length in the Premio Roma at the back-end.

One of the most painful sights of the whole season was watching an abject-looking Reference Point run the gauntlet of French boos and catcalls as he returned vanquished to be unsaddled. Whether this moronic and futile display of ill-feeling was inspired by chauvinism or by the loss of francs on the odds-on favourite is debatable but such a wretched exhibition of bad sportsmanship thoroughly tarnished the running of Europe's top race.

Eddery compared the winner favourably with Dancing Brave, and the colt came close to achieving a notable double when pipped by Theatrical in the Breeders' Cup Turf at Hollywood Park in November when Yorkshire Oaks and Prix Vermeille winner Bint Pasha and Sir Harry Lewis both flopped.

○**SHINING BRIGHT: Celestial Storm opens his short season with a convincing win in the Princess of Wales's Stakes. Also pictured is third-placed Mountain Kingdom.**
Picture: ALAN JOHNSON

Reference Point, subsequently found to have been suffering from an abcess on his foot, had run his last race but Triptych was not finished yet by a long chalk.

She went to Newmarket later in October, as though she had never had a hard race in her life, and beat Derby second Most Welcome in the Dubai Champion Stakes, with a below-par Mtoto out with the washing in eighth.

By-passing the Breeders' Cup,

○ SWEEPING UP: Moon Madness has made all the running in the Hoover Cumberland Lodge Stakes and stays on to beat **Knockando and Mashkour (right).**

Picture: EDWARD WHITAKER

Triptych tackled the Japan Cup in Tokyo at the end of November, where she was joined by Moon Madness and Mountain Kingdom, who had finished a good second to Reference Point in the St Leger.

Triptych sailed through her prep race over nine furlongs, winning by five lengths but when it came to the crunch, neither she nor Moon Madness found the Fates smiling on them.

○ **WELL DONE: Michael Roberts shows his delight at Mtoto's victory in the Coral-Eclipse Stakes.** Picture: GERRY CRANHAM

○ **DEE NOTICE: Sir Harry Lewis comes into his own, flooring the odds laid on Shady Heights in the Dee Stakes.** Picture: ALEC RUSSELL

Moon Madness, upset by the antics of an American horse Akabir in the adjacent stall, started slowly and then used up his speed in the first half of the race. At one stage Pat Eddery managed to build up a seven-length advantage on Moon Madness but this was quickly whittled away in the home straight and the Arundel colt faded into fifth.

The cards fell wrongly for Triptych too. Sent off at 4-5, she hung all the way on the firm going and was blocked attempting to make her run up the inside in the home straight. Well though she finished, she was never going to catch her compatriot Le Glorieux, who beat her three lengths into fourth, half a length in front of Moon Madness, with Mountain Kingdom about a length farther back in seventh.

○ **BINT SMASHER: A Group One win for Bint Pasha as she beats Blessed Event in the Yorkshire Oaks.**   Picture: JOHN CROFTS

And so even France's Iron Lady ended her season with a disappointing defeat, as had almost all the other middle-distance luminaries.

One notable exception was Henry Cecil's filly Indian Skimmer, who was unbeaten in five starts as a three-year-old and put up one of the season's most spectacular performances when she trounced France's brilliant miler Miesque by four lengths in the Prix de Diane Hermès at Chantilly in June.

Sadly, she was unable to race again to test her superb turn of finishing speed against the top-ranking colts. Who knows? Granted a full campaign, she might even have upstaged her stable-companion Reference Point and his strong supporting cast.□

○ **SPEED COUNTS: Mtoto lands the Prince of Wales's Stakes at Royal Ascot from Amerigo Vespucci and Gesedeh.**

Picture: PHIL SMITH

4 June – Epsom
GOOD　　　　　　　　　　　　　　　　　1m 4f

Hanson Trust Coronation Cup

1st £54,759 **2nd** £20,297.20 **3rd** £9,586.10 **4th** £3,997.70

1		**TRIPTYCH** 5 8-11	A Cruz **4-5F**
2	¾	**RAKAPOSHI KING** 5 9-0	S Cauthen **100-30**
3	nk	**ACATENANGO** 5 9-0	Pat Eddery **100-30**
4	3	**MAYSOON** 4 8-11	W R Swinburn **25-1**
5	20	**NISNAS** 4 9-0	T Quinn **20-1**

5 ran
TIME 2m 35.97s
1st OWNER: A Clore TRAINER: P Biancone, France
2nd OWNER: Lord Howard de Walden TRAINER: H Cecil
3rd OWNER: Gestut Fahrhof TRAINER: H Jentzsch, Germany
4th OWNER: Maktoum Al-Maktoum TRAINER: M Stoute

○ **TONY CRUZ**　　　　　　　　　Picture: KICKSPORTS

Triptych
(b m, 19-4-82)

		Nasrullah
	Never Bend	Lulun
Riverman (b 1969)		Prince John
	River Lady	Nile Lily
		Turn-to
	Hail To Reason	Nothirdchance
Trillion (b 1974)		Tulyar
	Margarethen	Russ-Marie

Bred by N B Hunt and E Stephenson, in United States $2,150,000 yearling Keeneland July Sale

Rakaposhi King
(b h, 14-4-82)

		Crepello
	Busted	Sans Le Sou
Bustino (b 1971)		Doutelle
	Ship Yard	Paving Stone
		Sicambre
	Shantung	Barley Corn
Supper Time (b 1974)		Relic
	Curfew Bell	Twilight Hour

Bred by E Cooper Bland: 52,000 gns 3yo 1985 Newmarket December Sale

Acatenango
(ch h, 13-4-82)

		Birkhahn
	Literat	Lis
Surumu (ch 1974)		Reliance
	Surama	Suncourt
		Combat
	Aggressor	Phaetonia
Aggravate (b 1966)		Mr Jinks
	Raven Locks	Gentlemen's Relish

Bred by Gestut Fahrhof, in West Germany

Maysoon
(b f, 20-3-83)

		Honeyway
	Great Nephew	Sybil's Niece
Shergar (b 1978)		Val De Loir
	Sharmeen	Nasreen
		Derring-Do
	High Top	Camenae
Triple First (b 1974)		Grey Sovereign
	Field Mouse	Meadow Song

Bred by Hesmonds Stud Limited: 540,000gns yearling Newmarket Highflyer Sale

4 July – Sandown Park
GOOD TO FIRM   1m 2f

Coral-Eclipse Stakes

1st £116,100 **2nd** £43,580 **3rd** £21,040 **4th** £9,280

1		**MTOTO 4 9-7**	M Roberts **6-1**
2	¾	**REFERENCE POINT 3 8-8**	S Cauthen **Evens F**
3	1½	**TRIPTYCH 5 9-4**	A Cruz **4-1**
4	10	**BELLOTTO 3 8-8**	Pat Eddery **6-1**
5	¾	**MILLIGRAM 3 8-6**	W R Swinburn **10-1**
6	12	**GULF KING 3 8-8**	P Cook **150-1**
7		**SHARP NOBLE 5 9-7**	G Baxter **66-1**
8		**MEDIA STARGUEST 3 8-8**	D Boeuf **200-1**

8 ran
TIME 2m 4.33s
1st OWNER: Sheikh Ahmed Al-Maktoum TRAINER: A Stewart
2nd OWNER: L Freedman TRAINER: H Cecil
3rd OWNER: A Clore TRAINER: P Biancone, France
4th OWNER: K Abdullah TRAINER: J Tree

○ **ALEC STEWART**   Picture: TONY EDENDEN

Mtoto
(b c, 1-4-83)

Busted (b 1963)	Crepello	Donatello
		Crepuscule
	Sans Le Sou	Vimy
		Martial Loan
Amazer (br 1967)	Mincio	Relic
		Merise
	Alzara	Alycidon
		Zabara

Bred by J Moore: 110,000gns yearling Newmarket Highflyer Sale

Reference Point
(b c, 26-2-84)

Mill Reef (b 1968)	Never Bend	Nasrullah
		Lalun
	Milan Mill	Princequillo
		Virginia Water
Home On The Range (br 1978)	Habitat	Sir Gaylord
		Little Hut
	Great Guns	Busted
		Byblis

Bred by Cliveden Stud

Triptych
(b m, 19-4-82)

Riverman (b 1969)	Never Bend	Nasrullah
		Lalun
	River Lady	Prince John
		Nile Lily
Trillion (b 1974)	Hail To Reason	Turn-to
		Nothirdchance
	Margarethen	Tulyar
		Russ-Marie

Bred by N B Hunt and E Stephenson, in United States: $2,150,000 yearling Keeneland July Sale

Bellotto
(b c, 27-4-84)

Mr Prospector (b 1970)	Raise A Native	Native Dancer
		Raise You
	Gold Digger	Nashua
		Sequence
Shelf Talker (b 1968)	Tatan	The Yuvaraj
		Valkyrie
	Melody Mine	The Doge
		Magic Melody

Bred by Glen Hill Farm, in United States: $700,000 yearling Keeneland July Sale

25 July – Ascot
SOFT   1m 4f

King George VI & Queen Elizabeth Diamond Stakes

1st £182,790 **2nd** £68,219.50 **3rd** £32,609.75 **4th** £14,030.75

1		**REFERENCE POINT** 3 8-8	S Cauthen **11-10F**
2	*3*	**CELESTIAL STORM** 4 9-7	R Cochrane **5-1**
3	*nk*	**TRIPTYCH** 5 9-4	A Cruz **5-1**
4	*5*	**MOON MADNESS** 4 9-7	T Ives **25-1**
5	*hd*	**TONY BIN** 4 9-7	M Jerome **100-1**
6	*¾*	**ACATENANGO** 5 9-7	C Asmussen **18-1**
7	*shd*	**SIR HARRY LEWIS** 3 8-8	J Reid **10-1**
8	*15*	**UNITE** 3 8-6	W R Swinburn **13-2**
9		**BOURBON GIRL** 3 8-5	Pat Eddery **40-1**

9 ran
TIME 2m 34.63s
1st OWNER: L Freedman TRAINER: H Cecil
2nd OWNER: R Duchossois TRAINER: L Cumani
3rd OWNER: A Clore TRAINER: P Biancone, France
4th OWNER: Lavinia, Duchess of Norfolk TRAINER: J Dunlop

○ **HENRY CECIL**   Picture: GEORGE SELWYN

Reference Point   (b c, 26-2-84)

Mill Reef (b 1968)	Never Bend	Nasrullah
		Lalun
	Milan Mill	Princequillo
		Virginia Water
Home On The Range (br 1978)	Habitat	Sir Gaylord
		Little Hut
	Great Guns	Busted
		Byblis

Bred by Cliveden Stud

Celestial Storm   (b c, 18-4-83)

Roberto (b 1969)	Hail To Reason	Turn-to
		Nothirdchance
	Bramalea	Nashua
		Rarelea
Tobira Celeste (b 1971)	Ribot	Tenerani
		Romanella
	Heavenly Body	Dark Star
		Dangerous Dame

Bred by North Ridge Farm, in United States

Triptych   (b m, 19-4-82)

Riverman (b 1969)	Never Bend	Nasrullah
		Lalun
	River Lady	Prince John
		Nile Lily
Trillion (b 1974)	Hail To Reason	Turn-to
		Nothirdchance
	Margarethen	Tulyar
		Russ-Marie

Bred by N B Hunt and E Stephenson, in United States: $2,150,000 yearling Keeneland July Sale

Moon Madness   (b c, 1-3-83)

Vitiges (ch 1973)	Phaeton	Sicambre
		Pasquinade
	Vale	Verrieres
		Calliopsis
Castle Moon (ro 1975)	Kalamoun	Zeddaan
		Khairunissa
	Fotheringay	Right Royal
		La Fresnes

Bred by Lavinia, Duchess of Norfolk

18 August – York
SOFT 1m 2f 110y

Matchmaker International

1st £129,949.20 **2nd** £48,426.36 **3rd** £23,088.18 **4th** £9,868.26

1		TRIPTYCH 5 9-3	A Cruz **13-8F**
2	2	ASCOT KNIGHT 3 8-10	W R Swinburn **6-1**
3	3	SIR HARRY LEWIS 3 8-10	J Reid **9-1**
4	½	MOTLEY 3 8-10	C Asmussen **25-1**
5	12	MOST WELCOME 3 8-10	Pat Eddery **15-2**
6	3	LOVE THE GROOM 3 8-10	W Carson **11-2**
7	nk	ALLEZ MILORD 4 9-6	G Starkey **7-1**
8	6	CHAUMIERE 6 9-6	T Ives **100-1**
9	3	SHADY HEIGHTS 3 8-10	M Roberts **14-1**
10	12	SHARP NOBLE 5 9-6	A McGlone **40-1**

10 ran
TIME 2m 15.53s
1st OWNER: A Clore TRAINER: P Biancone, France
2nd OWNER: Maktoum Al-Maktoum TRAINER: M Stoute
3rd OWNER: H Kaskel TRAINER: B Hills
4th OWNER: N B Hunt TRAINER: J Pease, France

○ **PATRICK BIANCONE** Picture: KICKSPORTS

Triptych
(b m, 19-4-82)

		Nasrullah
Riverman (b 1969)	Never Bend	Nasrullah
		Lulun
	River Lady	Prince John
		Nile Lily
Trillion (b 1974)	Hail To Reason	Turn-to
		Nothirdchance
	Margarethen	Tulyar
		Russ-Marie

Bred by N B Hunt and E Stephenson, in United States $2,150,000 yearling Keeneland July Sale

Ascot Knight
(b c, 17-4-84)

		Nearctic
Danzig (b 1977)	Northern Dancer	Nearctic
		Natalma
	Pas De Nom	Admiral's Voyage
		Petitioner
Bambee T T (ch 1973)	Better Bee	Triplicate
		S Bee
	Golden Beach	Djeddah
		Wise Ally

Bred by R Anderson, in Canada: $1,400,000 yearling Keeneland July Sale

Sir Harry Lewis
(b c, 24-1-84)

		Tom Rolfe
Alleged (b 1974)	Hoist The Flag	Tom Rolfe
		Wavy Navy
	Princess Pout	Prince John
		Determined Lady
Sue Babe (b 1978)	Mr Prospector	Raise A Native
		Gold Digger
	Sleek Belle	Vaguely Noble
		Sleek Dancer

Bred by J Allen and Regent Farm, in United States

Motley
(b c, 19-5-84)

		Royal Charger
Best Turn (b 1966)	Turn-to	Royal Charger
		Source Sucree
	Sweet Clementine	Swaps
		Miz Clementine
Tipping Time (b 1966)	Commanding	Knight's Romance
		Qualify
	Tipping	Khaled
		Fast Tip

Bred by N B Hunt, in United States

18 August – York
SOFT   1m 4f

Yorkshire Oaks

1st £48,573 **2nd** £18,064.65 **3rd** £8,582.33 **4th** £3,625.02

1		**BINT PASHA** 3 9-0	....	T Quinn **5-1**
2	1½	**BLESSED EVENT** 3 9-0	....	C Asmussen **5-1**
3	6	**BOURBON GIRL** 3 9-0	....	Pat Eddery **3-1**
4	2	**THREE TAILS** 3 9-0	....	W Carson **5-2F**
5	7	**EUROBIRD** 3 9-0	....	T Ives **7-1**
6	2	**DEBACH DELIGHT** 3 9-0	....	R Cochrane **40-1**
7	25	**ISLAND LAKE** 3 9-0	....	W R Swinburn **14-1**
8	½	**SHINING WATER** 3 9-0	....	S Cauthen **14-1**
9	3	**KNOWN LINE** 3 9-0	....	W Newnes **16-1**

9 ran
TIME 2m 38.45s
1st OWNER: F Salman TRAINER: P Cole
2nd OWNER: R Sangster TRAINER: B Hills
3rd OWNER: K Abdullah TRAINER: B Hills
4th OWNER: Sheikh Mohammed TRAINER: J Dunlop

○ **RICHARD QUINN**   Picture: TONY EDENDEN

Bint Pasha   (ch f, 7-3-84)

		Raise A Native
	Exclusive Native	
		Exclusive
Affirmed (ch 1975)		Crafty Admiral
	Won't Tell You	
		Scarlet Ribbon
		Ribot
	Graustark	
		Flower Bowl
Icely Polite (b or br 1979)		Sir Gaylord
	Royal Kin	
		Myth

Bred by Spendthrift Thoroughbred Breeding No 1, in United States: $220,000 yearling Fasig-Tipton Saratoga Sale

Blessed Event   (b f, 9-3-84)

		Northern Dancer
	Nijinsky	
		Flaming Page
Kings Lake (b 1978)		Baldric
	Fish-Bar	
		Fisherman's Wharf
		Tamerlane
	Dschingis Khan	
		Donna Diana
Friedrichsruh (b 1974)		Kaiseradler
	Friedensbotschaft	
		Friedenstaube

Bred by Swettenham Stud, in Ireland

Bourbon Girl   (b f, 9-2-84)

		Northern Dancer
	Nijinsky	
		Flaming Page
Ile De Bourbon (b 1975)		Misti
	Roseliere	
		Peace Rose
		Sir Gaylord
	Habitat	
		Little Hut
Fleet Girl (ch 1975)		Vaguely Noble
	Fleet Noble	
		Limey's Moppet

Bred by Juddmonte Farms

Three Tails   (b f, 3-3-84)

		Hugh Lupus
	Hethersett	
		Bride Elect
Blakeney (b 1966)		Hornbeam
	Windmill Girl	
		Chorus Beauty
		Derring-Do
	High Top	
		Camenae
Triple First (b 1974)		Grey Sovereign
	Field Mouse	
		Meadow Song

Bred by Hesmond Stud Limited: 290,000gns yearling Newmarket Highflyer Sale

17 October – Newmarket
GOOD TO SOFT   1m 2f

Dubai Champion Stakes

1st £80,600 **2nd** £30,280 **3rd** £14,640 **4th** £6,480

1		**TRIPTYCH** 5 9-0	....	A Cruz **6-5F**
2	2½	**MOST WELCOME** 3 8-10	....	Pat Eddery **17-2**
3	4	**SAINT ANDREWS** 3 8-10	....	Y Saint-Martin **12-1**
4	1½	**BLESSED EVENT** 3 8-7	....	C Asmussen **40-1**
5	shd	**RISK ME** 3 8-10	....	S Cauthen **6-1**
6	hd	**DON'T FORGET ME** 3 8-10	....	W Carson **12-1**
7	4	**MILL NATIVE** 3 8-10	....	W Newnes **33-1**
8	7	**MTOTO** 4 9-3	....	M Roberts **4-1**
9	2	**AMERIGO VESPUCCI** 5 9-3	....	G Starkey **100-1**
10	5	**GENOBRA** 3 8-10	....	J Reid **200-1**
11		**BOLD ARRANGEMENT** 4 9-3	....	T Ives **100-1**

11 ran
TIME 2m 10.98s
1st OWNER: A Clore TRAINER: P Biancone, France
2nd OWNER: E Moller TRAINER: G Wragg
3rd OWNER: Mme L Volterra TRAINER: J Beguigne, France
4th OWNER: R Sangster TRAINER: B Hills

○ **ALAN CLORE**   Picture: JOHN CROFTS

Triptych
(b m, 19-4-82)

Riverman (b 1969)	Never Bend	Nasrullah
		Lulun
	River Lady	Prince John
		Nile Lily
Trillion (b 1974)	Hail To Reason	Turn-to
		Nothirdchance
	Margarethen	Tulyar
		Russ-Marie

Bred by N B Hunt and E Stephenson, in United States $2,150,000 yearling Keeneland July Sale

Most Welcome
(ch c, 15-4-84)

Be My Guest (ch 1974)	Northern Dancer	Nearctic
		Natalma
	What A Treat	Tudor Minstrel
		Rare Treat
Topsy (ch 1976)	Habitat	Sir Gaylord
		Little Hut
	Furioso	Ballymoss
		Violetta

Bred by White Lodge Stud Limited

Saint Andrews
(b c, 22-3-84)

Kenmare (gr 1975)	Kalamoun	Zeddaan
		Khairunissa
	Belle Of Ireland	Milesian
		Belle Of The Ball
Hardiona (ch 1976)	Hard To Beat	Hardicanute
		Virtuous
	Mapiona	Tompion
		Marion Delorme

Bred by P, R and A Azam, in France: 125,000fr yearling Deauville November Sale

Blessed Event
(b f, 9-3-84)

Kings Lake (b 1978)	Nijinsky	Northern Dancer
		Flaming Page
	Fish-Bar	Baldric
		Fisherman's Wharf
Friedrichsruh (b 1974)	Dschingis Khan	Tamerlane
		Donna Diana
	Friedensbotschaft	Kaiseradler
		Friedenstaube

Bred by Swettenham Stud, in Ireland

● **JUST STROLLING: Paean makes light work of the heavy ground in the Gold Cup at Royal Ascot.**
Picture: MARK CRANHAM

CHAPTER 7

Stayers

by RON COX

○ **EARLY STRIKE: Sadeem reappears to beat Paean (left) and Kudz in the Insulpak Sagaro Stakes.**   Picture: GEORGE SELWYN

Stayers

by RON COX

A CRYSTAL BALL might have been of greater assistance than the form book when thoughts turned to the major staying races at the beginning of the 1987 Flat season, since there was no obvious successor when Longboat retired to stud in Australia.

By the end of the year matters were far from crystal clear. Gold Cup hero Paean had run his last race at Ascot; other pretenders had fallen by the wayside, and Buckley, winner of the Doncaster Cup and Jockey Club Cup, was beaten in handicap company on his final outing.

First clues came at Ascot, where the finish of the Insulpak Sagaro Stakes was fought out by Sadeem and Paean. Henry Cecil's Paean, with the benefit of a previous outing under a big weight in Newmarket handicap company was narrowly preferred in the betting, but it was Guy Harwood's lightly-raced colt Sadeem who produced the better turn of foot to beat Paean, on whom Steve Cauthen had gone for home nearly half a mile out, by three-parts of a length.

In less than two months they crossed swords again, but the circumstances were vastly different.

Sadeem, who had shown his ability to quicken at the finish of a fast-run race and shaped as though he would stay beyond two miles, next met Cecil's principal Cup candidate Bonhomie, who hit rock bottom in Sandown's Mappin and Webb Henry II Stakes, back-pedalling in the straight to finish a distant fifth. Sadeem, however, was unable to capitalise on the situation as Clive Brittain's Saronicos, moving up from the handicap ranks, got first run and held him at bay by a length and a half in record time. Giving 3lb, Sadeem was still the best horse at the weights and more than ever looked sure to

○ **HEADS DOWN: Saronicos battles on to beat Sadeem in the Mappin & Webb Henry II Stakes.**   Picture: ALAN JOHNSON

appreciate an even longer trip.

By contrast, the Yorkshire Cup 11 days earlier was very slowly run.

It signalled the beginning of the end for Valuable Witness, who trailed in sixth behind Verd-Antique. Ten days later in the Prix du Cadran at Longchamp, a lack-lustre fourth behind up-and-coming Spanish-trained Royal Gait was the best Valuable Witness could manage. Yet Valuable Witness started favourite for the Gold Cup less than a month later.

As the rain fell on Ascot so the money poured on Pat Eddery's mount who, ironically, would have run in the race with a major chance the previous year, when it was first opened to geldings, had the ground been in his favour. This time conditions were right, but sadly Valuable Witness was not. From five furlongs out, where Cauthen sent Paean past pace-making Caesar Imperator, the result was never in doubt. Revelling in the muddy ground, Paean steadily increased his lead on the home turn and came away in the straight for a stunning 15 lengths victory. It was the greatest winning margin since St Simon swept home by 20 lengths 100 years before.

○ **ALL LINED UP: Paean poses for the cameras after winning the Gold Cup at Royal Ascot.**   Picture: TONY EDENDEN

○ **TREBLE TONIC: Buckley completes a hat-trick by taking the Jockey Club Cup from Daarkom (left) and Lemhill (centre).**   Picture: ALAN JOHNSON

Sadeem, nothing like as effective in the testing ground, won the battle for runner-up honours with Saronicos, who plugged on to finish two lengths third. Valuable Witness, whose retirement was announced afterwards, showed none of his old sparkle and trailed in fourth. Cauthen switched from Bonhomie to Paean only hours before the race, his tactics could not be faulted. Bonhomie proved incapable of handling the heavy ground; he beat only Authaal and had run his last race.

Only days later Paean, a big, attractive son of Bustino, was found to be lame. A bowed tendon was diagnosed and retirement became a formality. Sold to a syndicate headed by Ronald Shaw, Paean stands at the Greenville House Stud, County Waterford.

Gold Cup form was not put to the test in the Goodwood Cup, where only five went to post, and on the strength of his close second to Arden

○ **UP FOR THE CUP: Honours in the Doncaster Cup go to Buckley, who beats the Sheikh Mohammed pair Sadeem and Kudz.**
Picture: JOHN CROFTS

in the Queen's Vase, John Dunlop's three-year-old Sergeyevich started favourite. The race provided a stirring finish and a record time. Sergeyevich, señt to the front two furlongs out by Willie Carson, did just enough to hold off Ascot Stakes third El Conquistator by three-parts of a length and they were well clear of the others.

Sergeyevich became the first of his age to win the Goodwood Cup since Proverb in 1973. But his victory was perhaps better remembered for the post-race remarks of Dunlop, a member of the British Pattern Race Committee, who called for a reduction of all Cup races to two miles, arguing that this would result in more competitive racing without sacrificing stamina.

Sergeyevich was the hot favourite for the Doncaster Cup, which also featured Sadeem, fifth in the 15-furlong Prix Kergorlay, Kudz for Henry Cecil, and the improving handicapper Buckley.

Two furlongs out an uneventful race came to life. Sadeem, who had been switched round tiring horses early in the straight, threw down a strong challenge on the outside but in doing so edged left and tightened up

○ **ALL THE WAY: Orban brings his stamina into play in the Hardwicke Stakes.**
Picture: PHIL SMITH

○ **NOT TOO FAR: Sergeyevich stretches out to beat El Conquistador in the Goodwood Cup.** Picture: JOHN CROFTS

Sergeyevich. Neither Kudz, trying for a run on the rails, nor Buckley had much room to manoeuvre. Sergeyevich could find no more, but when a gap did appear for Buckley entering the final furlong, he quickened smartly and held the persistent Sadeem (gave 3lbs) by a neck. Kudz was one and a half lengths away third, with Sergeyevich fourth.

Three weeks later Sadeem was out for revenge in the Jockey Club Cup at Newmarket, where he tackled Buckley at levels, Daarkom, who had beaten Buckley into sixth spot in the Ebor. Dry Dock, third in the St Leger; March Stakes winner Ala Hounak, and Angel City, game winner of the Lonsdale Stakes at York, comprised a powerful three-year-old challenge. Kudz, Saronicos and that doughty battler Lemhill were also present. But Buckley and Ray Cochrane were again equal to the task, striding clear on meeting the rising ground to put two lengths between themselves and Daarkom (rec. 3lbs).

Lemhill, running an excellent race, kept on well to narrowly deprive Angel City of third. Sadeem ran as though over the top; Dry Dock and Ala Hounak were other disappointments, but the former reportedly finished lame and it may be premature to write him off.

Luca Cumani had no hesitation in nominating the £40,000-added Cesarewitch as next stop for Buckley. The weights were already published and, with no penalty, Buckley looked the proverbial handicap 'snip'. But, not for the first time, the Handicapper and bookmakers were let off the hook. A substantial rise in the weights did not help Buckley and the dead ground finished him off. He struggled home under 9st 10lb in sixth place behind runaway eight-length winner Private Audition.

There seems little doubt that Buckley will play a prominent role in the Cup races in 1988, but the unpredictable British climate will have to be taken into account. Buckley is best on a sound surface, whereas Daarkom relishes some cut.

Dry Dock may yet make the grade provided he returns sound, and across the Channel there is a rising French star in Royal Gait. Bred in England and Spanish-trained when winning the Cadran, he joined John Fellows towards the end of the year and signed off with a spectacular eight-length victory in the Prix Royal-Oak. Another wet summer would bring him into the Gold Cup line-up with a major chance.

So despite John Dunlop's plea, there is every prospect of a competitive season ahead among the stayers. But the fact remains they are likely to remain flat racing's poor relations for the foreseeable future.

Even owner Lord Howard de Walden could not find a place for Paean alongside Derby winner Slip Anchor at his Plantation Stud. Like Le Moss and Buckskin, two notable Cup winners also standing in Ireland, Paean is at risk of becoming a sire of jumpers and all too soon a forgotten name. But there are 15 good reasons why Paean and the 1987 Gold Cup should be remembered. Let's wish them both well.□

18 June – Royal Ascot
SOFT   2m 4f

Gold Cup

1st £53,656.20 **2nd** £19,966.96 **3rd** £9,495.98 **4th** £4,032.86

1		**PAEAN** 4 9-0	S Cauthen **6-1**
2	*15*	**SADEEM** 4 9-0	G Starkey **7-2**
3	*2*	**SARONICOS** 4 9-0	C Asmussen **7-1**
4	*4*	**VALUABLE WITNESS** 7 9-0	Pat Eddery **100-30F**
5	*7*	**SATCO** 4 9-0	E Saint-Martin **6-1**
6	*3*	**CAESAR IMPERATOR** 4 9-0	R Cochrane **66-1**
7		**BONHOMIE** 4 9-0	W Ryan **8-1**
8		**AUTHAAL** 4 9-0	C Roche **9-1**

8 ran
TIME 4m 33.26s
1st OWNER: Lord Howard de Walden TRAINER: H Cecil
2nd OWNER: Sheikh Mohammed TRAINER: G Harwood
3rd OWNER: A Richards TRAINER: C Brittain
4th OWNER: S Niarchos TRAINER: J Tree

○ **LORD HOWARD de WALDEN**   Picture: TONY EDENDEN

Paean   (ch c, 4-4-83)

Bustino (b 1971)	Busted	Crepello
		Sans Le Sou
	Ship Yard	Doutelle
		Paving Stone
Mixed Applause (b 1976)	Nijinsky	Northern Dancer
		Flaming Page
	My Advantage	Princely Gift
		My Game

Bred by Lord Howard de Walden

Sadeem   (ch c, 25-5-83)

Forli (ch 1963)	Aristophanes	Hyperion
		Commotion
	Trevisa	Advocate
		Veneta
Miss Mazepah (b 1972)	Nijinsky	Northern Dancer
		Flaming Page
	Monade	Klairon
		Mormyre

Bred by King Ranch Inc, in United States: $155,000 yearling Fasig-Tipton Kentucky Summer Sale

Saronicos   (b or br c, 17-4-83)

Dalsaan (b 1977)	Habitat	Sir Gaylord
		Little Hut
	Dumka	Kashmir
		Faizebad
Gulf Bird (ch 1971)	Gulf Pearl	Persian Gulf
		Nan
	Cherry Bird	Abernant
		Jenny Wren

Bred by M O'Brien, in Ireland: 33,000gns Newmarket October Yearling Sale

Valuable Witness   (b g, 14-6-80)

Val De L'Orne (b 1972)	Val De Loir	Vieux Manoir
		Vali
	Aglae	Armistice
		Aglae Grace
Friendly Witness (b or br 1971)	Northern Dancer	Nearctic
		Natalma
	Alibi	Birkhahn
		Alouette

Bred by E P Taylor, in United States: $40,000 yearling Fasig-Tipton Kentucky Summer Sale

CHAPTER 8

Two-Year-Olds

by MELVYN DAY

● **TABLE TOPPER: Warning earns highest two-year-old honours by beating Always Fair in the Laurent Perrier Champagne Stakes.**

Picture: GERRY CRANHAM

○ **NO PROBLEMS:** Warning comfortably lands the odds laid on him in the P & OCL Richmond Stakes from Bellefella (left).
Picture: EDWARD WHITAKER

Two-Year-Olds

by MELVYN DAY

WARNING, unbeaten in four starts, earned the right to be regarded as the leading juvenile of 1987 with his performance in Doncaster's Champagne Stakes.

Guy Harwood's youngster made an impressive debut at Salisbury in June, winning easily by five lengths, and on his return to the Wiltshire track the following month, effortlessly doubled

his winning margin against three moderate opponents.

At the Goodwood festival meeting later in July he showed an exceptional turn of foot to beat six opponents in

○ **SO FAR, SO GOOD: Diminuendo went through her first season unbeaten in four races. Above – she is pushed out to beat What Speed in the Ewar Stud Farm Stakes at Newmarket. Below – she goes on to finish two lengths clear of Haiati in the Hoover Mile at Ascot.**   Pictures: ALAN JOHNSON/ALEC RUSSELL

the P & OCL Richmond Stakes. Already regarded by many as a leading contender for the juvenile crown, he underlined his potential as a high-class colt.

In what was to be his fourth and final outing of the season, in the Laurent Perrier Champagne Stakes, Warning took on Always Fair, who was unbeaten in his previous three starts, including the Coventry Stakes at Royal Ascot and Acomb Stakes at York. Opinion in the market was equally divided and both horses started at even money.

Steve Cauthen, deputising for the suspended Walter Swinburn on Always Fair, took up the running at halfway but Pat Eddery on Warning was tracking him and appearing to be going much better. At the furlong marker Eddery shook the reins and Warning immediately quickened clear, winning tidily by one and a half lengths. It was the best juvenile performance of the season.

Highest-rated filly is the French-trained Ravinella, who is placed just 1lb behind Warning. She started her career by winning a newcomers' event at Deauville in August and followed up by taking the Prix d'Arenberg at Longchamp in September by five lengths in a fast time. However, her best performance came on her third and final outing, in the Tattersalls Cheveley Park Stakes.

Ela Romara, then favourite for the 1,000 Guineas following her easy three-length win in the Lowther Stakes at York, was made even money favourite, with Ravinella at 9-2 and Prix Morny winner First Waltz at 11-2. Ravinella gave a breathtaking performance, coming from last to first. She sprinted past First Waltz in the final half-furlong to gain a comfortable one and a half lengths success. Ela Romara was beaten another two lengths into third, with Babita one and a half lengths away

○ **PAUSE FOR THOUGHT: Reprimand, at long odds-on for the Scottish Equitable Gimcrack Stakes, has to be shaken up to get the better of Intimidate (right).**

Picture: ALAN JOHNSON

○ **RAIDING PARTY: French-trained fillies are first and second in the Tattersalls Cheveley Park Stakes, as Ravinella (right) beats First Waltz. Ela Romara (centre) is third and Babita fourth.**   Picture: ALAN JOHNSON

fourth and Timely a further length back in fifth.

Babita is a useful yardstick in linking the fillies and the colts. In her previous race over six furlongs she finished one and a half lengths behind Magic Of Life, who in turn was beaten by an identical margin by comfortable winner Diminuendo in the Hillsdown Cherry Hinton Stakes at Newmarket's July meeting.

Magic Of Life disappointed on her next start but then went on to win a minor event at Windsor before beating Intimidate (gave 5lb) by threequarters of a length in the Rokeby Farms Mill Reef Stakes. In his previous race Intimidate had run Reprimand to one and a half lengths in the Scottish Equitable Gimcrack Stakes at York.

Diminuendo shares third place with stable-companion Sanquirico; both are unbeaten, in four and five outings respectively.

After completing her hat-trick in the Cherry Hinton, Diminuendo rounded off a fine first season by winning the Hoover Mile at Ascot, beating Haiati (rec 3lb) by two lengths, with Ashayer (rec 3lb) threequarters of a length back in third and Obeah (levels) a further three lengths away in fourth. The form of this race looks solid, as Obeah had previously won the Waterford Candelabra Stakes at Goodwood and Ashayer went on to win the Prix Marcel Boussac at Longchamp on Arc day.

Sanquirico's high rating was achieved on his final outing, in the Royal Lodge Stakes at Ascot, where he bravely repelled all challengers and had a head to spare over Undercut, with Alwuhush (rec 3lb) a neck away in third, Emmson (rec 3lb) a length back in fourth and Always Fair a disappointing four lengths further back in fifth.

Undercut did not race again but

○ **CUT ABOVE: Sanquirico has made all the running in the Royal Lodge Stakes and is about to hold Undercut (centre). Alwuhush (not in picture) came along to deprive Emmson (second left) of third place.** Picture: ALAN JOHNSON

○ **IN THE PICTURE: Sanquirico (second right) heads the line–up in the Anglia TV July Stakes.** Picture: EDWARD WHITAKER

Alwuhush and Emmson contested the William Hill Futurity at Doncaster, where Henry Cecil's Salse, winner of his previous three races, was 4-7 favourite. Alwuhush ran appallingly and finished last of six to Emmson, who beat Sheriff's Star by a neck, with Salse two lengths back in third. Emmson improved about 5lb on his Royal Lodge form and Salse was judged to have run 3lb below his previous best.

Sharing the same mark as Reprimand (whose Dewhurst Stakes outing was sadly called off) and Undercut is the French colt Fijar Tango, who won the Grand Criterium at Longchamp, beating Pasakos by two lengths, with the fillies Most Precious (rec 3lb) and Seattle Sangue (rec 3lb) two lengths further back in third and fourth.

Most Precious did not run up to her best here in the very soft ground. She had previously run Common Grounds to a neck in the Prix de la Salamandre, and Common Grounds recorded a rating of 120 when beaten a short neck by First Waltz (rec 3lb) in the Prix Morny at Deauville.

Balawaki, who had finished two lengths behind Common Grounds (gave 3lb) in the Prix Morny, also provides a useful link between English and French form. In his previous race Balawaki had beaten Oakworth (gave 1lb) by a head in the Prix Robert Papin. Oakworth had earlier finished a length second to Always Fair in the Coventry Stakes and on his final start was beaten a neck by Digamist in the Heinz "57" at Phoenix Park, so there exists a useful yardstick to the Irish juveniles, and for the second year running the Irish were not outstanding.

Leading Irish juvenile is Caerwent,

Vincent O'Brien's easy winner of the National Stakes at The Curragh in September, when he beat the English challenger Acajou by five lengths. Best of the rest appears to be Trusted Partner (113), an easy four-length winner of the C.L. Weld Park Stakes, and Peace Girl (110), who beat Classic Ruler (rec 1lb) by half a length in the Nishapour Curragh Stakes.

Not far behind the best of the English-trained two-year-olds are Gallic League, Glacial Storm and Carmelite House.

Gallic League won four of his six starts, including the Flying Childers Stakes at Doncaster's St Leger meeting and the Tattersalls Middle Park, in which he gained a comfortable one and a half length win over Rahy (111).

Glacial Storm's rating was earned

when beating Zelphi (114) by a length in the Matchmaker Horris Hill Stakes on heavy ground at Newbury in October.

Carmelite House — one of five Henry Cecil juveniles in my top 20 — underlined his Classic prospects with smooth wins at Kempton Park and Newmarket, on the latter occasion having six lengths to spare over his nearest rival, Mulia (rec 7lb).

Several horses lower down the handicap have every prospect of improving.

Tralos (108), trained by Guy Harwood, is considered in the same league as stable-companions Warning (126) and Undercut (121), though on the evidence of what he has beaten in his two races to date he cannot be rated within 13lb of that pair. Nevertheless Tralos won both his

● FLEET OF FOOT: Gallic League is in front from start to finish of the Flying Childers Stakes, with Tommy Daly (blinkers) closest to him at the winning post.

Picture: JOHN CROFTS

○ **ONE FOR ENGLAND: Ashayer plunders the Prix Marcel Boussac at Longchamp from Riviere d'Or and Harmless Albatross.**
Picture: PHIL SMITH

starts very easily and has to be respected.

Moogie (109) is another who must be considered a candidate for next season. She was an easy four-length winner of her maiden at Haydock Park in July and went on to beat Timely (rec 4lb) by a length at York in September. Timely was then narrowly beaten in the Moyglare Stud Stakes at The Curragh and ran a creditable fifth to Ravinella in the Cheveley Park.

Doyoun (108), trained by Michael Stoute, is another to keep an eye on in '88. He ran out a comfortable winner of a well-contested maiden race on his only start and has scope for further improvement. So too does Al Mufti (106), comfortable winner of the Duke Of Edinburgh Stakes, a race for newcomers, at Ascot in October.□

Rating	horse's name	sex	trained
126	Warning	C	GB
125	Ravinella	F	FR
122	Diminuendo	F	GB
122	Sanquirico	C	GB
121	Fijar Tango	C	FR
121	Reprimand	C	GB
121	Undercut	C	GB
120	Caerwent	C	IRE
120	Common Grounds	C	FR
120	Emmson	C	GB
119	Sheriff's Star	C	GB
118	First Waltz	F	FR
118	Gallic League	C	GB
118	Salse	C	GB
117	Always Fair	C	GB
117	Glacial Storm	C	GB
117	Alwuhush	C	GB
117	Pasakos	C	FR
117	Intimidate	C	GB
116	Carmelite House	C	GB

30 September – Newmarket
GOOD TO FIRM 6f

Tattersalls Cheveley Park Stakes

1st £53,292 **2nd** £19,666.10 **3rd** £9,608.05 **4th** £4,203.85

1		**RAVINELLA** 2 8-11	G W Moore	**9-2**
2	1½	**FIRST WALTZ** 2 8-11	M Philipperon	**11-1**
3	2	**ELA ROMARA** 2 8-11	Paul Eddery	**Evens F**
4	1½	**BABITA** 2 8-11	G Stevens	**100-1**
5	1	**TIMELY** 2 8-11	S Cauthen	**9-1**
6	4	**AIM FOR THE TOP** 2 8-11	W R Swinburn	**8-1**
7	¾	**RIMSH** 2 8-11	Pat Eddery	**12-1**
8		**MADAME DE SEUL** 2 8-11	P Bloomfield	**20-1**

8 ran
TIME 1m 14.26s
1st OWNER: Ecurie Aland TRAINER: Mme C Head, France
2nd OWNER: Sir Robin McAlpine TRAINER: E Bartholomew, France
3rd OWNER: E Moller TRAINER: G Wragg
4th OWNER: Saeed Manana TRAINER: C Brittain

○ **CRIQUETTE HEAD** Picture: MARK LEECH

Ravinella
(b f, 25-4-85)

		Native Dancer
Mr Prospector (b 1970)	Raise A Native	Native Dancer
		Raise You
	Gold Digger	Nashua
		Sequence
Really Lucky (b 1978)	Northern Dancer	Nearctic
		Natalma
	Realty	Sir Ivor
		Reveille

Bred by Societe Aland, in United States

First Waltz
(b f, 25-4-85)

Green Dancer (b 1972)	Nijinsky	Northern Dancer
		Flaming Page
	Green Valley	Val De Loir
		Sly Pola
Fell Sweep (b 1979)	Huntercombe	Derring-Do
		Ergina
	Syrona	Salvo
		Matchmo

Bred by Sir Robin McAlpine, in France

Ela Romara
(b f, 23-4-85)

Ela-Mana-Mou (b 1976)	Pitcairn	Petingo
		Border Bounty
	Rose Bertin	High Hat
		Wide Awake
Romara (ch 1976)	Bold Lad	Bold Ruler
		Barn Pride
	Peaceful	Crepello
		Look Away

Bred by White Lodge Stud Limited

Babita
(28-4-85)

Habitat (b 1966)	Sir Gaylord	Turn-to
		Somethingroyal
	Little Hut	Occupy
		Savage Beauty
Barbara Zapolia (b 1974)	Great Nephew	Honeyway
		Sybil's Niece
	Bonifacia	Botticelli
		Buontalenta

Bred by Spendthrift Farm, in Ireland: $35,000 yearling Keeneland July Sale

3 October – Newmarket
FIRM   6f

Tattersalls Middle Park Stakes

1st £46,224 **2nd** £17,256.70 **3rd** £8,253.35 **4th** £3,555.95

1		**GALLIC LEAGUE 2** 9-0	S Cauthen **6-4F**
2	1½	**RAHY 2** 9-0	W R Swinburn **9-4**
3	4	**PERSIAN HEIGHTS 2** 9-0	R Cochrane **7-2**
4	hd	**GOLDEN GARTER 2** 9-0	W Carson **50-1**
5	2½	**DIGAMIST 2** 9-0	Pat Eddery **5-1**

5 ran
TIME 1m 13.95s
1st OWNER: R Sangster TRAINER: B Hills
2nd OWNER: Maktoum Al-Maktoum TRAINER: M Stoute
3rd OWNER: Prince Yazid Saud TRAINER: G Huffer
4th OWNER: Tony Wong TRAINER: M Brittain

○ **BARRY HILLS**   Picture: GEORGE HERRINGSHAW

Gallic League
(br c, 24-3-85)

Welsh Saint (b 1966)	St Paddy	Aureole
		Edie Kelly
	Welsh Way	Abernant
		Winning Ways
Red Rose Bowl (gr 1980)	Dragonara Palace	Young Emperor
		Rubys Princess
	Loren	Crocket
		Gallissa

Bred by N Abbott: 24,000gns Newmarket October Yearling Sale

Rahy
(ch c, 18-2-85)

Blushing Groom (ch 1974)	Red God	Nasrullah
		Spring Run
	Runaway Bride	Wild Risk
		Aimee
Glorious Song (b 1976)	Halo	Hail To Reason
		Cosmah
	Ballade	Herbager
		Miss Swapsco

Bred by Hill 'N Dale Farm, in United States: $2,000,000 yearling Keeneland July Sale

Persian Heights
(ch c, 29-4-85)

Persian Bold (br 1975)	Bold Lad	Bold Ruler
		Barn Pride
	Relkarunner	Relko
		Running Blue
Ready And Willing (b 1971)	Reliance	Tantieme
		Relance
	No Saint	Narrator
		Vellada

Bred by The Bamstead Manor Stud: 25,000gns yearling Newmarket Highflyer Sale

Golden Garter
(ch c, 9-4-85)

Ballacashtal (ch 1977)	Vice Regent	Northern Dancer
		Victoria Regina
	Swiss Roll	Counterpoint
		Revolve
Blue Garter (ch 1978)	Targowice	Round Table
		Matriarch
	Blue Rag	Ragusa
		Blue Butterfly

Bred by J Danks: 4,000gns Newmarket October Yearling Sale

24 October – Doncaster
GOOD   1m

William Hill Futurity Stakes

1st £48,384 **2nd** £18,177.20 **3rd** £8,788.60 **4th** £3,890.20

1		EMMSON 2 9-0	W Carson **7-1**
2	*nk*	SHERIFF'S STAR 2 9-0	A Clark **17-2**
3	*2*	SALSE 2 9-0	S Cauthen **4-7F**
4	*10*	TOP CLASS 2 9-0	G Starkey **66-1**
5	*nk*	ILISHPOUR 2 9-0	R Cochrane **12-1**
6	*3*	ALWUHUSH 2 9-0	T Ives **3-1**

6 ran
TIME 1m 42.66s
1st OWNER: Sir Michael Sobell TRAINER: W Hern
2nd OWNER: Lavinia, Duchess of Norfolk TRAINER: Lady Herries
3rd OWNER: Sheikh Mohammed TRAINER: H Cecil
4th OWNER: M Lemos TRAINER: C Brittain

○ **DICK HERN**   Picture: MARK LEECH

Emmson
(b c, 11-2-85)

Ela-Mana-Mou (b 1976)	Pitcairn	Petingo
		Border Bounty
	Rose Bertin	High Hat
		Wide Awake
Happy Kin (b 1975)	Bold Hitter	Bold Ruler
		Batter Up
	Gay Niece	Sir Gaylord
		Great Niece

Bred by Ballymacoll Stud Farm Limited

Sheriff's Star
(gr c, 27-4-85)

Posse (ch 1977)	Forli	Aristophanes
		Trevisa
	In Hot Pursuit	Bold Ruler
		Lady Be Good
Castle Moon (ro 1975)	Kalamoun	Zeddaan
		Khairunissa
	Fotheringay	Right Royal
		La Fresnes

Bred by Lavinia, Duchess of Norfolk

Salse
(b c, 24-2-85)

Topsider (b 1974)	Northern Dancer	Nearctic
		Natalma
	Drumtop	Round Table
		Zonah
Carnival Princess (b 1974)	Prince John	Princequillo
		Not Afraid
	Carnival Queen	Amerigo
		Circus Ring

Bred by Oxford Stable, in United States: $190,000 yearling Keeneland September Sale

Top Class
(b c, 6-5-85)

High Top (b 1969)	Derring-Do	Darius
		Sipsey Bridge
	Camenae	Vimy
		Madrilene
Cassina (b 1977)	Habitat	Sir Gaylord
		Little Hut
	Cesarea	Raeburn
		Jibuti

Bred by M McCalmont: 64,000gns Newmarket October Yearling Sale

— CHAPTER 9 —

Breeders' Cup

by HOWARD WRIGHT

● **HEADING FOR GLORY: Miesque and Freddie Head after morning work at Hollywood Park in preparation for the Breeders' Cup.**
Picture: GEORGE SELWYN

○ **PAT'S DAY: Theatrical and Pat Day are just too good for Pat Eddery's mount Trempolino in the Breeders' Cup Turf race.**
Picture: STEVE STIDHAM

Breeders' Cup

by HOWARD WRIGHT

ON ANY NORMAL DAY the scintillating success of Miesque in course record time would have been the climax. But this was Breeders' Cup Day 1987, an occasion when the leaders of two generations met, and those who were privileged to be there knew they had witnessed something out of the ordinary.

The Breeders' Cup Classic was one of those races which come along only rarely; it promised much and delivered more.

Ferdinand, winner of the 1986 Kentucky Derby, met Alysheba, his 1987 successor, and 57,357 turned up at Hollywood Park, California, to watch.

The minority of Europeans in the crowd – punters and professionals alike – could have been excused for regarding this as no more than a

dirt-track supporting act. After all, even allowing for individual inclinations, no-one from this side of the Atlantic could have failed to appreciate the star quality of the marvellous Miesque as she whipped a Mile field bursting with talent.

Heroine of the Anglo-French 1,000 Guineas double, Miesque had been disappointing when beaten by Milligram at long odds-on for the Queen Elizabeth II Stakes at Ascot in late-September. She had a point to prove.

The Michael Stoute pair, Milligram and Sonic Lady, who finished at either end of Miesque at Ascot, were sent to California a month before the Mile's 21 November starting date; Miesque went out with a week to spare. The bulk of the other European-based runners left on the Tuesday prior to

the Saturday target, but their departure was delayed for several hours by transport problems.

Bint Pasha lost enough weight between leaving her Berkshire stable and arriving in quarantine to reckon she was beaten before the start of the Turf race, and Bold Arrangement had to get over the equine equivalent of jet-lag in time for the Classic. Both are seasoned travellers, but both trailed the field, so the debate about the best time to ship Breeders' Cup horses, which bubbled in the wake of Dancing Brave's demoralising defeat in 1986, will go on until Breeders' Cup V at Churchill Downs in November '88.

The chances are that more European trainers will examine the Stoute-Boutin schedules; but they will also have to ponder more seriously the aspects of quality and experience.

That intrepid globetrotter Clive *rittain sent two runners: Cruise Ship, *ho finished plumb last in the *uvenile, and Bold Arrangement, who *eat only the tailed-off invalid *kywalker in the Classic. And in the print, with one exception, it was the *ame story for Britain, as Sharp *omance finished 12th, seven lengths *ff the 11th and six lengths in front of *3th and last Governor General. Only *ylvan Express covered himself with *ny semblance of Sprint glory. He ran *n stoutly in the straight under Steve *authen to take eighth place, about a *ength and a half away from a $50,000 *ick-up for fifth prize and not much *nore than five lengths behind the *nuch-vaunted Groovy, who for the *econd year running failed to break as *uickly as was intended and this time

○ **CLEAR CUT: There's no doubt about the winner of the Breeders' Cup Sprint as Very Subtle romps home four lengths clear.**   Picture: STEVE STIDHAM

EPITOME OF SUCCESS: Smiles all round as Pat Day and Epitome come back after landing the Breeders' Cup Juvenile *illies' race.   Picture: GEORGE SELWYN

went down by four lengths to the three-year-old Very Subtle and Pat Valenzuela.

Cauthen thought Sylvan Express would have got into the money had he had more experience of American dirt racing. The opinion came too late to be of any use in 1987 but it may be priceless in '88, given the right horse.

Only in the Mile did British hopes come anywhere near realisation, as Sonic Lady battled on into third place for Laffit Pincay. But even here there was disappointment, as Milligram and Pat Eddery staved off last place by a rapidly disappearing neck.

British journalists arrived on Tuesday night, after their own dose of technical delays, and were out on the track early next morning to find the bustling yet informal training area bathed in sunshine but the Stoute camp swamped in anxiety. Sonic Lady breezed along but Milligram was missing from the gallops sheet; she had walked out slightly lame. For 48 hours her recovery from a bruised hoof was monitored by Stoute and Press in equal proportions. Even on the morning of the race she was being given the ice-bucket treatment; it got her to the races but it did not get her into the picture.

○ **FOLLOW MY LEADER: Miesque has company on her way to the start of the Breeders' Cup Mile.** Picture: GEORGE SELWYN

○ **FIRST CLASS: Trainer D Wayne Lukas lands his second win on the card as Success Express takes the Breeders' Cup Juvenile.** Picture: GEORGE SELWYN

Meanwhile, Miesque, Francois Boutin and Freddie Head appeared in the expectant area of the training barns. Miesque, smallish and unprepossessing, looked nothing special as she was led round in morning temperatures gently wafting up towards 80 degrees. Boutin and Head searched beyond outward appearances and said Miesque was in the same mood and form as when she won the English and French Guineas. So it proved.

Never worse than fifth in the 14-runner field, Miesque relaxed as connections hoped she would, and having thrust aside the unwelcome and unhelpfully wayward attentions of the leader, Show Dancer, on the last bend, she swept clear in a matter of strides. At the post Miesque was three and a half lengths in front; Head was

○ **TOP SPEED: Very Subtle romps away with the Breeders' Cup Sprint.**   Picture: GEORGE SELWYN

waving in salute, and the Europeans were on top of the world.

The Mile had demonstrated the strength of European-trained horses on turf; the coming Turf race itself could hardly do anything else, since most of another maximum line-up of 14 had been or still are based on this side of the Atlantic.

Victory went to Theatrical (like Miesque a product of Nureyev), who when trained in Ireland two years previously had been Lester Piggott's last Epsom Derby ride. Now he was heading from five Grade One stakes wins in the year, and made it six under a supremely confident ride from Pat Day, who took up the running at the mile mark and kept just enough in reserve to shade out by half a length the Arc de Triomphe-winning combination of Pat Eddery and Trempolino. Village Star, from the Trempolino stable of Andre Fabre, was third, a respectful three and a half

lengths away.

France had saved the day, and Day himself was having an afternoon to remember. He had already won the Juvenile Fillies race on Epitome, who made up eight lengths on the leader in the straight to pip Jeanne Jones and Bill Shoemaker by a nose. Shoemaker had still not won a Breeders' Cup race; nor had 74-year-old trainer Charlie Whittingham. And it looked like staying that way.

Whittingham's five-year-old mare Infinidad started odds-on for the Distaff but finished only fourth as D Wayne Lukas, saddling half the six-runner field, landed a one-two with all-the-way-winner Sacahuista (Randy Romero) and Clabber Girl. Lukas, whose love-hate relationship with the American racing Press kept British observers amused and amazed, went on to take the Juvenile with Success Express (Jose Santos). He can now dream of a first Kentucky Derby

victory, but suddenly, as Breeders' Cup Day rallied to its seventh and final fling, the reality of America's premier Classic became apparent.

Bill Shoemaker, 56, against Chris McCarron; Charlie Whittingham against another peerless trainer, Jack Van Berg; and ultimately Ferdinand against Alysheba: it proved an occasion to savour as the powerful Ferdinand held off the athletic Alysheba by a nose in a contest set up by strong running from the start of Judge Angelucci and Candi's Gold.

Half a furlong from home Ferdinand led on the rails and Alysheba was making his run on the outside. At the line neither jockey was certain which had won. The photo-finish gave it to Ferdinand, but there were other winners – Hollywood Park, Breeders' Cup, and every one of those 57,357 there to see it.□

○ **IT WAS LIKE THIS, GUV'NOR: Tyrone Williams uses the sign language universal to jockeys as he explains to Patrick Haslam exactly how the race developed.**
Pictures: TONY EDENDEN

CHAPTER 10

Jockeys
by LAWRENCE WADEY

○ **A DAY'S WORK: Mark Birch, after morning exercise with Peter Easterby's string. He notched a personal best 92 winners in 1987.**

Picture: ALEC RUSSELL

Jockeys

by LAWRENCE WADEY

AN AMERICAN as a British institution: it is a situation Steve Cauthen would have been long odds to attain at the tail-end of 1985, when the Press in this country was ablaze with his personal problems.

His career as a top Flat jockey could not be guaranteed, as he spent three weeks in a Cincinatti hospital sorting out weight and related alcohol problems.

Even at the end of the 1986 season

the difficulty of controlling the pounds was evident as he put up overweight to ride at 9st. Shortly after the term closed he was around the 10st mark. And in trying to find a solution Cauthen was "flipping", the American term for thrusting his fingers down his throat every time he had eaten.

The doubters and detractors were out in force again, mentioning not just the "munchies" but also the Moet.

But they were reckoning with the spirit which had already triumphed over adversity.

At Belmont Park, New York, on 23 May 1977, the 17-year-old Cauthen took an horrific spill as Bay Streak snapped a foreleg and fell entering the stretch. As two other horses tumbled over them, Cauthen had his consciousness knocked from him, his right wrist and three fingers broken, his ribs bruised and face lacerated. A mere 31 days later he was back on the aptly-named Little Miracle. It was not the victory but the manner which revealed much about the Kentuckian's inner nerve. Ignoring the easy option of a wide run, Cauthen swept Little Miracle between horses for a length and a quarter success. So when, in November 1986, Cauthen vowed during a stint in Hong Kong: "I will be doing my damndest to win back the title," the warning was there for all to heed.

Bookmakers remained sceptical and laid 6-1 even to those in the know. The ensuing tussle even cut through family ties, as Pat Eddery's brother Robert, in his capacity as travelling head lad at Charles St George's Sefton Lodge yard, spent much of the season preparing, indeed supervising, several Cauthen winners at the racecourse. By the end of June, the Derby tucked snuggly and proudly under his belt, Cauthen led Eddery by 13, propelled by his own desire and Henry Cecil's incomparable training ability.

Though briefly headed as the titantic, engaging contest drew to a close, Cauthen finally secured the crown when Vague Discretion got up close home at Doncaster on the last day of the season.

Cauthen's score, 197, was the highest since Sir Gordon Richards' final jockeys' title in 1953, and the margin of two the narrowest since Piggott beat Breasley by the same in 1963.

Cecil summed up: "I really admire him, the way he's taken the bull by the horns and pulled himself together. It was really very important to us that he should win the championship having sorted himself out." If the British Open would not be the same without Nicklaus and Palmer, then British Racing would sorely miss Cauthen's digital deftness and quartz-like timing.

With 1,080 winners and three championships to his name since arriving nine years ago as a fresh-faced teenager from Kentucky, Cauthen is now a British sporting institution. The bookmakers quickly drew swords for the season ahead. Eddery, whom they favoured for most of 1987, has a host of potentially brilliant three-year-olds to ride and is again a shade of odds on.

○ **UP AND COMING: Dana Mellor, one of the rising stars among the girls.**
Picture: TONY EDENDEN

○ RISING STAR: Ray Cochrane topped 100 winners for the first time. He shows his style and strength on Then Again (No 4) to beat Water Cay in the Queen Anne Stakes.

Picture: GERRY CRANHAM

○ **TOP OF THE CLASS: Gary Bardwell, champion apprentice.**
Picture: GEORGE HERRINGSHAW

The value about Cauthen (7-4) has gone. But what about Ray Cochrane at 12-1?

Cochrane's first season with Luca Cumani yielded an admirable 111 winners, and with Cumani's star in the ascendency he has increased his string by 20 to 140, Cochrane may be the liveliest outsider to break the Cauthen-Eddery monopoly in the foreseeable future.

While attention was focussed so sharply on the race for the 1987 title itself, no-one suffered more than the effervescent Willie Carson, who recorded his 16th century of winners in 17 seasons when Pamusi won for Dick Hern at Newmarket on 31 October.

It would take a brave man to back against Carson making it 17 out of 18, but his title-chasing days seem to be over.

Mark Birch, Cock of the North, was another who deserved but received scant attention for his personal best tally of 92. With top Southern yards far more frequent and powerful in their forays North, this was a particularly tenacious effort, the highest total by a Northern-based rider since Edward Hide topped the 100 mark seven years previously.

○ **MAKING PROGRESS: Gary Carter, leading apprentice in 1986, joined the senior ranks and numbered the Old Newton Cup on Pipsted among his 50 winners.**
Picture: ALEC RUSSELL

○ **CENTURY BREAKER: Ray Cochrane rode more than 100 winners for the first time, helped by such power-packed finishes as that on Infamy (nearside) over Balabina at Doncaster.**   Picture: MARTIN LYNCH

Michael Hills continued the excellent progress he has made since taking the apprentices' crown in 1983, registering 75 successes. When his guv'nor Jeremy Hindley retired from training at the end of the season Hills made the not-altogether unexpected move to his father Barry's Manton stable. There he will share the mounts with Cash Asmussen, retained by Robert Sangster, and Eddery, who will continue his association with Khalid Abdullah.

Gary Carter, was another former champion apprentice to catch the eye, notching 50 wins and in his first season on senior terms, including the Cesarewitch. They did not go unnoticed by Mahmoud Fustok, who

signed up Carter to ride the 20 well-bred juveniles with which he has set up Mohammed Moubarak as his private trainer in Newmarket.

In Gary Bardwell, whose 27 wins beat Tony Culhane by three for the apprentices' title, there emerged one of the most engaging young talents for years. Attached to Mick Ryan since leaving school, he was partly helped by Philip Robinson's August departure to Hong Kong.

Bardwell's ability and charisma defies his stature, and was encapsulated during and after the Ayr Gold Cup. Tagged the "Angry Ant" in the weighing room, he conjured a devastatingly effective late burst from Not So Silly to get up on the line.

Asked on television by a stooping Brough Scott how angry he was in those final moments, Bardwell — all 4ft 11in of him — chuckled: "Very, angry indeed."

Among the girls, Dana Mellor's nine successes came in a rush towards the end of the season, earmarking her as an apprentice of some talent for the coming season, and Kim Tinkler came of age as a professional, her tally of 21 being the highest a woman jockey has achieved.

They did themselves proud, but the boys still rule the roost, none more proudly in 1987 than Steve Cauthen, the man who clambered to his feet, dusted himself over, and beat the best.□

● BIRD'S-EYE VIEW: Balthus is a 50-1 winner of the William Hill Cambridgeshire, beating Pictograph (red cap) and Terminator (yellow). The favourite Shabib finishes fast on the far side for fourth place.
Picture: ALAN JOHNSON

CHAPTER 11

Handicaps

by WILL O'HANLON

○ **ON TARGET: Star Of A Gunner (centre) has the William Hill Lincoln Handicap in his sights. Mystical Man (right) was kept out of second place by Vague Shot, who raced on the stands side.**
Picture: TONY EDENDEN

Handicaps

by WILL O'HANLON

ALEC STEWART, named Young Trainer of the Year in the Glen International Awards, marked his coming of age in 1987 with Mtoto's famous victory in the Coral-Eclipse Stakes at Sandown Park. But of only marginally less significance in the 32-year-old Scot's season were wins by Daarkom in the Tote-Ebor at York and Waajib in the Schweppes Golden Mile at Goodwood.

The margin between success and failure in top handicaps is razor thin,

yet it is remarkable how often the cream rises to the top.

Many a master-trainer has cut his teeth on handicaps — Michael Stoute with Alphadamus and Blue Cashmere, Henry Cecil with Orosio, Luca Cumani with Century City, Free Guest *et al*.

So for Stewart to exhibit that now all-too-rare skill of laying out a horse for a key target, as he did with Daarkom in the Ebor, and to overcome adversity in achieving that

goal, is to show a special talent.

Daarkom had come from a long way off the pace to finish third in the 1986 Ebor, but that campaign was generally marred by the colt's habit of trying to take a nip out of his fellow competitors. The talent was there if only it could be harnessed, and gelding was the obvious course of action for Daarkom.

The four-year-old displayed none of his wayward tendencies when scoring under 9st 10lb on his reappearance at

Brighton in May. But he was off the course for three months after damaging his off-fore fetlock joint, forcing Stewart to send him directly to York without another run.

As Ebor day neared, stable confidence mounted that the gelding, despite his lay-off, would go to York in peak condition and he was heavily-supported in the ante-post market. But that confidence was suddenly shaken as Yorkshire was hit by an August monsoon which left the Knavesmire resembling a trampled bog. Daarkom was presumed not to like soft ground, and who knows, perhaps he does not. But he still proved much too good on the day, launching an irresistible run up the middle to forge clear at the distance and won by two and a half lengths. Mudlark Pipsted, who had found conditions perfect for him in the quagmire that was Royal Ascot (where he won the King George V Handicap) came from a long way back to take second place, but was never a

BETTER LUCK: Vague Shot (left) goes one better in the Royal Hunt Cup, beating Granny's Bank and Gold Prospect (right).

Picture: TONY EDENDEN

○ **STARRING ROLE:** Gary Carter makes a point about his 50-1 win on Private Audition in the Tote Cesarewitch.
Picture: GERRY CRANHAM

threat to the winner. Daarkom went on to finish a very creditable second to Buckley in the Group Three Jockey Club Stakes at Newmarket in October.

The Schweppes Mile at Goodwood in July was the first handicap with win prize-money in excess of £50,000 sanctioned by the Jockey Club. With typical enterprise, Stewart set out to grasp the golden purse with Waajib, who had already run third in a Pattern race in Ireland (and who would later win the Group Three Prix du Rond-Point at Longchamp).

Undeterred by the fact that Waajib was set to carry 9st 10lb at Goodwood, Stewart and the tactically-astute Michael Roberts went to war. Waajib is a slightly tricky ride in that he needs to be held up to the last moment. He had been unfortunate in the Pacemaker International at Phoenix Park to find himself in front after Teleprompter and Polonia, who had gone off at a suicidal pace, fell in a heap with two furlongs still to run. Waajib was then picked off close to home by Fair Judgment and Stately Don. Roberts (who did not ride him in Ireland) was determined not to find himself in the same position at Goodwood.

It takes nerves of steel to play the waiting game in a 20-runner handicap, and Roberts cannot have ridden a much better race all year as he produced Waajib to lead with 100 yards to go. Even then, it could be argued that he delivered Waajib's challenge a couple of strides too soon, as Boot Polish was closing rapidly at the line, hotly pursued by Genghiz and Rhazali. Waajib held on by a neck, though Boot Polish can be adjudged an unlucky loser (one of several for Bill Watts in a season of might-have-beens) as he had to be switched round a wall of horses to deliver his run.

Waajib's win was the best possible outcome to this initial running of the "Schweppes", as it will encourage the training elite to try their luck in the white-hot competition which well-framed handicaps provide.

One aspect of British Flat racing which needs corrective treatment is the deep-rooted resistance among top

○ **CLOSE CALL: Roushayd (white blaze) leads in the last strides to beat Bocatower and Wolsey (centre) in the Tote Festival Handicap at Ascot.**
Picture: GEORGE SELWYN

○ **EXPERIENCE COUNTS: Daarkom is followed home by the three-year-olds Pipsted (centre) and Ala Hounak (rails) in the Tote-Ebor Handicap.** Picture: JOHN CROFTS

○ **BIGGER THE FIELD: Bel Byou (right) justifies favouritism in the Wokingham Stakes, beating Dorking Lad (noseband) and 27 others.** Picture: TONY EDENDEN

○ **GOLDEN BOY: Top apprentice Gary Bardwell drives Not So Silly into the lead to win the Ladbroke Ayr Gold Cup from Serve N' Volley.**
Picture: ALEC RUSSELL

trainers to running horses in handicaps. The racing public likes to see (and gets with its chasers and hurdlers) competitive weight-adjusted racing, with horses from the upper strata put to the test against their inferiors.

The Schweppes afforded that opportunity, as did the Tote Festival Handicap at Ascot in September. The latter, worth £64,000 to the winner, would probably have fallen to a Group horse had Trampship, winner of the Park Hill Stakes at Doncaster on her previous start, not come into season before the start and refused to take part. Her absence was quickly forgotten (except by her hapless army of ante-post backers) as Roushayd won a pulsating race in the final stride from Bocatower, with Wolsey a further head away third.

Michael Stoute, with three runners, Luca Cumani and Guy Harwood (two apiece) and Henry Cecil (one) gave an emphatic endorsement to this innovative handicap, showing that the big battalions can be persuaded to have a go when the price is right.

A race which the Jockey Club

Handicappers must approach with trepidation is the Extel Stakes for three-year-olds at Glorious Goodwood. In theory this should be one of the keenest contests for progressive young horses in the calendar, but contemptuously easy wins by the Cumani-trained Free Guest and Fish 'N' Chips in recent years have proved acutely embarrassing.

No sooner had the Cumani tide been stemmed (1987 representative Norman Invader finished ninth) than another of their old tormentors, Paul Cole, appeared with the aptly-named Broken Hearted. This was not a race so much as a ceremonial procession, with the lightly-raced son of Dara Monarch cruising to the front two furlongs out and winning hard-held from Random Rover.

Broken Hearted had subsequent Arc winner Trempolino four lengths away in third when taking the Group Two Prix Guillaume d'Ornano at Deauville two weeks later. While that was not Trempolino's best form (he reportedly hurt himself in the race), it once again underlined the Extel's status as a springboard for Pattern-race success, as Free Guest and Celestial Storm had previously illustrated.

Cole, unrivalled in his exploitation of sprint handicap talent over the years, showed he has lost none of his skill in that department with his handling of four-times winner Bel Byou. The Try My Best colt landed a massive gamble in the Wokingham at Royal Ascot and was subsequently a shade unlucky not to add to his successes in Listed races abroad.

But if Bel Byou's win that soggy June day at Ascot took many thousands of pounds out of the ring, the bookmakers more than made amends later in the season when a trio of 50-1 big-race winners had punters reeling.

The Peter Calver-trained Madraco was the first "skinner" for the books, showing vastly improved form to win the William Hill Stewards' Cup at Goodwood in July. No one can predict for sure what effect blinkers will have on a horse's performance. Madraco

had been mulish when tried in them at Nottingham in June so Calver quickly dispensed with them for the Goodwood race — with electrifying results.

Blinkers had exactly the opposite effect on Jeremy Glover's gelding Balthus in the William Hill Cambridgeshire at Newmarket. They roused this potential giant-killer from his slumber, and with Dean McKeown riding a perfectly judged race on the ex-Cumani gelding, Balthus prevailed by half a length from Pictograph to give ex-jump jockey Glover the greatest day of his life.

Blinkers played no part in the third 50-1 shock, Private Audition's astonishing eight-length rout of 27 opponents in the Tote Cesarewitch. Favourite Buckley could not handle the softish ground, and several fancied runners ran out of steam some way from home — not many horses stay a testing two-and-a-quarter miles these days. An intelligent reading of the situation by Gary Carter shot Private

Audition clear with three furlongs to run, and it was simply no contest thereafter as Mark Tompkins gained the biggest success of his training career.

No review of the 1987 handicap season would be complete without mention of Not So Silly, snapped up for 2,600gns by Alan Bailey out of an Ayr seller in March. The gelding went on to win six more times, returning to the Scottish track to record his most notable win in the Ladbrokes Ayr Gold Cup, where he just snatched victory from Serve 'N' Volley.

Handicap trainer of the year? Without a doubt, that has to be Gerald Cottrell, a 62-year-old Cullompton farmer who turned to training late in life. Cottrell looked to have a star in the making in the spring of 1986 in Governor General. But that horse was to prove something of a wayward talent and, in retrospect, it may have been a blessing in disguise when he was moved to David Elsworth's stable.

○ **SPOT THE WINNER: It's Madraco (noseband, towards right), who strikes a blow for the North by winning the William Hill Stewards' Cup at 50-1.**
Picture: TONY EDENDEN

This allowed Cottrell to concentrate on his less talented, but fiercely determined, bunch of sprint handicappers. Gallant Hope, Ever Sharp, Young Inca and Stock Hill Lass enjoyed a remarkable run, pocketing 14 handicaps at five and six furlongs.

But even that outstanding achievement was overshadowed by Stock Hill Lass's final win in the one-mile Geoffrey Hamlyn Handicap at Kempton Park on 4 September. A mile was previously thought to be beyond the mare's capability, but with a £50,000 bonus on offer if she could achieve the treble of Kempton Park wins, Cottrell and his team set to with a will to transform their six-furlong racer into a miler.

A third at Sandown Park two weeks before Kempton convinced them they were on the right lines, and the mare brought off the coup in great style, beating Bold Pillager by an emphatic three lengths. Truly the stuff of which dreams are made!□

○ **SPOT THE WINNER: It's a dead heat between Brave Dancer (stars on sleeve) and Wolsey (dark cap) – but only after Knockando (going out of official photo-finish picture) is relegated to third at a Stewards' inquiry.**

— CHAPTER 12 —

Trainers
by J. A. McGRATH

● **TEAM WORK: Michael Stoute, with assistant James Fanshawe, Milligram's lass Sira Hornsby, and chief work rider Cliff Lines.**
Picture: GEORGE SELWYN

○ **GOING UP: Paul Cole and stable jockey Richard Quinn continued their climb up the ladder. Until December, Cole was leading British-based trainer for prize money earned in Ireland and overseas.**   Picture: TONY EDENDEN

Trainers

by J. A. McGRATH

HENRY CECIL might not have started the trend for trainers to spend more time in their stables than on racecourses, but he has played his part in making that approach popular.

His theory is simple. "I feel my time is more profitably spent at Warren Place than on racecourses," he says. "I would like to be with my horses 24 hours, if possible."

When he can train a record-breaking 180 winners in a season, take the title with stake money in excess of £1.8 million, and clinch two Classics as well as the King George VI, it is hard to say he is doing the wrong thing. And with satellite coverage to the professional in the comfort of his office or home just around the corner, the day may be coming when more trainers are seen even less on the racecourse.

Without delving too deeply into what may be possible in the 21st century, the point underlined by Cecil's approach is that a trainer spends too much time travelling, merely to supervise and observe first-hand.

Racing in Britain is not centralised, it is commonplace for jockeys, and many trainers, to travel 50,000 miles a year in the course of their job. It is possible for these professionals to spend almost one-third of their time during a season locked away in a car!

Racecourse reporters are likely to be the only ones to display concern at the trend towards a Cecil-like absence.

One worrying day at Chepstow last year we went through the card; not one winning trainer out of six was there to greet his horse. What's more fate stepped in and ruled that all "winning" assistant trainers and travelling head lads had sworn an oath of secrecy.

Since Cecil prefers to be at home looking after the inmates at Warren Place, it is particularly significant when he does go racing. He will be at all the big ones, Newmarket, Ascot, Sandown Park, York and the like, but when he elects to journey to Leicester on a wet, miserable Saturday night in June, it is time to sit up and take notice.

Last year we sat up, and it was not long before it came to everyone's notice why the champion trainer had selected such an unlikely venue for a Saturday night out.

Diminuendo was making her debut in the Sports Final Stakes, for maiden two-year-old fillies. Starting 3-1 on, she did not let down her trainer – nor her owner Sheikh Mohammed – when she scooted away from moderate opposition to win by ten lengths. Diminuendo went on to far better things and looks one of the brightest filly prospects for Warren Place for 1988.

○**MEL BRITTAIN had a marvellous season.**   Picture: ALEC RUSSELL

After the event, Cecil conducted his post-race interview with Pressmen who appeared to spring from nowhere to hear what he had to say. He had his back to the second-placed Benediction in the small enclosure in front of the weighing room, and determined to attract the attention of the champion trainer, the filly kept poking her nose into the middle of Cecil's back.

With a smile, Cecil broke off and allowed Benediction to nuzzle under his arm before giving the filly a generous pat. That simple episode said something about Cecil's love of horses – even one who has taken a 10-length drubbing from one of his own!

The fact that 40 per cent of Cecil's runners were winners in 1987 is testimony to his genius. But there is more – a lot more – to the Cecil success story.

He is ambitious and loyal, qualities which drove him to smash John Day's long-standing record of 146 winners in a season. They also enabled Steve Cauthen to call on ammunition into the late, dark months of his tense title battle with Pat Eddery, a tribute to Cecil's training skills in being able to keep his big string on the go to the end of the season.

Reference Point, with wins in the Derby, King George VI and Queen Elizabeth Diamond Stakes and St Leger, provided highlights of the Cecil year.

Bringing back Reference Point to win the Mecca-Dante Stakes at York, after the colt had been operated on for a sinus problem in the off-season, was a brilliant performance. And having the colt spot-on for the Derby was another king-sized feather in his cap.

If there was one slight disappointment, it must have been that Indian Skimmer, the filly dubbed "the grey shadow" by admiring scribes, missed the chance to build on her record of five wins in the second half of the season. Having beaten the brilliant Miesque pointless in the Prix de Diane Hermes at Chantilly, she suffered shoulder problems which forced her on to the sidelines.

Cecil has already said he is looking forward to Indian Skimmer clashing again with Miesque in 1988.

○**MICHAEL STOUTE trained the Princess Royal's first Ascot winner, Ten No Trumps.**   Picture: TONY EDENDEN

Michael Stoute, with 105 winners, was the other trainer to smash the £1m stakes barrier in win money.

Unite carried Sheikh Mohammed's colours to victory in the Gold Seal Oaks at Epsom. The same race was marred by the Cecil-trained Scimitarra breaking down and being pulled up over a furlong from the finish.

Luca Cumani, now firmly established in the upper bracket of trainers, finished third with win money of £530,250 and 83 victories to his credit.

It was a memorable season for Barry Hills when he trained 96 winners from Robert Sangster's Manton stable, the year after Michael Dickinson had been replaced.

Sangster had boldly – and publicly – set Hills a target of 70 winners for the season, which he passed with several weeks remaining. Crowning achievement was the win of Sir Harry Lewis in the Budweiser Irish Derby in soft ground at The Curragh.

Alec Stewart, the young Newmarket-based trainer, caught continued attention with his expert handling of Mtoto, who proved a giant-killer in beating Reference Point and Triptych in the Coral-Eclipse Stakes at Sandown Park in July.

Stewart will go a long way, but like every other trainer in the lists, he will find Henry Cecil, with 180 winners to prove the point, hard to topple.□

— CHAPTER 13 —

France

by DESMOND STONEHAM

○ **GUINEAS GLORY: Miesque follows up her English 1,000 Guineas win by beating Sakura Reiko in the French equivalent, the Poule d'Essai des Pouliches.**
Picture: JOHN CROFTS

France

by DESMOND STONEHAM

THE OUTSTANDING PERFORMER in France, and possible worldwide, during 1987 was Miesque, who was so profoundly appreciated by her talented trainer Francois Boutin. In a period of under eight months, the daughter of Nureyev performed on eight occasions and won five races in the Grade or Group One category.

True, she was beaten by Indian Skimmer when conditions were against her in the Prix de Diane Hermes, but Miesque went on until the end of the season, by which time she had proved herself the best miler in the world.

Owned and bred by Stavros Niarchos, Miesque will remain in training during 1988 and it can only be hoped that a second clash with Indian Skimmer is on the horizon.

Miesque reeled off the English and French 1,000 Guineas, the Fresnay-le-Buffard (ex-Jacques la Marois), the Moulin de Longchamp and finally an amazing victory in the Breeders' Cup Mile at Hollywood Park.

Although Boutin understood the filly to perfection, her engagement in the Breeders' Cup was decided only at the last moment by Niarchos, who saw his magnificent filly just twice, in defeat in the Diane and victory in the Moulin de Longchamp.

Nureyev was also responsible for the talented Soviet Star, who after taking the French 2,000 Guineas and Swettenham Stud Sussex Stakes, was firmly put in his place by Miesque in the Moulin.

Owned by Sheikh Mohammed and trained by Andre Fabre, Soviet Star ended the season on a high note by easily defeating the Prix d'Ispahan hero Highest Honor in the Prix de la Foret.

Fabre, who will campaign Soviet Star again in 1988, reached the high point of his career when he saddled Trempolino to win the Arc de Triomphe in the hands of Pat Eddery.

Virtually ignored in the betting, Trempolino crushed Dancing Brave's course record when taking the Arc, and the son of Sharpen Up ended his season by running a gallant second to Theatrical in the Breeders' Cup Turf.

Trempolino matured throughout the season and really only needed a truly-run mile and a half to show his best. His progress is well demonstrated in the formbook. Trempolino was narrowly beaten by Natroun in the Prix du Jockey-Club but subsequently reversed the form in both the Prix Niel and the Arc.

Two horses virtually unbeatable over distances of around ten furlongs in 1987 were Groom Dancer and Triptych, who was also greatly aided by some cut in the ground.

Groom Dancer dominated Trempolino in the Prix Lupin, before failing to stay the distance of the Epsom Derby. He then won the Prix Daphnis, was withdrawn from the Matchmaker International at York because of soft ground, unshipped his rider at the Phoenix Park and took the Prix du Prince d'Orange before his stamina again ran out in the Arc.

The amazing Triptych began her year by picking up the Prix Ganay and then reeled off victories in the Coronation Cup, Matchmaker International, Dunnes Stores St Bernard Champion Stakes and Dubai Champion Stakes for the second consecutive year.

Brilliantly trained by Patrick Biancone, Triptych then went to Japan and after winning the Fuji Stakes, was unlucky in the Japan Cup which unfortunately for her was run on a firm surface. Triptych does not truly stay a mile and a half and although the world's stock markets have added doubt to her future, she should still again be carrying Alan Clore's colours in 1988.

A vastly underrated horse in France during 1987 was the Spanish-owned Royal Gait, who was the only stayer in

○ **STAR TURN: The French 2,000 Guineas (Poules d'Essai des Poulains) falls to Soviet Star, who beats Noble Minstrel.**   Picture: JOHN CROFTS

○ **TAKE THAT: Indian Skimmer slams Miesque (striped sleeves) in the Prix de Diane Hermes (French Oaks).**
Picture: GEORGE SELWYN

Europe to pick up a pair of Group One events. A 5,500 gns unraced two-year-old at the Doncaster Sales, Royal Gait took the Prix du Cadran and ended his year by trotting up in the Prix Royal-Oak (French St Leger).

If Royal Gait had been entered in the Gold Cup at Ascot, he would have tested Paean, but the five-year-old gelded son of Gunner B will have his chance in 1988 and will be a tough adversary, particularly if the ground is testing.

Yves Saint-Martin's retirement from the saddle is a great loss, not only to French racing but the sport throughout the world. Happily the 46-year-old Frenchman will be around in other capacities in the future.

His career spanned 30 years, during which he won every important race, including the inaugural running of the Breeders' Cup Turf on Lashkari, which he considers to be his finest moment. His most satisfying victory came when he took the 1970 Arc de Triomphe on Sassafras, who outstayed the hot-favourite Nijinsky and Lester Piggott.

With over 3,300 victories to his credit, Saint-Martin will be remembered as a rider for his balance and poise. As a person, he is a man with dignity, humour, kindness and

○ **BOWING OUT: Yves Saint-Martin, who retired from the saddle, and Natroun, after the Prix du Jockey-Club.** Picture: DAVID HASTINGS

warmth, with a word for everybody, not just the most important.

His place as jockey to the Aga Khan will be taken by the talented Dominique Boeuf, whose best victories in 1987 came with Groom Dancer. Very few young jockeys are making the grade in French racing and

Boeuf will have a challenge on his hands. It is to be hoped that he succeeds when many others, finding that success and wealth come too quickly, have not.

The two-year-old season in France can only be described as moderate, with the exception of Ravinella, who

○ **GRAND CRITERIUM: Fijar Tango beats Pasakos.** Picture: JOHN CROFTS

○ **PRIX DE LA SALAMANDRE: Common Grounds beats Most Precious and Miss Boniface.** Picture: JOHN CROFTS

○ **INTO GEAR: Trempolino gives Pat Eddery a hat-trick of Prix de l'Arc de Triomphe wins by beating Tony Bin.**

Picture: DAVID HASTINGS

○ **PRIX MORNY: First Waltz (left) beats Common Grounds.**   Picture: JOHN CROFTS

staked her claim to the 1988 Classics in the Tattersalls Cheveley Park Stakes at Newmarket.

Ravinella is one of many highly talented two-year-olds in the stable of Criquette Head, who, barring ill luck, should hit the headlines in many European Classics this season, particularly with her fillies.

Criquette's only decent three-year-old in 1987, Ofanto, had training problems, but this season she will have strength in depth, with the likes of 1,000 Guineas hope Ravinella, Most Precious and Riviere d'Or, plus the colts In Extremis, Nabis and Radjhasi.

Once again France's top two-year-old race, the Grand Criterium, may prove a poor guide for the future. The useful but not brilliant Fijar Tango was the winner.

The Criterium de Saint-Cloud, a Group One race for the first time, may be no help either. This went to Waki River, who for much of the season had in-and-out form but a fairly impressive autumn.

After one year as a trainer in France, John Hammond has a chance in a lifetime now he has been sent some 45 horses owned by Daniel Wildenstein. The 27-year-old Englishman took the Prix Corrida with Bonshamile and the Prix Chloe with Swept Away, to give him a couple of Group victories in his first season.

Only the Board of Directors of Trusthouse Forte know the true reason why they withdrew sponsorship of the Arc de Triomphe. After six

○ **FIGHTING POLICY: Risk Me rattles Soviet Star, with Bengal Fire third, in the Prix Jean Prat.**   Picture: JOHN CROFTS

years they had cemented their name to Europe's richest race. But Trusthouse Forte's loss is the gain of the Italian hotel group Ciga, who signed up to sponsor the Arc for the next six years at a cost of £2.5m.

The Aga Khan is a major shareholder in Cigahotels and he is intending to make the Arc weekend into a festival of French racing as a way of promoting the already excellent reputation of the company.

Gary Moore became French champion jockey, following in the footsteps of Cash Asmussen, who took the title in 1985 and 1986. Moore will be back in 1988, as will the talented Tony Cruz, whose association with Biancone is extremely firm.

But nothing enthralled the French racing public more in 1987 than the brilliant riding of Pat Eddery, who rode nearly every Sunday for Andre Fabre. Trempolino was the icing on a cake which contained more than 20 winners.□

○ **LUCKY FOR SOME: Bint Pasha races away with the Prix Vermeille, chased by Three Tails.**   Picture: JOHN CROFTS

4 October – Longchamp
GOOD TO FIRM   1m 4f

Trusthouse Forte Prix de l'Arc de Triomphe

1st £423,280 **2nd** £169,312 **3rd** £84,656 **4th** £42,328

1		**TREMPOLINO** 3 8-11	Pat Eddery	**20-1**
2	2	**TONY BIN** 4 9-4	C Asmussen	**29-1**
3	3	**TRIPTYCH** 5 9-1	A Cruz	**5-1**
4	hd	**MTOTO** 4 9-4	M Roberts	**63-10**
5	3	**TABAYAAN** 3 8-11	W R Swinburn	**63-10**
6	2½	**ORBAN** 4 9-4	G Starkey	**25-1**
7	5	**TERESA** 3 8-8	G W Moore	**43-1**
8	5	**REFERENCE POINT** 3 8-11	S Cauthen	**7-10F**
9	1½	**NATROUN** 3 8-11	Y Saint-Martin	**63-10**
10	ns	**SHARANIYA** 4 9-1	A Lequeux	**63-10**
11	2½	**GROOM DANCER** 3 8-11	D Boeuf	**10-1**

11 ran
TIME 2m 26.3s
1st OWNER: P de Moussac TRAINER: A Fabre
2nd OWNER: Allevamento White Star TRAINER: L Camici, Italy
3rd OWNER: A Clore TRAINER: P Biancone
4th OWNER: Sheikh Ahmed Al-Maktoum TRAINER: A Stewart, Britain
Pari-Mutuel (including one franc stake): Win 21.00; places 4.20, 4.40, 2.00;
dual forecast 203.30.

○ **ANDRE FABRE**   Picture: TONY EDENDEN

Trempolino   (ch c, 17-3-84)

Sharpen Up (ch 1969)	Atan	Native Dancer
		Mixed Marriage
	Rocchetta	Rockefella
		Chambiges
Trephine (b 1977)	Viceregal	Northern Dancer
		Victoria Regina
	Quiriquina	Molvedo
		La Chausee

Bred by Maryland Stud, in United States

Tony Bin   (b c, 7-4-83)

Kampala (b 1976)	Kalamoun	Zeddaan
		Khairunissa
	State Pension	Only for Life
		Lorelei
Severn Bridge (ch 1965)	Hornbeam	Hyperion
		Thicket
	Priddy Fair	Preciptic
		Campanette

Bred by P O'Callaghan: 3,000gns Goffs Irish National Foal Sale

Triptych   (b m, 19-4-82)

Riverman (b 1969)	Never Bend	Nasrullah
		Lalun
	River Lady	Prince John
		Nile Lily
Trillion (b 1974)	Hail To Reason	Turn-to
		Nothirdchance
	Margarethen	Tulyar
		Russ-Marie

Bred by N B Hunt and E Stephenson, in United States: $2,150,000 yearling Keeneland July Sale

Mtoto   (b c, 1-4-83)

Busted (b 1963)	Crepello	Donatello
		Crepuscule
	Sans Le Sou	Vimy
		Martial Loan
Amazer (br 1967)	Mincio	Relic
		Merise
	Alzara	Alycidon
		Zabara

Bred by J Moore: 110,000gns yearling Newmarket Highflyer Sale

Quiz of the Year

by HOWARD WRIGHT (Answers on page 274)

1. How did De Rigueur follow the example of No Bombs?
2. Why did Peter Scudamore fall foul of the Leopardstown Stewards in February?
3. Who took over sponsorship of the Schweppes Gold Trophy at Newbury?
4. Paul Barton retired early in the year; on which horse did he win the Welsh National?
5. The 1978 Coventry Stakes runner-up went chasing last season; name him.
6. In which state did Michael Dickinson begin his US training career?
7. What do the initials SIS stand for?
8. Which trainer won with his first runner, Have Faith at Kempton Park on 27 February?
9. Which horse won the first race at the Cheltenham NH Festival meeting?
10. Who rode Taberna Lord to win the Coral Golden Hurdle Final?
11. Where was trainer Arthur

○ **Fighting out Question 47.**   Picture: JOHN CROFTS

Stephenson when his horse The Thinker was winning the Tote Cheltenham Gold Cup?
12. How many winners did Irish-based trainers saddle at the Cheltenham NH Festival?
13. Which horse, placed at the Cheltenham NH Festival last season, won the 1984 Newbury Autumn Cup?
14. Four winners at the 1987 Cheltenham NH Festival meeting had previously won at the corresponding fixture; name them.
15. Who trained the first winner of the 1987 Flat season in Britain?
16. Name the horse who started favourite for the Lincoln Handicap and Royal Hunt Cup, and won neither.
17. Which horse started favourite for the Seagram Grand National?
18. Who was the only woman to ride in the Seagram Grand National?
19. Name the only owner, apart from Jim Joel, to win the Derby and Grand National in the last 50 years.
20. Which of Maori Venture's stablemates also completed the course in the 1987 Seagram Grand National?
21. Which horse ran in both the Whitbread Trophy and Grand National?

22. Which trainer had the first win of his career with Tricky Note at Newmarket in April?
23. Who trained the Jameson Irish Grand National winner Brittany Boy?
24. The Gordon Richards Stakes was run for the first time in 1987; what was its previous name?
25. What was the amount of Guy Landau's claim when he won the Whitbread Gold Cup on Lean Ar Aghaidh?
26. Who gained the first success of his training career with Sanamar at Pontefract in April?
27. What was Miesque's winning distance over Milligram in the General Accident 1,000 Guineas?
28. Milligram was Michael Stoute's fifth 1,000 Guineas runner-up; name the others.
29. Which horse was promoted to third in the General Accident 2,000 Guineas on the disqualification of Most Welcome?
30. Name Willie Carson's 2,000 Guineas winners before Don't Forget Me.
31. Which trainer had the first success of his career with Romantic Prince at Haydock Park in May?
32. Which two colts lost their unbeaten records behind Reference Point in the 'Ever Ready Derby?

○ **Backing into Question 54?**
Picture: EDWARD WHITAKER

33. Name the owner of the filly who came between a one-two in the Gold Seal Oaks for Sheikh Mohammed with Unite and Three Tails.
34. Ray Cochrane and Luca Cumani shared two winners on the opening day of Royal Ascot; name them.
35. Who trained his first winner when Vague Shot landed the Royal Hunt Cup?
36. Name William Jarvis's first Royal Ascot winner.
37. Which horse started favourite for the Gold Cup?
38. Who rode the winner of the Wokingham Stakes?
39. Steve Cauthen was leading jockey at Royal Ascot with seven winners; name the only other riders with more than one winner at the meeting.
40. How many Royal Ascot winners did Sheikh Mohammed own?
41. Which jockey had his first ride in Britain on Perion to finish second in the King's Stand Stakes?
42. For which three trainers has Triptych raced?
43. Which two Group One races did Risk Me win?
44. Which Derby did Vincent O'Brien win for the seventh time with Baba Karam in July?
45. Which course celebrated 100 years of racing in July?
46. Name the Princess Royal's first winner at Ascot.
47. Who trained Sheikh Mohammed's three runners in the Swettenham Stud Sussex Stakes?
48. Who is Clerk of the Course at Goodwood?

49. Who said: "Two miles and five furlongs is too far for any horse on the Flat."?
50. What was the new job Joe Mercer took on in the summer?
51. On which course did Steve Cauthen gain his 1,000th victory in Britain in August?
52. Name the runner-up to Triptych in the Matchmaker International.
53. Reprimand was Henry Cecil's second winner of the Gimrack Stakes; name the first.
54. Which brothers finished first and second in the Lowther Stakes?
55. Where is the Roman Warrior Shield run?
56. How much did Stock Hill Lass earn as a bonus for winning at Kempton Park in September?
57. Which anniversary did Doncaster Bloodstock Sales celebrate by sponsoring the Scarbrough Stakes?
58. Dawn's Delight became the sixth horse this century to win the Portland Handicap twice; when was his previous victory?
59. Which horses started joint favourite for the Laurent Perrier Champagne Stakes?
60. Who rode Gulf King into last place in the Holsten Pils St Leger?
61. Name the last horse before Reference Point to win both the Derby and St Leger.
62. Brent Thomson parted company from two trainers in the autumn; who were they?
63. Who was due to sponsor the Dewhurst Stakes for the first time?
64. Which trainers were responsible

○ **Answer to Question 35.**
Picture: BESPIX

for the 50-1 winners of the William Hill Cambridgeshire and Tote Cesarewitch?
65. Who won the Long John Scotch Whisky International European Apprentice Championship?
66. Jeremy Hindley announced his retirement in October; how many Classics did he win in Britain and Ireland?
67. Name the trainers of Pat Eddery's three consecutive Prix de l'Arc de Triomphe winners.
68. Which jockey started the last week of the Flat season leading the championship race?
69. Who rode the last winner of the Flat season in Britain?
70. How many jockeys rode 100 winners or more during the Flat season in Britain?
71. Who was the Flat Season's leading trainer, based on win money, not located in Newmarket?
72. Which horses won most races during the Flat season?
73. What was the illness from which Dancing Brave was found to be suffering in November?
74. Daniel Wildenstein has appointed an Englishman to be his principal trainer in France in 1988; who is he?
75. Name the four European-raced horses who won prize money in the Breeders' Cup Mile.

○ **Half of Question 43.**
Picture: JOHN CROFTS

Downfall of Lester Piggott

by TIM RICHARDS

THE SENTENCE

Before Mr Justice Farquharson

Regina

v

Lester Keith Piggott

Mr A. Hidden QC and Mr P. Rook appeared for the prosecution.
Mr J. Mathew QC and Mr J. Bevan appeared for the defendant.

Mr Justice Farquharson said in sentencing: "Lester Keith Piggott, I suppose that the arguments in your favour could scarcely have been put more attractively than they have during the course of the afternoon, and indeed during the course of the day, because the Prosecution have spoken so well of you in your career having regard to your fame. I take that very much into account.

"Perhaps more than anything I take into account the substantial repayments you have made to the Inland Revenue, including the amounts covered in this indictment.

"I, of course, pay attention to the fact that you have admitted these offences, which I emphasise are offences of dishonesty.

"It is right perhaps, also for me to recognise that a lot of the dishonesty in which you have engaged in your failure to own up to the Inland Revenue as to your various assets, has taken place in a climate where cash payments are not infrequent and often not accounted for. I repeat, those matters are very much in my mind.

"On the other hand your fame has resulted in you having a quite enormous income. Tax gathering must depend, must it not, on the honesty of all of us when the demands come in. Up and down the country those who only have a tiny proportion of what you enjoy pay up and loyally meet their obligations.

"So how can I pass over your case when you had the resources to meet the heavy demands that no doubt would have been made upon you, and still have a large amount of money to look after yourself and your family.

"One might have been able to accede to the submission made by Mr Mathew if when the matter really came up to the boil in April 1986 or February 1986, you then revealed all

these bank accounts and the monies that they held. But not only did you not reveal them to the Revenue, you did not even tell your own professional advisers until finally it was forced out in December of last year.

"If I was to pass over this it would be an invitation, I feel, for other people to be tempted to dishonour their obligations and try and cheat the Revenue.

"In the result I am going to impose terms of imprisonment upon you on counts six, eight and nine amounting to three years. On the remaining counts of the indictment there will be sentences of two years, all of those will run concurrently.

"You must pay the costs of £34,000 of the prosecution, and there will be a fine which in the circumstances is a nominal one of £5,000 on each of those counts with which the Company is also indicted, that is counts three, four, five, six and ten. The Company itself will be fined the sum of £100 on each of these counts."

The pity was not that he was found out, but that he did it at all. The mystery was why he did it.

To amass millions of pounds, hoard them in bank accounts under false names all over the world and hardly spend a penny was futile. Like Lester Piggott, most people love money, but for the majority it has a use. Piggott did not seem to know what to do with his. Beyond his beloved horses there was a shallow life, sadly deprived of the riches which money cannot buy. Presumably, he drew comfort and security from the knowledge that there, stashed away, were millions of pounds for the proverbial (and highly unlikely) rainy day.

All his waking hours have been sheltered in the world of racing, which by its nature is insular. Born into and brought up in racing, he was for 40 years totally dedicated to riding the best horse in as many races as possible. Real life, as most of us know it, passed him by.

But racing must not kid itself; justice was done when Judge Farquharson sentenced Piggott to three years in prison for his massive tax evasion.

Cries of sympathy for the defendant and foul against the Judge reverberated round racing. They pose several questions, not least whether the sport is an accessory to the fact.

At 3.30 p.m. on Friday 23 October 1987, Piggott left the dock in Ipswich Crown Court. As he passed his wife Susan, hesitating for a split-second to offer an apologetic glance, he was again centre stage in a life that is legend. As always he showed no apparent emotion, not a flicker in those vacant, staring eyes as every pace of his loneliest walk was closely followed by 100 eager journalists, stunned into disbelief by the reality that the greatest racing legend of their time was on his way to jail.

But Piggott has never allowed the pressures brought about by his legion of followers to break down his barriers. Were it Epsom, Newmarket or Longchamp, the 11-times champion jockey always isolated himself from the tensions of riding the big-race favourite.

Perhaps he genuinely believed himself the great untouchable.

He sold his services to the highest bidder, so often wealthy, famous and influential members of society. They paid him in the belief that without his celebrated artistry they would not enjoy the heady social accolades which go with winning races.

Their hero salted away the rewards, gifts from great people that could not be snatched back by lesser beings, Piggott reasoned mistakenly.

It was the birth of Piggott "the obsessive hoarder of money", to quote defence counsel Mr John Mathew QC. Yet not one of these owners of stature managed to break

○ **JUST CHECKING: Susan Piggott arrives at Highpoint Prison to visit her husband Lester.** Picture: MAIL NEWSPAPERS

○ **MORNING WORK-OUT: Lester Piggott on the laundry run.** Picture: MAIL NEWSPAPERS

into Piggott's introverted character to explain the error of his ways. Or perhaps the partially-deaf Piggott did not want to hear what they had to say.

The black economy is endemic to a sport in which so much unaccountable money changes hands so frequently.

While Piggott began his service at Her Majesty's pleasure, some of his fellow trainers and jockeys were investigated by the Inland Revenue. Some agreed settlements and paid up.

Piggott was given three chances, the first back in 1971, to come clean but each time he laughed at the taxman. Inevitably the time came for the laughing and lying to stop.

Now he is the frightening example the Revenue wanted to expose before the rest of racing, in order to shake more cash from their back pockets.

I am not holier than thou, witness the tax man who knocked on my door to present an unpaid bill of £200 plus interest. I paid up, grudgingly like the rest. The lesson to us all is that Lester Piggott was destroyed by his own greed.

● **CHANTILLY FACE:** Sheikh Mohammed greets his French Oaks winner Indian Skimmer, while in the background Henry Cecil discusses the race with Steve Cauthen.
Picture: GERRY CRANHAM

Owners

by EMILY WEBER

○ **ON SONG: Bluebird, disappointing towards the end of the season, still kept Robert Sangster in the limelight by winning the King's Stand Stakes at Royal Ascot.**
Picture: PHIL SMITH

Owners

by EMILY WEBER

THE CHORUS OF PRAISE for Henry Cecil and Steve Cauthen clouded another record in 1987: that of the man who had contributed so largely to their achievements.

Sheikh Mohammed, with 76 winners of 126 races worth £1,232,287, broke both his 1986 record of 119 races won, and his 1985 one for prize money.

It is a fact of life that owners get little credit for their horses when things go right, and the richer the owner the more reluctantly the praise flows. If things go wrong, gloating is almost embarrassingly thinly veiled.

Luckily, the very rich tend not to be over-sensitive about such things but to the families of Sheikh Mohammed and Khalid Abdullah in particular, for their decision to race the best bloodstock in the world in Britain, we

owe an irredeemable debt of gratitude.

Of all Sheikh Mohammed's good horses in 1987, the best was the grey filly Indian Skimmer, who managed only fourth in her one juvenile run, and wintered so badly that it was not until the spring that she turned into a swan.

She won all her five outings, ending with a four-length defeat of Miesque in the Group One Prix de Diane Hermes. The sight of her clear at the distance was one of the great memories of 1987. Sadly her season lasted no longer than that golden day in June, for she met with a setback soon after. All being well, she should be back in 1988.

Sheikh Mohammed also owned the season's leading sprinter, Ajdal, ironically turned down by Vincent

O'Brien as a yearling. Ajdal gained two of his owner's four British Group One successes, in the Norcros July Cup and William Hill Sprint Championship. Unite, in the Gold Seal Oaks, and Soviet Star, trained in France by Andre Fabre, in the Swettenham Stud Sussex Stakes, provided the other two. There were 16 Pattern-race wins in the Mohammed colours.

His two-year-olds were led by Reprimand, who had been well fancied to win the abandoned Dewhurst Stakes, and is expected to prove outstanding in 1988.

The disappointment of Sheikh Mohammed's year had to be that Sonic Lady never recovered her three-year-old brilliance. She struggled gamely to win the Child Stakes at Newmarket, a race not run to suit her, but was a shadow of her old self.

Another bad moment came in full view of the Epsom crowd and the television cameras when Scimitarra fractured a fetlock in the Oaks. She had looked likely to become a leading middle-distance filly; now her future is at stud.

Following Sheikh Mohammed in the owners' table was leading British-based owner Louis Freedman, with a numerically modest 13 races from his four winners.

Reference Point contributed £683,028 of the £741,042 total with his five wins, including the Ever Ready Derby, Holsten Pils St Leger and King George VI and Queen Elizabeth Diamond Stakes. Although apparently rated rather high among recent Derby winners by some experts, my guess is that his comparative rating will have slipped in a few years' time. We must have a 'star' thrust upon us every season, it seems, and Reference Point, hardy and genuine as he was, uneasily carried the mantle in 1987.

His claims to greatness lay in his three-length defeat of Celestial Storm and Triptych on soft ground in the King George. But Celestial Storm's best run came when breaking the Newmarket July course record for a

○ **WORRYING TIMES: Discussing Scimitarra's injury in the Oaks are, from left, owner Sheikh Mohammed, racing manager Anthony Stroud, trainer Henry Cecil and vet James Crowhurst.**   Picture: ALEC RUSSELL

mile and a half on fast ground in the Princess of Wales's Stakes: he had been flattered by his second to Triptych in the previous year's Champion Stakes, the latter having been in front plenty long enough.

As for Triptych at Ascot, the soft ground which suits her so well over a mile and a quarter saps her stamina at the highest level over two furlongs farther, and any comparison with Dancing Brave using the Ascot run as a yardstick must surely be suspect.

Unlike Louis Freedman, Robert Sangster had no great torch-bearer in 1987. Up from sixth place to third, with long-time friend Barry Hills replacing Michael Dickinson at Manton, he nearly trebled his winners of the previous year and more than doubled the prize money, with 73 wins worth £468,289.

Yet the season was not one of unmitigated joy for Sangster. In spite of winning eight Pattern races, he had no genuinely top-class animal after Bluebird, trained in Ireland by Vincent O'Brien, went the wrong way once he had won the King's Stand Stakes. But his other Group One success, by Gallic League in the Tattersalls Middle Park Stakes, was more encouraging: he looks destined to go to the top as a sprinter, and there were good end-of-season wins from juveniles Glacial Storm and Sparrow's Air.

There was no Dancing Brave for Khalid Abdullah in 1987, and he slipped from the second place he had held for the previous three years down to fourth, with 51 races worth £348,573. He held an enviably strong

hand with his two-year-olds, headed by Warning, with Tralos, Undercut and Digamist backing him up.

Searching for plaudits in the Press for fifth-placed owner Alan Clore is like looking for an ill-turned phrase from John Oaksey, but he did us all a huge favour by keeping the incomparable Triptych in training as a five-year-old.

Whatever his financial problems, Clore is an enthusiast who seems genuinely to care about his horses, and believes their place is on a racecourse.

Triptych did him proud in 1987, with the ground at last coming right for her. Her Group One wins included the Hanson Trust Coronation Cup, Matchmaker International and Dubai Champion Stakes. She will be back once more in 1988, although she will be lucky if underfoot conditions favour her quite as much again.

If, looking at the list of leading owners, it seems that only the richest can hope to get a look-in, it is worth casting slightly lower down the list to consider the achievements of Full Circle Thoroughbreds, a company which won 17 races in 1987 and finished 13th in the numerical table. Their members pay around £1 a day for the privilege, and the sight of them crowding into the winner's enclosure is increasing.

Whether the participant is Sheikh Mohammed or the 12-year-old-boy who sold his boat to join a racing syndicate shows that not every owner counts the cost of his enthusiasm. We should be glad so many are still willing to pay the price.□

○ **KHALID ABDULLAH and trainer Guy Harwood (right) in the place of honour.**
Picture: TONY EDENDEN

● **GRANDSTAND VIEW: Looking down
on the action at York.**
Picture: GERRY CRANHAM

CHAPTER 15

The North

by RAY GILPIN

○ **WIDE BERTH: Treasure Hunter (left) and Lindsay Charnock lift the Newcastle 'Brown Ale' Northumberland Plate.**
Picture: ALEC RUSSELL

The North

by RAY GILPIN

As 1987 faded into the record books the North was left reflecting on a relatively successful and certainly eventful year, but still hoping for a better future. Shrewd marketing helped boost crowds without the overall quality of racing necessarily being improved, and several courses positively encourage quantity rather than quality. It might be argued that attendance figures suggest racegoers do not care about the standard of racing, but the appearance of Messrs Cauthen and Eddery doubled attendances at Edinburgh and Hamilton Park in the last weeks of the season, leaving no doubt there is a bigger spectator market to be captured with the bait of good horses and top jockeys.

The removal of on-course betting tax gave the ring a boost, and starting-price reporter Brian Lumley recalled that Reference Point was backed at 14-1 on at York! But things could be better, not least if some of the major owners on the Flat were to spread their equine cream beyond the bounds of Newmarket and Lambourn. It is not a new plea, but the North must not give up hope that one day it will receive a positive response. How Northern trainers would relish the presence of a decent horse or two in their yards, instead of "having to make the best of a poor lot."

Putting the great divide into perspective, did Mel Brittain's 57 winners with a string of bargain-buys rate alongside Henry Cecil's 180 from a huge team of blue-bloods?

Was Mark Birch's feat of coaxing 92 successes out of· mostly moderate horses any less impressive than the scoring rate of Cauthen and Eddery on the best that money can buy?

Boosting prize money does help the cause but the biggest plums at York, Doncaster, Chester, Haydock Park etc provide more pickings for the leading Southern stables.

Northern trainers did win three races at the York May meeting but it tells the tale in that one was a maiden event and the others handicaps; and the sole Northern success at the York August fixture was in a seller.

And having failed to hold the raiders on the home front, Northern trainers had little hope of beating them to any great degree on their own patch. There was not one runner from the North in the five Classics and not a single Royal Ascot prize came back up the A1.

Still, there were several highlights on the Flat, and Birch's gallant but unsuccessful bid to reach a century for the first time in his career was one of them. He had his fifth Northern championship sewn up in August, and though only fifth in the overall championship, was the leading English-born rider. And it gave him great pleasure to keep the South at bay on Swingit Gunner in the·William Hill November Handicap on the last day of the season.

○ **BIG GUN: K-Battery, trained by Bill Elsey, was the North's only Pattern-race winner on the Flat in 1987.**

Picture: TONY EDENDEN

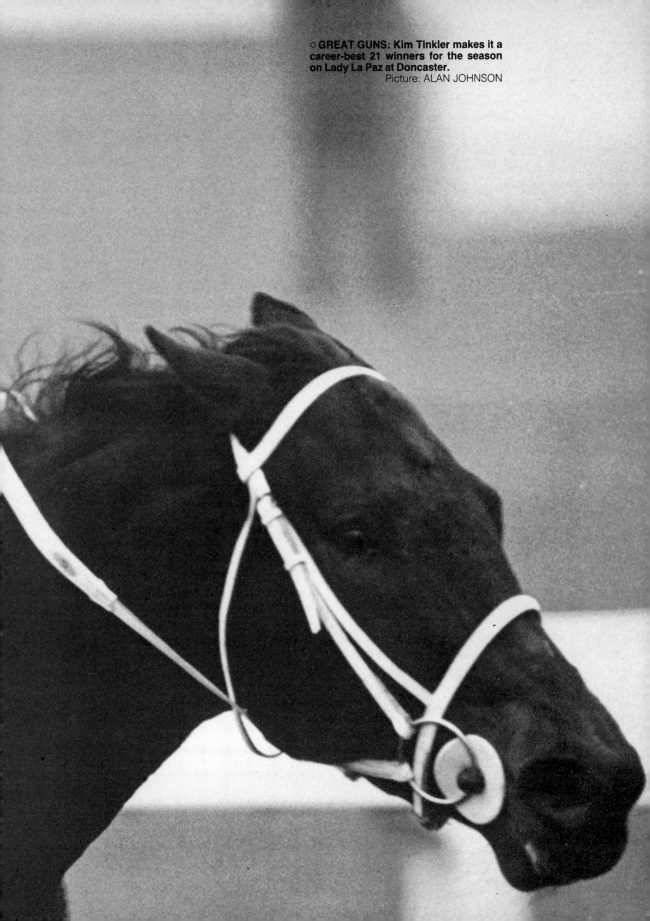

○ **GREAT GUNS: Kim Tinkler makes it a career-best 21 winners for the season on Lady La Paz at Doncaster.**
Picture: ALAN JOHNSON

○ **LAST BLOOD: To the North, as Swingit Gunner (left) beats Mr Pintips and Osric (centre) for the William Hill November Handicap.**
Picture: ALEC RUSSELL

Lindsay Charnock and John Lowe again proved a match for the best lightweights in the country, while John Carroll and Tony Culhane are youngsters with a future.

Swingit Gunner was trained by Colin Tinkler, and he and brother Nigel showed they are on the way up, enjoying their best seasons with 31 winners each. Richard Whitaker also set a new high of 33.

Nigel's wife, Kim, emerged easily the top woman rider with 21 winners, most for the successful Full Circle Throroughbred owners' group. Bill Watts was unlucky not to win a top-class event with Oakworth, whose

season was cut short through injury. And he was sad to see Teleprompter retire and leave his yard, but what memories Lord Derby's gelding left behind.

K-Battery bowed out too, Bill Elsey having done well to pick up a couple of Group races with him.

Peter Easterby was top trainer numerically with 68 winners but they earned only £205,997, scant reward for a long campaign, with his first winner on March 28 and last on November 7.

There has never been any reluctance on Steve Norton's part to travel and his boldness was rewarded

with two successes in Ireland with Just Class.

Haydock Park's realigned bend had the thumbs up and an earlier introduction of a straight six furlongs helped the Vernons Sprint achieve Group One status. At nearby Chester — its tight circuit unmatched for excitement and atmosphere — a magnificent new structure emerged from the ashes of the burned County Stand.

Not for the first time — and doubtless not for the last — the North's most memorable moment was in the jumping arena where multi-million dollar cheque books do not rule the roost and the area matches the rest of the country with its chasers and hurdlers year after year.

The sight of The Thinker and Ridley Lamb battling up the snowbound Cheltenham hill to take Gold Cup glory will never be forgotten. It was a first Gold Cup winner for that incomparable character Arthur Stephenson, who elected to go to Hexham rather than Cheltenham on the big day!

'W.A.' has saddled 100 winners or more a season no fewer than seven times since 1959, a magnificent feat. But the Gold Cup at last forced him to concede that big fish can be sweet too.

The Thinker helped Stephenson and owner Tom McDonagh into second place respectively in the trainers' and owners' list. But Stephenson's 65 winners earned a mere £202,776, more than a quarter of that courtesy of the Gold Cup. Martin Pipe's 106 successes earned £166,926, hammering home the point that few get rich in the winter game.

The North struck three other Cheltenham Festival blows. The Waltons from Morpeth took the National Hunt Handicap Chase with Mighty Mark, while Gordon Richards struck with Tartan Tailor. And there was another family affair when Nigel Tinkler sent out Full Circle Thoroughbred's The Ellier to give syndicate ownership another shot in the arm by winning the Kim Muir Memorial Chase.

As the jumping season moved on, April showers brought their share of sad moments amid the roars of triumph.

There was disappointment when Stephenson, though never having won

a Grand National, decided it was not in The Thinker's best interests to send him to Aintree. And there was tragedy when Dark Ivy was fatally injured at the sixth fence in the National. The Ellier, who finished seventh at Aintree, was destroyed two weeks later after breaking a leg at Wetherby.

Forty-eight hours before the National, Wayward Lad's success in the Whitbread Gold Label Cup was greeted with almost as much enthusiasm as the big winner. It proved to be his swan song, only to be followed by the Dickinson family's being forced to go to 42,000gns to dissolve a partnership in the old warrior. The possibility that one of Wayward Lad's owners might send him point-to-pointing had stunned trainer Monica Dickinson. His appearance at the Doncaster Sales put an end to that idea, and Wayward Lad was sent across to Fair Hill in Maryland where he joined his former trainer Michael Dickinson.

Another Dickinson star, Badsworth Boy left the scene too, having re-written the record books when winning the Queen Mother Champion Chase three years in a row — 1983, 84 and 85.

A return to his native Ireland reaped rich reward for Jimmy FitzGerald when Forgive'N Forget lifted Leopardstown's Vincent O'Brien Gold Cup. But Gordon Richards' 59 winners at home earned more than the 73 sent out by FitzGerald, whose run rate slowed considerably in the New Year after 52 wins by the end of Boxing Day.

There were hopes at one stage that Mark Dwyer might take the jockeys'

championship but his challenge failed because of the numbers game. Dwyer rode 81 winners, 42 adrift of Peter Scudamore, but the latter had 241 more rides and Dwyer at least had the satisfaction of a better winning average. Among the amateurs Jamie Osborne emerged as a rising star and Anthea Farrell (nee Beaumont) impressed, particularly on her father Peter's exciting chaser J-J-Henry.

Racing's image was done no favours when Graham Bradley was banned for three months for failing to gain the best possible placing on Deadly Going at Market Rasen. Nevertheless he, Dwyer, Lorcan Wyer and Chris Grant in particular are Northern-based riders who are a match, pound for pound, for any.

For other jockeys it was time to call it a day. Ridley Lamb, Maurice Barnes, Steve Youlden, Derek Oldham and Robert Earnshaw all decided to hang up their boots for a variety of reasons. Earnshaw switched to training and Happy Voyage opened his account at Nottingham on 20 November. And you would have thought Shelbourne had won the Scottish National by the reception he received when giving Jonjo O'Neill his first training success at Ayr on January 30. Edinburgh's new jumping track, brainchild of Clerk of Course David McHarg, proved a tremendous success. There is no more exciting jumping course for spectators and the Scottish roar of 'away ye certainty' when the favourite clears the last in front is an experience those north of the Border will savour for years to come.□

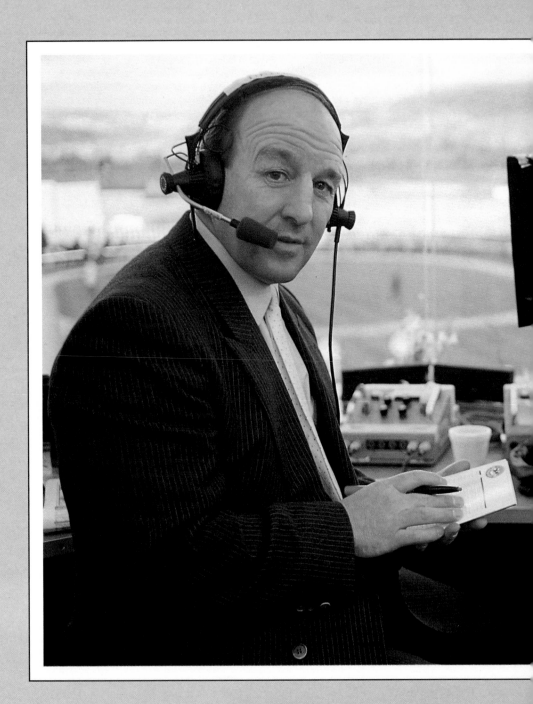

Racing and Broadcasting

Racing and Broadcasting

by RICHARD PITMAN

CONTRARY TO popular belief, both the BBC and Channel 4 consider horse racing an important part of their sporting output with recent cuts more of a trim than a scalpeling job. Now, with the emergence of Satellite Information Services providing pictures of non-networked racing, the sport has never been better served.

On BBC the only noticeable loss has been the Chester May fixture, the Corporation's best meeting for bringing live racing into non-converted racegoers' homes. The tight, ever-turning track meant that coverage brought more close-up action than normal. From Chester, housebound viewers could see flared nostrils and working muscle, and watch the plot being hatched.

On the plus side, BBC coverage in 1988 has expanded in Ireland, with Leopardstown in January, Punchestown in February and Fairyhouse in April all featuring top chases. The Budweiser Irish Derby has the whole stage on 25 June, while the inaugural Cartier Million shares air space with Chepstow on 1 October (subject to finalisation of contracts).

In all, 89 meetings are due to be covered in 1988 by the BBC (to 84 by Channel 4), including the Cheltenham and Aintree Festivals, Royal Ascot and Glorious Goodwood. The only Saturdays when no racing is scheduled are 6 February, 14 May and 2 July.

BBC camera work and production makes the licence fee look good value. The major bone of contention with the viewing public seems to be the use of frequent close-up shots in tight finishes which ignore the rest. But as it would be impossible to please everybody if the opposite were the norm, there would be a lobby against long-distance finishes giving a picture not dissimilar to flies on a window. With the machinery now available to produce instant replays, relevant happenings ignored in live coverage can be brought to viewers' attention when reviewing the last few furlongs.

Coverage of Saturday racing on BBC has been pruned to the bare essentials, with this just one of a plethora of sports featured during the afternoon. When the occasion merits, previews, paddock coverage and relevant interviews are given air space, but run-of-the-mill contests are limited to the race itself and essentials. The pattern is unlikely to change much in the coming year.

What may well be different though, is the content of the Seagram Grand National show. This year producer Fred Viner steps down after almost two decades of calling the shots. His successor is Grand Prix producer Keith Mackenzie, and although it is doubtful whether he will make significant changes initially, there could be much greater involvement from Grandstand's editor and producer on the two warm-up days.

Channel 4's changes have been far more obvious, especially the decision to concentrate on a single meeting every Saturday instead of the old ITV Seven from two meetings. It's swings and roundabouts: a single meeting can be covered in greater detail, with time for interviews and filmed stories to placate the purist; coverage of two meetings appeals more to the betting man whilst costing more to stage.

Now the rival channels have settled down to their concept of how much racing can be televised without over-egging the pudding, it seems we do fare rather well.

Channel 4 have the best of the Flat-race action, with a clean sweep of the British Classics, York, Epsom, Doncaster, Newcastle, Sandown Park, Kempton Park and Newmarket. But Goodwood, Ascot and Haydock Park rest firmly with the BBC giving them a good bite at the Flat.

Over the sticks the opposite is true, with Channel 4 nibbling at the Beeb's hold over the top steeplechases. Channel 4's contract with Ayr, Sandown and Kempton gives them enough muscle to hold up their end

during the winter.

I cannot envisage the likes of Ascot wishing to swop channels for mere money; nor is it likely the BBC will enter into an auction involving huge sums to secure any Classics. So the status quo looks like being maintained – or does it?

With SIS gathering momentum, it could be in a position, in the not-too-distant future, to supply either or both networks with pictures for the existing production and presentation teams to use.

After getting over the expected initial teething problems, the SIS service is a good one, and at present efforts are being directed towards supplying those betting shops which have signed up to take the service.

In one respect the gradual switch-on to shops has been a blessing, as improvements are being carried out while the bulk of suscribers are in the wings. Standards of racecourse commentary did not reach broadcasting quality in some cases, and studio routine also needed refining.

From early-1988 the plan is to cover two horse-race meetings every day to give continuous live action from every part of Britain. It is also the intention of SIS to help promote all-weather tracks here, to maintain a constant supply of the racing with which the British public are familiar.

SIS executives are also interested in helping racecourses stage a regular seventh race to reduce the number of oversubscribed novice hurdles and bumpers events. The estimated 1.5m viewers in betting shops each day should be an attractive incentive to sponsors who might be persuaded to fund this extra race.

At the end of December 1987, SIS contracted to take live coverage of, or to record, the 30 days which RTE televise in Ireland. This will give British race fans a chance to see Cheltenham Festival hopes before they pop up in March. The same will be true of Irish Classic hopes coming over the water.

Stage One in SIS development is obviously to sell what is on offer at present, but you do not need three A-levels to realise the potential of packaging racing to Europe or perhaps even to the 24-hour a day gambling mad town of Las Vegas.

Have no fear, televised horse racing is unlikely to take a back seat to the minority sports. It is an important part of the network schedule and the lifeblood of SIS. Punters and enthusiasts alike have never had a better chance to evaluate their sport from pictures than they have today.□

Peter O'Sullevan

by JOHN OAKSEY

IMAGINE A RACE MEETING on television with no mention of betting, no pre-race market moves, no idea of prices before the race, and after it no starting-price return.

"Life before McCririck" I suppose you would call it and some misguided souls might even consider that an advantage. But not many.

This, believe it or not, was the BBC's inflexible rule until as late as August 1958. It was only then, for the first time, that they reluctantly allowed their commentators even to admit that betting was taking place.

No-one has ever accused Peter O'Sullevan of ignoring betting and he had been campaigning for years in his Daily Express column to bring the Corporation up to date. During those early racing programmes, he always tried to stop talking when any useful mention of betting or prices was audible over the public address system.

"Sometimes you could hear the bookies themselves," Peter says, "and I would shut up as quickly as possible to let the poor viewers listen. The snag was that my producer used to wonder what was happening. 'What the hell's wrong?' he would shout down the headset. 'Why don't you keep talking?' Somehow I don't think I ever got around to explaining my motive!"

In the end it was not so much the efforts of their chief commentator as the appearance of competition which changed the BBC's policy. When John Rickman and Tony Cooke came on the screens of Associated Rediffusion in 1957, their ITV employers had no inhibitions about the "evils" of gambling. The commercial channels immediately began giving out starting prices and were soon developing betting shows and other pre-McCririck trimmings.

So what were they like, those early, black and white years? The man to ask is clearly Peter O'Sullevan, whose career with the BBC began straight after the war, first as "racereader" to Raymond Glendenning or more frequently Peter Dimmock, and then, more and more, on his own account, using what has been, as long as I can remember, the inimitable, instantly-recognisable "voice of racing".

A bronchial chest kept Peter out of the Army so he spent the War in the Rescue Service, digging people out of bombed houses in his beloved Chelsea throughout the Blitz and, even more unacceptable he says, during the buzz-bomb attacks of 1944, the year he joined the Press Association.

In 1950, when Cyril Luckman retired and Clive Graham became The Scout on the Daily Express, Peter was quickly persuaded to join him. "They didn't know it, but I had already written for them," he remembers. "One weekend Clive somehow got marooned in Paris, at a party too good to leave I suspect. He cabled me in London, 'Urgent. Please cover Salisbury tomorrow. Will pay in Brandy!' It is always easier writing someone else's piece and no-one seemed to mind."

So began the close, friendly and famous partnership which was to last until Graham's death.

At the beginning, however, it seemed far from certain that Peter's employers would see the two jobs, journalism and commentating, as

○ **John Oaksey on duty.**
Picture: ALAN JOHNSON

compatible. "Your value to the paper will be completely lost if this goes on," editor Authur Christiansen wrote after hearing Peter had done a trial racecourse commentary at Goodwood in 1952. He was, it seems, convinced that racegoing readers of the Express, having heard the O'Sullevan comments live on a racecourse, would refuse to pay for them in the morning paper!

As it turned out, of course, quite apart from his often genuinely exclusive reports, Peter is one of the very few racing journalists in my time whose tips were well worth taking note of. Since his work for the BBC also made him famous throughout the racing world, I doubt whether any newspaper editor has got things much more comprehensively wrong than Christiansen on that occasion!

From 1946 Peter O'Sullevan began

working regularly for BBC TV. The Derby had occasionally been televised before the War but when two steeplechases and a hurdle race were covered live at Sandown on 24 January 1948, it was believed to be the first broadcast of its kind in the world. From then on, in those early post-War, pre-competition days, a surprising number and variety of meetings were covered by the BBC.

By modern standards, understandably, broadcasting facilities were fairly primitive. "As long as you were on the racecourse they reckoned you were sure to be able to see everything," Peter says. "There was seldom a 'position' or any cover to speak of, and after standing out in the rain all day at Sedgefield, you really felt you had earned your fee."

Clive Graham who had joined the Daily Express in 1931 and remained with it all his working life, became the BBC's paddock commentator in the 1950s. Although he did not believe in, or seem to need, a lot of homework, the job has never been done better on any channel, certainly never with such a mixture of wit, charm and encyclopaedic knowledge of the sport.

As an assistant commentator, on the other hand, Clive seems to have had his limitations. Peter asked him to help at one of his first Grand Nationals, and since no special viewpoint had been prepared, decided to climb on the corrugated iron roof of a public lavatory near their first-fence

position. It was just as the National field bore down on them, not the easiest moment for a young commentator, that Clive made his first and only contribution. "Christ", he said. "I'm falling off this effing roof."

Such disorganised scenes seem a world away now, as you talk to Peter O'Sullevan in his elegant London flat, surrounded by the paintings, drawings and bronzes of his late, great friend John Skeaping.

They met in 1940, through a greyhound which John was training and whose owner wanted it put down because of the War. On Peter's insistence, John sent the dog from Exeter, and though not interested in chasing anything at first, Slim, Rosebud or Rainbow — his name depended on which of the various suburban "flapping" tracks he was gracing — became so speedy that his exploits, mostly at Staines, kept his one-dog, owner-trainer in funds for several years.

Nowadays, Peter's string is reduced to one, small, vociferous poodle, but he has always loved dog-racing and commentated on all the early Greyhound Derbys. At the first, in 1957, the crew held an elaborate afternoon rehearsal, only to find in the evening that they had forgotten there would be a crowd between them and the action. Both commentator and cameras finished perched insecurely on a pile of wine crates.

A deep love of animals and dislike of people or things which cause them pain has always been central to Peter O'Sullevan's philosophy. In 1979, under an Express headline "Backed any beaten horses lately?", he launched an eloquent campaign against the excessive use of the whip, which was then and, I'm sorry to say, is once again, commonplace in this country. Peter, whose views were supported by such stylists as Joe Mercer and Johnny Gilbert, had been impressed by the much stricter (and more strictly enforced) rules on the whip in Scandinavia.

Nor is his sympathy confined to racehorses. On a visit to Morocco in January 1983, he was horrified by the condition of the horses, ponies and donkeys on the streets and beaches of

Agadir. In December that year, he raised £36,833 in an auction at the Horserace Writers' Association lunch, and dividing that sum between the International League for the Protection of Horses and the Brooke Hospital in Cairo, he inspired the opening of a special Veterinary Centre at Agadir.

Without spending gigantic sums, Peter O'Sullevan has had remarkable success as an owner, and no-one who heard him will forget the scarcely believeable blend of accuracy and detachment with which he described on television the Cheltenham and Haydock Park triumphs of Attivo and Be Friendly. Not at all surprisingly, they are among his favourite memories.

Of course, even for someone who does his homework as thoroughly as Peter, luck occasionally runs out. One foggy day at Hurst Park for instance, the camera suddenly chose as "the leader" a grey horse who had been pulled up first time round and was lobbing home in his own time. Peter, who was describing a hard-fought battle over the last three fences between the three actual leaders, found to his horror that his commentary bore no relation to the only picture viewers were being offered.

Television has not always been flavour of the month with the powers that be in racing and it was a very special tribute to Peter O'Sullevan's unique record of service to the sport that as a still-working commentator, he should be elected to the Jockey Club.

No United States Senator ever looked the part of an elder statesman much better – with that elegant snow-white hair and wise, slightly battered face.

If the Jockey Club Stewards have any sense, they will listen very carefully to the opinions of a man who has loved, watched and adorned British racing for forty years. And whether they follow Peter's advice or not, the deep, clear, gravel voice in which it is given will conjure up enough golden memories to raise the hair on the back of some eminent necks.□

○ **PETER O'SULLEVAN**
Picture: STEWART KENDALL

— CHAPTER 17 —

Sires

by ADRIAN COOK

● **NOT FORGOTTEN: Mill Reef, who died in 1986, was the Flat season's leading sire.**

Picture: GERRY CRANHAM

○ **LIKE FATHER . . .:** Don't Forget Me arrives at Coolmore Stud to be greeted by his sire Ahonoora.

Sires

by ADRIAN COOK

REFERENCE POINT'S magnificent victories ensured that Mill Reef headed the British and Irish sires' list for the second time and helped his sire to a record prize-money total of almost £1,250,000.

The former National Stud stallion, who died in February 1986, had an advantage of almost £500,000 over Riverman, who like Mill Reef is a son of the champion US 1962 two-year-old Never Bend.

But once more the most dominant figure on the leading sires' table was the outstanding Canadian-bred Northern Dancer, whose retirement from active stud duty was announced in April.

He finished 11th leading sire while 10 of his sons and grandsons figured in the top 30: Nureyev, Be My Guest, Danzig, Kings Lake, Try My Best, Ile de Bourbon, Storm Bird, Nijinsky, Lomond and Golden Fleece.

Northern Dancer's retirement was sandwiched between the deaths of Mill Reef and Habitat, so that within

an 18-month period the stud careers of the three most influential sires in British and Irish racing since 1970 has come to an end.

Their influence will live on. Northern Dancer has founded his own dynasty while Habitat became the leading broodmare sire in 1987 and Mill Reef has numerous successful sons at stud.

Mill Reef's previous Derby winning son, Shirley Heights, has already sired a Derby winner in Slip Anchor. Besides Shirley Heights, Glint of Gold, Pas De Seul, Moulton and Main Reef were other sons of Mill Reef to have Pattern winners during the year.

By his victories in the Ever Ready Derby, King George VI and Queen Elizabeth Diamond Stakes, and Holsten Pils St Leger, Reference Point established himself as the best son of his sire.

And although Milligram finished only second in the English and Irish 1,000 Guineas, she laid claim to be regarded as his best daughter when

she won the Queen Elizabeth II Stakes and Waterford Crystal Mile.

Other excellent three-year-olds by Mill Reef were the Gran Premio d'Italia winner Ibn Bey and the Tara Sires Desmond Stakes winner Entitled, while the older pair Big Reef and Verardi also won Pattern races in Italy.

The Gainesway stallion Riverman enjoyed an excellent year, finishing high on the sires' lists in Britain and Ireland, France and the United States.

His most successful runner in Europe was Triptych, who did better than ever at the age of five and included the Prix Ganay, Matchmaker International, Dunnes Stores St Bernard Champion Stakes and Dubai Champion among her string of big-race successes.

The unbeaten St James's Palace Stakes winner Half A Year and the Trusthouse Forte Diadem Stakes winner Dowsing were other British Pattern-race scorers for him.

The French-trained three-year-old filly River Memories stood up well to a tough season to win four major prizes, including the Prix Maurice de Nieuil at Saint-Cloud and Rothmans International Championship at Woodbine in Canada.

Riverman's leading US winners included the Graded stakes winners Rivlia, Akabir and Adorable Micol. He also enjoyed considerable success as a broodmare sire, while his son Irish River enjoyed his most successful year at stud.

Third on the table was Nureyev, who also headed the French sires' list and did well in the US too. It is to be hoped he makes a full recovery from the serious leg injury he sustained in May.

He had six individual Pattern race winners in Europe, headed by the Classic-winning pair Miesque and Soviet Star, who won eight Group One races between them.

The others were last year's champion miler Sonic Lady, the French juveniles Movieland and Pasakos, and Stately Don, who won a Group Three in Ireland before winning the Grade One Arlington Stakes and Hollywood Derby in the States.

Also in the States, Theatrical finally came into his own as a five-year-old. He had been runner-up in the Sweeps Derby at three and Breeders' Cup Turf at four, but in 1987 he went from strength to strength and his successes included the Man O'War Stakes, and Turf Classic and Breeders' Cup Turf.

For the third year in succession the dual Arc winner Alleged finished in the top four and once more he had a European Classic winner to his name.

Following Law Society and Leading Counsel in 1985 and Midway Lady in 1986 came Sir Harry Lewis, who took the Budweiser Irish Derby.

Fair Judgment, Sharaniya and Jurado were other European Pattern race winners for him while Kazaroun, Mister Big Louie, Lord Justice and Safety Catch were all Group-placed.

In America he got only his second Graded stakes winner on dirt when Fiesta Gal proved herself a leading three-year-old filly when winning the Mother Goose Stakes and CCA Oaks.

For the second year in succession the leading domestically-based sire was Ahonoora, who just edged out Be My Guest.

Ahonoora was bought by Coolmore Stud and Segenhoe Stud in July for £7m, and is to stand a season in New Zealand this autumn after covering in Ireland.

Standing alongside him in 1988 at Coolmore will be Don't Forget Me, who became the first since Right Tack in 1969 to win both the English and Irish 2,000 Guineas.

Nashamaa, Princess Athena, Ginny Binny and Noora Abu were other notable runners by this former Irish National Stud sire, whose fee has risen from IR£2,750 in 1984 to IR£45,000 in 1988.

Another Coolmore resident, Be My Guest, enjoyed his best season since he won the sires' championship in 1982 with his runners headed by the Derby and Champion Stakes runner-up Most Welcome.

He was one of four Pattern-race winners for his sire, following the fillies Invited Guest (in France), Intimate Guest and Guest Performer, while Daarkom and Media Starguest were other important winners for him.

The leading British-based sire was Kris, champion sire of 1985, who got his third Classic winner in three crops when Unite completed the Oaks double at Epsom and The Curragh, following the Classic successes of Oh So Sharp and Flash of Steel.

His three-year-olds also included Scimitarra, who was badly injured when favourite for the Oaks, and the Group-race winning French-trained pair Swept Away and The Scout.

In the Prix de la Salamandre winner Common Grounds he has a major contender for Classic honours in 1988, and as the only one of the top 12 sires to be British-based he is justifiably recognised as Britain's top sire.

Busted owed his return to the top ten for the first time since 1979 to the top-class mile and a quarter performer Mtoto, who completed a hat-trick of Pattern race wins with his Coral-Eclipse success over Reference Point.

Buckley also did his now-retired sire proud by winning the Doncaster and Jockey Club Cups. Other sons of Busted, Bustino and Labus, and his grandson, Akarad, all had notable winners, while Busted also enjoyed notable success as a broodmare sire.

Ela-Mana-Mou enjoyed an extremely successful second half of the season and the successes of Emmson in the William Hill Futurity and Eurobird in the Jefferson Smurfit Memorial Irish St Leger hoisted him to ninth on the sires' table.

The Lowther winner Ela Romara, Grand Prix de Deauville and Prix Kergorlay scorer Almaarad and the Prix de Flore winner Only A Rumour were others who showed that the Airlie stallion is good value at his IR£15,000 covering fee.

Blushing Groom topped the two-year-old sires' list thanks to the Heinz 57 Phoenix Stakes success of Digamist. That victory also helped him into tenth place overall.

The King Edward VII and Gordon Stakes winner Love the Groom also did well here while Groom Dancer, Luth Dancer, Nashmeel, Malakim and Blushing John helped their sire into the top ten in France and Ifrad took Grade One honours in the USA.

Four-times champion Northern Dancer owed the bulk of his earnings here to Ajdal, who proved himself a champion when it was discovered that sprinting was his game.

The five-year-old mare Northern Aspen became Northern Dancer's 30th Group or Grade One winner when winning the Gamely Handicap in May and he also enjoyed success as a broodmare sire with his daughters producing such as Ravinella, Half A Year, Digamist and Magic of Life.

Completing the top dozen is the recently-exported 2,000 Guineas winner Known Fact, who will stand at Juddmonte Farm, Kentucky in 1988.

His first two crops have been mainly disappointing but his third includes the unbeaten Warning, ante-post favourite for the 2,000 Guineas following his wins in the P & OCL Richmond and Laurent Perrier Champagne Stakes.

With 15 individual winners at home and abroad he was represented by more two-year-old scorers than any other sire and already more members of his third crop have won than of his second.

The sire with the most individual winners in Britain and Ireland was Taufan, who had 29 firsts, including the smart miler Pasticcio and successful sprinters such as Royal Fan, Ingabelle, Clear Her Stage and Nafuat.

The sire whose progeny won the most races (46) was the consistently successful Dominion. His leading winners included the smart juveniles Peace Girl and Classic Ruler, three-year-olds Belle Poitrine and Just Class, and older performers such as Governor General and Sprowston Boy.

The first-season sires' title went to Northern Dancer's son Lomond, whose winners included three Pattern-winning fillies in Ashayer, Flutter Away and Lomond Blossom.

He was chased hard by Nijinsky's son Caerleon, who had the Irish Pattern winners Caerwent and Careafolie to represent him, and by Kris's brother Diesis, sire of Diminuendo and Carmelite House.

All three have leading Classic contenders and are likely to be challenging established names at the top of the sires' table in 1988.□

CHAPTER 18

Bloodstock Sales

by TONY MORRIS

○ **ROUND FIGURES: The scene during the Goffs Million Sale.**

Picture: GERRY CRANHAM

Bloodstock Sales

by TONY MORRIS

THIS WAS A SEASON OF progress on the yearling sales front, most significantly at the quality end of the market. Most substantial gains were recorded at Tattersalls' Highflyer auction and at Goffs in October, when the innovation of the much publicized "Million" sale proved a resounding success.

But while the advances were welcome, in most cases they did not go far enough to suggest that thoroughbred breeding was once more a profitable business. On the contrary, a majority of the 1987 yearlings were sold at under their production cost, the third consecutive season that sorry state of affairs had existed.

Once more there was no reason to blame the buyers, who were always willing to pay realistic prices for racing potential, who were content to pay rather more than last year for the

better-quality stock, and who wanted just as many yearlings as in 1986. It was hardly their fault if their acceptance of 3,082 Flat-bred yearlings in the 11 major auctions accounted for only 73.3 per cent of what they were offered.

Over the last few seasons the volume of demand has been quite steady, and a fair "rule of thumb" might be that there is generally a market for 3,000 British and Irish yearlings. The suppliers have yet to adjust to that level of demand, to the sad extent that more than a quarter of the 1987 yearling crop went unwanted. That ratio can be expected to rise again this autumn after another record foal crop.

With a quarter of their produce rejected, and half of what was sold returning a net loss, breeders generally did not have a lot to enthuse

about in the 1987 market, for all the statistical progress.

At year's end two insults were added to the injuries.

The announcement of the fees for stallions to cover in 1988 was met with general dismay, the scale being patently too close to that which offered scant hope of a return to profitability in the previous season. Less than half the horses who covered for excessive amounts in 1987 were reduced in price for 1988, and as many as 20, in defiance of the state of the market, had their fees raised – such as Dominion and Lomond by more than 50 per cent, and Ahonoora by more than 100 per cent.

Breeders were clearly going to have their work cut out when trying to select value-for-money sires for their yearlings of 1990 – if they elected to stay in the business.

The mid-December ruling by the Law Lords that stud buildings were no longer exempt from rating, as they had been under an Act of Parliament passed more than half a century ago, inevitably threatened many small British operations and promised to impose yet another heavy burden on an industry already under-encouraged and actively penalized by Government.

The repercussions of the ruling will be strongly felt in and beyond the bloodstock business, because it effectively rubber-stamped the arbitrary actions of ratings officers who held no authority from Parliament to levy the charge.

Certainly there was plenty to cause concern among thoroughbred breeders about the events of 1987. But things could have been much worse. The fact that British- or Irish-bred horses won four of the five Classics, plus the Eclipse and the "King George" provided an agreeable climate for the autumn yearling sales, and the timing of the worldwide stock market crash, with the major auctions already over, could hardly have been more propitious.

Doncaster provided an excellent beginning to the sales series, with a slight drop in the percentage of lots sold as the only disappointment. Both turnover and average were the second best on record, while the median (6,200gns) advanced beyond the previous best of 1984.

The St Leger sale, which outstrips all others in the production of two-year-old winners, got most things right in 1987 and that rise in the median is a sure indication the occasion is gaining popularity with vendors and buyers alike. Doncaster's first five-figure average, which seemed to be close five years ago, could become a reality in 1988.

The highest-priced lot of the sale was a Welsh Saint colt, knocked down to the week's biggest spender, Newmarket trainer Ian Matthews. The 51,000gns youngster from Robin

○ **TOP TEAM: Khalid Abdullah (right) gets the views of agent George Blackwell (centre), trainer Jeremy Tree (left) and manager Grant Pritchard-Gordon.**
Picture: GERRY CRANHAM

○ **IAN MATTHEWS spent heavily at the Doncaster Yearling Sales.**
Picture: TONY EDENDEN

and Scarlett Knipe's Cobhall Court Stud was one of 11 Matthews bought during the five-day auction.

Only one of the five major yearling sales failed to register a higher aggregate in 1987 than in 1986. That was the Tattersalls (Ireland) sale at Ballsbridge, which suffered an inconsequential loss while recording satisfactory compensating gains in terms of average and median.

The two-day catalogue was remarkable in that the second session, apparently the better on paper, proved distinctly disappointing, with an abundance of poor individuals and a third of the lots sold realizing under IR2,000gns. But the late deterioration in trade was not sufficient to prevent overall progress, although the average still lagged behind the levels set from 1981 to 1984.

Top price here was IR36,000gns, given by Philpotstown Stud owner Cathal McCarthy for a bay son of first-crop sire Precocious out of Arenetta, from an old-established and successful Kildangan family.

As commonly expected, the abandonment of the select session at Tattersalls' Highflyer sale provided a considerable boost to trade. A strong catalogue overall and the strongest-ever demand in the middle market yielded vast increases in average and

median prices, both to record levels. The turnover was still five million guineas short of 1984's all-time high, but in that season of ultimate irrationality 70 more yearlings had been sold.

To nobody's surprise, the Highflyer auction was dominated by the Maktoum family, who bought 25 of the 40 lots sold in the ring for 200,000gns and more, who acquired at least 68 yearlings and contributed 12,638,000gns (40 per cent) to the week's proceeds, and whose average purchase cost 185,853gns, compared with 73,124gns for the rest of the catalogue.

Among the Maktoum buys was the season's top-priced yearling, a 780,000gns colt bought for Sheikh Hamdan from Hubbards Lodge Stud. This was the very last Mill Reef

yearling to go to auction, and if some felt that his pedigree on the dam's side did not read exceptionally, nobody disputed that he was a fine individual and a grand mover.

The oddest feature of the 1986 Highflyer Sale had been that the highest-priced lot, a 600,000gns Nureyev colt out of Etoile de Paris, had not even come to Newmarket. But at least the details of that private transaction were released by Tattersalls.

In 1987 there was official silence over an equally significant deal involving an absentee from the sale-ring. A bald end-of-business statement recorded only that there had been three private sales for a total of 756,900gns during the week, and it took a little detective work to learn that one of the transactions concerned

○ **MAN IN A MILLION: Jonathan Irwin, whose idea for the Million Sale at Goffs had immediate effect.**
Picture: GERRY CRANHAM

the withdrawn Northern Dancer filly out of Where You Lead, apparently sold to Alan Clore for 725,000gns. No confirmation was obtainable from the auctioneers.

The Highflyer results were excellent, but Tattersalls had to give best to their Irish rivals for the success story of the year. That award surely goes to Kill for an outstanding occasion which took aggregate and average prices beyond even the 1984 records.

The dramatic upsurge owed all to the concept of the "Million", a seven-furlong race scheduled for Phoenix Park in 1988 with a million punts in prize money and entry restricted to 250 specially nominated Goffs' yearlings. The impact made by this innovation, brainchild of Goffs'

managing director Jonathan Irwin, may be gauged from the fact that the 232 "Million" yearlings realized IR21,356,500gns, whereas the other 467 sold during the four-day auction fetched IR5,243,950gns between them.

Best of all was a first-crop son of the exceptional El Gran Senor, whose price of IR780,000gns (given by George Blackwell on behalf of Khalid Abdullah) was the highest for a Kill yearling since Authaal set his European record of IR3,100,000gns in 1984. The colt is out of Vive La Reine, a sister to Vaguely Noble whose previous successful products include the Champagne Stakes victor R.B. Chesne.

Tattersalls' October Sales, last of the five major yearling auctions, is

generally regarded as the most significant in the series. More than any other, this one tells the story of how trade is for the majority of those who deal in bloodstock, and in 1987 it had its good points and its bad points.

The biggest-ever catalogue duly delivered the expected highest-ever aggregate, but the average and median figures advanced only by slim margins, and a distinct sex bias was noted, with the median for colts at 12,000gns and the median for fillies at a less satisfactory 9,200gns.

Only four of the 860 lots sold reached six figures, with a top price of 140,000gns for the grey colt by Busti-no out of Nicholas Grey sold by Hesmonds Stud to Lady Beaverbrook.□

Yearling Sales 1987

	Catalogued	Offered	Sold	Aggregate	Average	Median	Per cent sold
DONCASTER ST LEGER	445	406	332	2,790,200 +16.8%	8,404 +8.8%	6,200 +10.7%	81.8 −1.3%
BALLSBRIDGE SEPTEMBER	338	310	230	1,144,900 −3.3%	4,977 +5.1%	4,000 +14.3%	74.2 −2.5%
NEWMARKET HIGHFLYER	426	389	325	31,430,900 +17%	96,710 +28.2%	56,000 +36.6%	83.5 −5.3%
GOFFS OCTOBER	874	802	699	26,600,450 +64.6%	38,055 +51.2%	15,000 +27.1%	87.1 +8.2%
NEWMARKET OCTOBER	1,097	1,009	860	13,319,829 +14.3%	15,488 +9.2%	10,500 +5%	85.2 −2.9%
DONCASTER OCTOBER	313	274	197	500,530 +71.5%	2,541 +23.6%	1,700 +11.8%	71.9 +4.9%
NEWMARKET AUTUMN	296	265	210	685,235 −8.5%	3,263 −0.6%	2,000 −28.6%	79.2 −3.4%
DONCASTER NOVEMBER	63	52	37	69,120 +12.5%	1,868 +24.7%	1,300 +8.3%	71.1 −2.1%
BALLSBRIDGE NOVEMBER	77	58	22	50,670 −60.1%	2,303 −7.6%	1,375 −27.6%	37.9 −39.4%
NEWMARKET DECEMBER	243	188	136	1,072,150 −7.5%	7,883 −20.4%	5,400 −22.8%	72.3 −3.7%
GOFFS DECEMBER	69	54	34	110,100 +16.8%	3,238 −55.4%	2,600 −7.1%	63 +27.9%

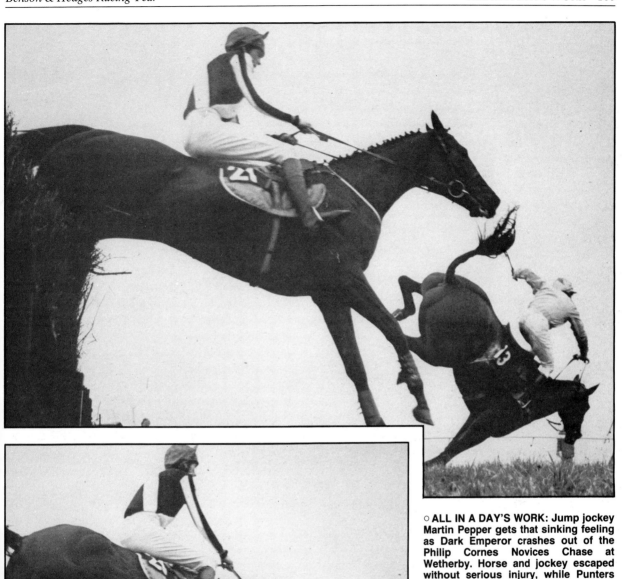

○ **ALL IN A DAY'S WORK: Jump jockey Martin Pepper gets that sinking feeling as Dark Emperor crashes out of the Philip Cornes Novices Chase at Wetherby. Horse and jockey escaped without serious injury, while Punters Lad and Peter Hobbs scrambled along their way.** Pictures: ALAN JOHNSON

CHAPTER 19

Melbourne Cup

A personal view by J. A. McGRATH

○**WORTH THE EFFORT: Larry Olsen, who shed stones to make a riding comeback, returns in triumph on Kensei.**
Picture: GEORGE SELWYN

Melbourne Cup

A personal view by J. A. McGRATH

KENSEI's Melbourne Cup win at Flemington in November was a readily acceptable result.

Prize money of A$1.25 million was on offer, thanks to second-year sponsorship by Foster's, but it was by no means a vintage running of the two-mile handicap.

Kensei would never be rated the best winner of the past decade. He would be considered easily superior to Robert Sangster's 1980 winner

Beldale Ball but not in the same class as Gurner's Lane (1982) or the amazing Kiwi (1983).

Yet even if the class was questionable, the tradition of the great race was upheld, with Kensei having been purchased as a yearling in New Zealand by a six-man syndicate for a mere NZ$3,750 a share.

The Melbourne Cup might be a two-mile handicap, often the target for moderate and suspect stayers, but there is no danger of this great race becoming the poor man's Cesarewitch, run Down Under just before the start of each summer.

No, it still remains the hardest race to win on the Australian calendar, and the reason is, quite simply, tradition.

Melbourne Cup tradition in Australia is no less established than Derby tradition in England.

The concept of running the Melbourne Cup, a 3,200 metre handicap on the Flat (usually on fast ground) every November, is no less crazy than the best three-year-olds in the world racing for the Derby around tricky Epsom, with its deceiving turns,

○ **STRIKING FOR HOME: Kensei makes his victory run to beat Empire Blue and Rosedale (left).**   Picture: GEORGE SELWYN

○ **NEARLY THERE: Kensei holds off the late efforts of Empire Blue (almost hidden) and Rosedale.**   Picture: GEORGE SELWYN

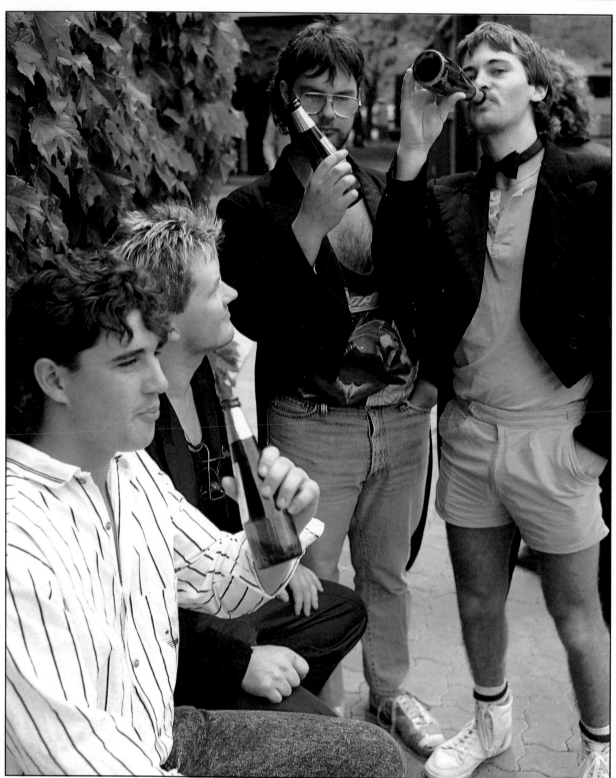

○ **MAN'S WORLD: Time to recharge the batteries at the Melbourne Cup meeting.**

Picture: GEORGE SELWYN

○ **JOLLY GREEN GIANT: It takes all kinds to make up the Melbourne Cup crowd.**   Picture: GEORGE SELWYN

gradients and downhill runs, as early in the year as June.

The Melbourne Cup is still the race that every owner in Australia and New Zealand wants to win, and many are prepared to shell out big money on a suitable handicapper just to have a runner.

No one would spend around £100,000 – in Australian terms over $200,000 – just to have an active interest in the Cesarewitch.

It is tradition that makes the Melbourne Cup the race it is today. To Australians, it is more than just a horse race. It is a national event celebrated by everyone, and owning a winner of the Cup is akin to becoming part of the country's history.

In 1987 Rosedale, formerly with John Dunlop, finished third in the Melbourne Cup under top weight of 8st 11lb, giving European form followers some idea of the calibre of stayer competing in Kensei's year.

Rosedale, whose sole English victory was earned at Bath, plugged to the line to take the minor money, beaten a length and a half and a short head by Kensei and Empire Rose.

Bart Cummings, now the five-year-old's trainer, following in the footsteps of Dunlop at Arundel and Charlie Whittingham in America, considers Rosedale will develop into a good stayer in Australia, given time.

But as we raised our glasses to Kensei after the Melbourne Cup, we also spared a thought for Neville Voigt, trainer of the fourth horse Balciano.

Voigt trained Kensei earlier in the stayer's career, before the horse chipped a bone in his knee and was then in plaster for six months.

He told me dejectedly: "It was nothing to do with me but I feel the owners blame me (for the injury) just the same." Even among the losers there is a story!□

○ **CUP HEROES: Winning trainer Les Bridge and jockey Larry Olsen.**
Picture: GEORGE SELWYN

○ **COMING BACK: Domus is set to return after an injury which curtailed his three-year-old career.** Picture: MARK LEECH

Twenty to Follow in 1988

by RACING POST TEAM

The Racing Post team of form experts has put together a list of 20 horses to follow on the Flat in 1988. Some of the names are familiar; some are not. They have been researched with one aim – to look for horses likely to show improvement, and provide a profit for backers, in the season ahead.

Last year's list yielded a level-stake profit of 13 points, with 14 horses winning 22 races. The most successful were Mischievous Miss (three wins, at 13-2, 6-1 and 3-1) and One To Mark (at 9-1 and 5-1).

ASL (USA)
3 gr.f. Caro – Call Me Goddess (Prince John)

Little went right for John Dunlop last year but his horses came with a flourish late in the season and Asl looked to be a filly with a future when storming home by three lengths at Leicester in October.

She was one of three Arundel juveniles to win over seven furlongs at the meeting, but Asl impressed her trainer the most, so much so that she may be a candidate for the fillies'

Classics this year. Asl should stay a mile and a quarter, and may get farther.
J. Dunlop, Arundel

BRIGHT-ONE
3 b.f. Electric – Lady Doubloon (Pieces of Eight)

This daughter of the talented but enigmatic Electric was a handful when she first came to Alec Stewart's yard. But she gradually settled down, and ran once at the backend of last season in a seven-furlong maiden at

Leicester, where she took time to find her stride but came home in good style to be third to Baby Marie.

The form is nothing special, but Bright-One has ability and a win in modest maiden company this spring should see her start her handicap career on an attractive mark.

A. Stewart, Newmarket

CHARMER

3 b.c. Be My Guest – Take Your Mark (Round Table)

Charmer's debut second to Undercut at Salisbury in June looked rather disappointing at the time since he went there with an impressive home reputation. In spite of his backward appearance, he even touched odds-on to beat Harwood's Goodwood winner. He could never get near the more-forward Undercut, yet subsequent events showed that run was no disgrace.

Charmer resembled the finished article a good deal more when he reappeared four months later at Newmarket. Kefaah was preferred in the market but Charmer was always going the better, staying on stoutly over the seven-furlong trip to hold the favourite by threequarters of a length.

Dick Hern rates Charmer very highly. This good-looking colt should be suited by distances in excess of a mile, and it will be a big disappointment if he fails to live up to his trainer's expectations.

W. Hern, West Ilsley

DOMUS

4 gr.c. Kalaglow – On The House (Be My Guest)

Domus did not have the chance to show his true worth last season. In his second race he sustained an injury to a joint which kept him off the course for the remainder of the year.

Geoff Wragg's colt looked very impressive on his debut in a 20-runner maiden at Newmarket in April, where he comfortably beat Bay Window by four lengths. The form does not look particularly special, but there was a lot to like about the way Domus quickened clear in the last two furlongs.

Wragg has been pleased with his progress through the winter and is

satisfied the injury was not serious enough to affect him this year. Domus could prove good enough to make his mark in Pattern races at around a mile.

G. Wragg, Newmarket

ERADICATE

3 b.c. Tender King-Pushkar (Northfields)

The discrepancy of the two sides of the straight at Newcastle were well illustrated at last season's late-August meeting. Every winner on the straight track raced on the far side, which appeared to be around ten lengths faster. So it was surprising that on the second day of the meeting Tony Ives chose to race on the unfavoured stands side on Eradicate in what appeared an ordinary maiden race. That he failed to win was not surprising, but in finishing second to the useful Puetorillo, beaten only three lengths, Eradicate proved there were races to be won with him.

He confirmed that view by beating some second-rate Newmarket raiders in the mud at Redcar in late-October on his only subsequent start. As he is likely to start the season on a low mark, he can pick up a few races before the Handicapper catches up with him.

P. Calver, Ripon

HAPPY CAVALIER

3 b.g. King of Spain – Happy Donna (Huntercombe)

It would be optimistic to say Happy Cavalier will turn out as good as Felipe Toro, who won five times for Peter Easterby in 1986, but his career has followed similar lines so far.

He has run only in conditions races, showing a little ability in the last of his three runs at Catterick in November, and thus should go into handicaps on a good mark. A son of sprinter King of Spain, who has made a good start at stud, and out of a mare that was speedy too, Happy Cavalier is the type

20 To Follow

ASL	—3yo—	J Dunlop
BRIGHT-ONE	—3yo—	A Stewart
CHARMER	—3yo—	W Hern
DOMUS	—4yo—	G Wragg
ERADICATE	—3yo—	P Calver
HAPPY CAVALIER	—3yo—	M H Easterby
INFANTA REAL	—3yo—	M Stoute
LORD LAMMAS	—3yo—	A Stewart
LUSTRE	—3yo—	M Stoute
MARKSTYLE	—3yo—	S Norton
MASTER ENGINEER	—3yo—	R Whitaker
MEDIA STARGUEST	—4yo—	L Cumani
NEW TRENDS	—3yo—	L Cumani
RED GLOW	—3yo—	G Wragg
REPRIMAND	—3yo—	H Cecil
SHEHIYR	—3yo—	R F Houghton
SMART ROBERTO	—3yo—	J Dunlop
TOPGLOW	—4yo—	A Stewart
WOOD CHANTER	—4yo—	J Dunlop
YACHTSMAN	—3yo—	H Cecil

to do better at three and is sure to be well placed by his canny trainer.

M. H. Easterby, Great Habton

INFANTA REAL

3 ch.f. Formidable – Alteza Real (Mansingh)

Infanta Real's fast-time wins at Yarmouth and Doncaster strongly suggest she is a top-class sprinter in the making. Following a pleasing first run at Windsor behind Jeremy Tree's good filly Magic Of Life, Infanta Real impressed clock-watchers with an all-the-way three-length victory over six furlongs at Yarmouth.

Not surprisingly, she found the drop to five furlongs no problem in quite a well-contested Listed race at Doncaster on her final start, where she was always close up, led two furlongs out and ran on well to beat J Cheever Loophole (himself no slouch) by two and a half lengths.

Infanta Real, a strongly-made filly, looks the sort to train on, and with the champion sprinter title up for grabs, she could take high rank.

M. Stoute, Newmarket

LORD LAMMAS

3 gr.c. Tap On Wood – Seriema (Petingo)

Lord Lammas had one educational run last season, finishing a highly promising sixth to Buzzards Crest at Leicester after a slow start. He was picking up ground hand over fist in the final furlong.

Lord Lammas comes from a high-class family: he is out of a half-sister to High Hawk, and is half-brother to Infamy, who improved throughout last season and won five races in succession.

Alec Stewart, gaining new admirers by the year, has a similar, highly effective approach to placing his horses as Luca Cumani. Lord Lammas is sure to be campaigned in his class, starting at a modest level, and he looks well worth following.

A. Stewart, Newmarket

LUSTRE (USA)

3 b. or br.f. Halo – White Star Line (Northern Dancer)

Lustre did not reveal her full potential as a two-year-old and could

well develop into a leading Classic prospect. Michael Stoute's filly looked potentially smart in both races, finishing a highly commendable third to Bluebook and Ela Romara at Newmarket, and following up by beating Silent Sister a neck at Lingfield Park, where she found six furlongs barely far enough.

She comes from a high-class family, and being stoutly bred on the dam's side (White Star Line won the Kentucky Oaks), she should be suited by a mile and a quarter and more as a three-year-old.

Lustre may have the class and constitution to develop into an Oaks filly if she manages to stay a mile and a half. She is definitely one to keep a close eye on.

M. Stoute, Newmarket

MARKSTYLE

3 b.c. Moorestyle-Alicia Markova (Habat)

This cheaply-bought colt is unlikely to be a world beater, and after two runs as a two-year-old he appeared to be no better than a plater, finishing unplaced in auction races at Ripon and Nottingham.

However, he left that form well behind on soft ground at Pontefract in the autumn, battling on well to win a graduation race by half a length from Shoe Lane over six furlongs. His style of racing suggests he will need much farther to realise his true potential.

Steve Norton rarely overtrains his juveniles and it is a fair bet there will be plenty of improvement in Markstyle. He looks sure to pay his way in small Northern handicaps, particularly when there is some give in the ground.

S. Norton, High Hoyland

MASTER ENGINEER

3 ch.c. Music Boy-Penny Pincher (Constable)

At 58,000gns this colt was one of the most expensive horses in Richard Whitaker's stable last season, and he repaid not one penny. But there is every chance he will rectify matters this season.

He was working in great style at home, managing to hold his own with such stars as his brother Clantime and

the Group-placed Orient. He ran once, starting favourite, but finishing only sixth of 11 in a small race at Hamilton in September.

Whitaker reckoned he would need the run, and his fears were justified, for after showing plenty of early speed Master Engineer tired in the closing stages, the testing ground finding him out.

With some clever placing, this colt could be a money-spinner over sprint distances next season.

R. Whitaker, Wetherby

MEDIA STARGUEST

4 ch.c. Be My Guest – Diomedia (Sea-Bird)

Media Starguest improved throughout last season, stamping himself a very useful sort, and he looks capable of developing into one of this year's leading older horses.

Luca Cumani's colt won three minor events and was fourth in the King Edward VII Stakes at Royal Ascot before finishing a good fourth to Roushayd under a big weight in the Tote Festival Handicap at Ascot. He rounded off the season by winning the Listed Breeders' Cup Classic Trial at Newmarket and the Cenotaph Stakes at Doncaster, the latter in great style from Celtic Ring.

Media Starguest stays a mile and a half but will probably prove most effective over slightly shorter distances this season. He has more improvement in him and his stable have particularly high expectations.

L. Cumani, Newmarket

NEW TRENDS (USA)

3 b.f. Lyphard – My Bupers (Bupers)

Luca Cumani's New Trends showed plenty of talent in some encouraging home work before she made her debut in the Blue Seal Stakes at Ascot. The high-class performance she put up there to beat Michael Stoute's well-regarded newcomer Dabaweyaa by two and a half lengths came as no great surprise to connections.

Her subsequent length second to Sparrow's Air when a hot favourite for the seven-furlong Radley Stakes at Newbury four weeks later was on the face of it disappointing, but she was given plenty to do in the testing

○**HEADLINE MAKER: Media Starguest won the last race of the 1987 season and can carry on where he left off.**
Picture: ALAN JOHNSON

conditions and only narrowly failed to get up.

New Trends is a sister to Guy Harwood's good colt Lyphard's Special, and has the scope to develop into a 1,000 Guineas prospect, although she will stay farther in due course. Cumani has had near-misses in the Guineas with Konafa and Freeze The Secret; New Trends could be the sort to provide compensation.

L. Cumani, Newmarket

RED GLOW
3 b.c. Kalaglow – Cherry Hinton (Nijinsky).

Red Glow is a robust colt with plenty of scope who could develop into a leading handicapper this season. He is highly regarded by his trainer and showed plenty of promise in his only race last season.

Red Glow, a son of the Hoover Fillies Mile winner Cherry Hinton and a half-brother to the smart Cherry Ridge, showed up well for a long way when sixth to easy winner Carmelite House in the Houghton Stakes at Newmarket, where he needed the race. Geoff Wragg's colt, who is likely to stay at least a mile and a quarter, has a deal of improvement in him.

G. Wragg, Newmarket

REPRIMAND
3 b.c. Mummy's Pet – Just You Wait (Nonoalco)

Reprimand is already a Pattern race winner, but the manner of his victory in the Gimcrack Stakes at York, where he had to be rousted to overhaul Intimidate, did not convince everyone that he is a colt with Classic potential.

However, the best is yet to be seen of this imposing individual, who retired unbeaten. He won on his debut at Ascot and went on from York to land a minor Lingfield contest by seven lengths.

Subsequently prepared for the Dewhurst Stakes, Reprimand was reportedly working in tremendous style for his intended clash with Warning. The abandonment of the Newmarket feature delayed that mouth-watering prospect, but Reprimand remains on course to meet

○ **CLASSIC TYPE: Reprimand went through his first season unbeaten and may take high honours in 1988.** Picture: ALAN JOHNSON

Guy Harwood's colt in the 2,000 Guineas.

Although Reprimand is by the sprinter Mummy's Pet there is stamina on the dam's side, and he will stay the Guineas trip. There are plenty at Warren Place who fancy he will emerge the stable's top colt this year.

H. Cecil, Newmarket

SHEHIYR
3 gr.c. Hotfoot – Shaiyra (Relko)

The much-touted Cecil newcomer Moscow Society grabbed all the attention before the start of the Whatton Stud Stakes at Nottingham in October and was sent off at 5-2 on. Shehiyr, a backward, still unfurnished, grey son of Hotfoot was easy to back at 12-1, but he came back the star, eclipsing Moscow Society by a convincing three lengths.

The margin would have been greater had not Billy Newnes eased down Shehiyr with his race won, and the other ten runners were strung out like washing. Soft ground probably contributed to the defeat of Moscow Society, who may yet live up to his reputation, but Shehiyr looks an even brighter prospect for 1988. He is a half-brother to the good miler Shaikiya but promises to stay farther.
F. Johnson Houghton, Didcot

SMART ROBERTO
3 b.c. Roberto – Night Fire (Cannonade)

Smart Roberto, a big, strong colt, has the makings of a useful middle-distance handicapper. Not seen out until September, he showed plenty of ability in a seven-furlong graduation race at Ascot, leading two furlongs out and staying on well when headed to finish a close third behind the useful Sheriff's Star.

Smart Roberto did all that was required of him when landing the odds in a mile maiden race in heavy ground at Haydock the following month, making all and beating White Sapphire by four lengths. He has the scope to improve considerably.
J. Dunlop, Arundel

TOPGLOW
4 b.c. Kalaglow – Lady Gaylass (Sir Gaylord)

Alec Stewart did this list proud last year, sending out Just David to win the Chester Cup at 10-1. Just David will again be one to keep an eye on, but an even more lucrative prospect from a yard which does exceptionally well with older horses may be the once-raced four-year-old Topglow.

Topglow had a hopeless draw and tired as lack of hard condition told from two out when a promising fifth to Media Starguest in a minor event over a mile at Leicester in April, beaten about five and a half lengths. He was off with a cracked cannon bone afterwards, but he is now fully recovered and is the subject of

○ **TOP NOTE: Wood Chanter (right), who gets off the mark in a Newmarket maiden race, looks set for better things in 1988.**   Picture: ALAN JOHNSON

encouraging reports from Newmarket.

He will need two more runs before he is handicapped, and then should quickly make up for lost time at around a mile and a quarter.
A. Stewart, Newmarket

WOOD CHANTER
4 gr.c. Vitiges – Castle Moon (Kalamoun)

Wood Chanter, included in this list last year on the strength of one promising run as a juvenile, was unable to fulfil anything like his true potential owing to a troublesome knee injury. But he is thought to have overcome his problems and should start to make up for lost time.

Winner of a Newmarket maiden in August, Wood Chanter was the least experienced in the line-up for the William Hill November Handicap three months later. But, after some encouraging work-outs with his brother Moon Madness at Arundel, Wood Chanter carried plenty of stable confidence. In finishing fifth to Swingit Gunner, he ran considerably better than his final position suggests,

having had to weave his way through the field after meeting interference on the home turn.

He has the makings of something better than a handicapper and we have no hesitation in putting his name forward again.
J. Dunlop, Arundel

YACHTSMAN (USA)
3 b.c. Robellino – B F's Sailingal (Sail on-Sail on)

Yachtsman is a brother to useful Faustus, and looks every bit as genuine and keen a galloper as his former stable-companion. Yachtsman was not tried too highly in his first season, but hinted that better things were in store when picking up minor seven-furlong events at Newcastle and Doncaster in October, stretching out in great style to beat Vayrua by four lengths in a big field on the latter course.

The Doncaster form worked out well and Yachtsman, who is sure to be suited by a mile, looks the sort to make an even better three-year-old.
H. Cecil, Newmarket

CHAPTER 20

Ireland – The Flat

by TONY O'HEHIR

• **FLAT OUT: Sir Harry Lewis beats Naheez for the Budweiser Irish Derby.**　　Picture: GERRY CRANHAM

○ **FULL MARKS:** Michael Kinane gets top billing for his riding of Flutter Away (left) as she wins the Moyglare Stud Stakes from Fairy Gold (noseband), Timely (right) and Thaidah.
Picture: CAROLINE NORRIS

Ireland – The Flat

by TONY O'HEHIR

1987 was far from being Vincent O'Brien's best year training but it marked a significant improvement on the previous year when his Ballydoyle stables were struck by a virus.

The recovery in O'Brien's fortunes enabled him to finish champion trainer for the 12th time, with earnings of IR£463,602 from 43 races.

Biggest contributor to the total was Caerwent, who lifted IR£104,950 when he won the GPA National Stakes at The Curragh in September.

Caerwent, owned and bred by Edmund Loder, easily won that Group One event by five lengths but the opposition was sub-standard and Ireland's best two-year-old may lack the scope to make him a strong Classic contender.

Caerwent's National Stakes victory ended in a two-year Group One famine in Ireland for O'Brien, who last achieved a win in the top bracket with Law Society in the 1985 Irish Derby.

Abroad the gap was longer. When Bluebird, now standing at Coolmore Stud, won the King's Stand Stakes at Ascot in June, he became O'Brien's first Group One winner in England since Sadler's Wells won the 1984 Eclipse Stakes.

Bluebird and Caerwent were ridden by Cash Asmussen, who in his first and only season as O'Brien's stable jockey finished runner up to Michael Kinane in the championship.

Succeeding Pat Eddery placed Asmussen in the hot seat and his quiet style did not always please the punters. His 62 winners from 185 rides was an impressive strike rate but the contract was ended in January 1988 and John Reid took over.

In the Classics, English stables went one better than in 1986 and only Eurobird's St Leger win prevented a clean sweep by the visitors.

In May, Don't Forget Me, trained by Richard Hannon, became the first horse since Right Tack in 1969 to complete the Newmarket-Curragh 2,000 Guineas double when he held Entitled by half a length.

A reception unprecedented at The Curragh, and more associated with an Irish winner at Cheltenham, greeted Willie Carson's mount on his return to an unsaddling enclosure thronged by the family and friends of his Cork owner, Jim Horgan.

That Classic was an unhappy occasion for Walter Swinburn, who cost Ajdal third place, and himself a fine of IR£500 when he forgot to weigh in.

In the 1,000 Guineas a week later Swinburn and Michael Stoute, who won three Irish Classics the previous year, were narrowly touched off when Forest Flower (Tony Ives) short-headed Milligram.

But there were no problems for Stoute and Swinburn in the Oaks in July when Unite easily added that prize to her English Oaks win, when she beat Bourbon Girl and Eurobird by three lengths and four.

Budweiser Derby day in June will be remembered for the confusion that reigned following a hoax bomb scare which delayed the start of the race for 49 minutes. When it finished, the

○ **FIRST AND SECOND: Caerwent, Ireland's leading two-year-old, and Cash Asmussen, runner-up in the jockeys' championship.** Picture: CAROLINE NORRIS

smiles were on the face of Manton's new boss Barry Hills, whose Sir Harry Lewis revelled in the soft ground and beat Naheez by threequarters of a length.

For jockey John Reid, who has an amazing record in big Irish races, it was the richest win of his career and for US owner Howard Kaskel the IR£331,000 earned was enough to top the owners' list.

Eurobird's appearance and form showed marked improvement in the second half of the season and she was at her peak on Leger Day when she slammed Spruce Baby by eight lengths. Her win achieved Irish Classic firsts for her jockey, Asmussen, and trainer, John Oxx, for whom her success was the highlight of his best season, during which his horses won 54 races.

The Classic breakthrough is one all trainers cherish and in Oxx's case there was added significance in Eurobird's runaway win. Nine years previously his father John and Eurobird's owner Gerald Jennings lost the Irish Oaks in the Stewards' room when their Sorbus was disqualified in favour of Fair Salinia.

That was an extremely controversial decision and Eurobird coming good on the big day was delayed compensation for both families. Unfortunately Oxx senior, trainer of Sorbus and Classic winners, died in May and missed his son's big day.

Post St Leger celebrations contributed to a bizarre happening in the next race, when Oxx's Excellenza, ridden by Asmussen, lost the

○ **ENGLISH ONE-TWO: Digamist (blinkers) pips Oakworth for Ireland's richest two-year-old prize, the Heinz '57' Phoenix Stakes** Picture: CAROLINE NORRIS

○ **DUAL CONTROL:** Don't Forget Me adds the Irish 2,000 Guineas to his English Classic by beating Entitled and Ajdal. Picture: GERRY CRANHAM

Cesarewitch when the Stewards discovered she raced without the blinkers which were declared.

Ireland's other Group One event open to older horses went to France when Triptych landed the Dunnes Stores Phoenix Champion Stakes. Her neck win from Entitled gave jockey Tony Cruz a perfect introduction to Irish racing.

The Park's Heinz 57 Phoenix Stakes lacked the class of the previous year and ended in a photo-finish involving arch rivals Pat Eddery and Steve Cauthen. Eddery, on Jeremy Tree's Digamist, beat Cauthen on Oakworth a neck.

If there was an award for the ride of the year, Michael Kinane would get my nomination for his superb handling of Flutter Away in the Group One Moyglare Stud Stakes at The Curragh. Kinane, who retained his title and won his fourth championship with 86 winners, is often taken for granted in his home country, where there is a tendency automatically to equate the Weld stable jockey job with the riders' crown.

○ **SAME AGAIN: Unite, winner of the Epsom Oaks, takes the Irish equivalent, beating Bourbon Girl.**
Picture: CAROLINE NORRIS

Not only is Kinane Ireland's best, but he is more than capable of holding his own at the highest international level. He has seldom ridden better than on the September Sunday in question, when his power-packed finish got Flutter Away up in the last few strides to beat Fairy Gold and Timely two short heads.

At Royal Ascot in June Kinane wore the colours of the Moyglare Stud when he and Weld struck with Big Shuffle in the Cork and Orrery Stakes.

Weld, runner up to O'Brien in the prize-money list, trained 31 more winners than the Ballydoyle maestro.

○ **TROUBLE LOOMING: Eurobird lands the Jefferson Smurfit Memorial St Leger, but in the excitement of victory connections forgot to declare blinkers for their next runner.**
Picture: CAROLINE NORRIS

○ **CLASSIC BLOOM: Forest Flower (noseband) short-heads Milligram for the Goffs 1,000 Guineas. Taking Steps (left) is third.**
Picture: CAROLINE NORRIS

And in Pattern winners Careafolie, Trusted Partner and Flutter Away, and maiden winners Clash of Ideas and Safety Catch, his three-year-olds of '88 could make a big impression.

Kinane will be a warm order to retain the jockeys' title this year, when two of his main rivals will have new jobs. Stephen Craine, runner-up to Kinane in '86 and fourth in '87, is to ride as stable jockey to Tommy Stack, whose expanded string will include approximately 40 choicely-bred two-year-olds. And Kevin Prendergast, who trained 53 winners, will have David Parnell as his number one for the new campaign.

In October Prendergast revealed that Parnell would replace Gabriel Curran, whose 21-year association

with the stable included three Classic winners: Nebbiolo (2,000 Guineas), Northern Treasure (Irish 2,000 Guineas) and Arctique Royale (Irish 1,000 Guineas).

Parnell represents the younger generation of Irish jockeys and has the polished talent to make it in the big league. Like Kinane and Craine he is a former champion apprentice, a role filled in 1987 by Kevin Manning, who topped the boys' list with 33 winners.

At the end of August, the cut-off date for qualification to ride in the Long John Scotch Whisky European Apprentice Championship, Manning had earned the right to represent his country. But his boss Jim Bolger made it known that he considered an alcoholic drinks firm to be

inappropriate sponsors of such a series and refused Manning permission to travel. With stablemate Willie Supple also ruled out, and Kieran Fallon too old to compete, Eddie Leonard grabbed the chance and beat rivals from eight countries to become the second Irish winner of the series.

Bolger's year had many positive aspects, most notably Polonia's emergence as a star sprinter.

Polonia, like Ajdal, started the year as a Classic contender and it was not until late August that she reverted to sprint distances over which she completed a hat-trick, climaxed by a dramatic win under Christy Roche in the Prix de l'Abbaye at Longchamp in October. She started late in 1987; it may be a different story in '88. □

1987 Irish Flat Statistics

Owners

	Win stakes IR£	Horses	Races
Howard Kaskel	331,000	1	1
Alan Clore	267,000	1	1
Sheikh Mohammed	233,839	19	27
Robert Sangster	227,752	18	27
Khalid Abdullah	164,950	1	1
Gerald Jennings	144,436	1	4
Allen Paulson	129,554	8	17
Stavros Niarchos	128,656	10	16
Edmund Loder	118,780	2	5
Oliver Murphy	117,305	1	3

Trainers

	Win stakes IR£	Horses	Races
M V O'Brien	463,602	25	43
D Weld	432,088	50	74
B Hills	367,080	3	3
J Oxx	351,730	36	54
P Biancone	267,500	1	1
J Bolger	250,694	40	62
J Tree	164,950	1	1
K Prendergast	118,488	40	53
R Hannon	107,717	2	2
M Stoute	101,000	1	1
C Collins	98,027	25	31
I Balding	92,000	1	1

Jockeys

	1	2	3	Unpl	Total	%
M J Kinane	86	64	68	247	465	18.2
C Asmussen	62	43	15	65	185	33.5
C Roche	54	57	53	201	365	14.8
S Craine	47	49	40	278	414	11.3
P Shanahan	46	27	35	228	336	13.7
D Gillespie	39	45	44	273	401	9.7
K Manning	33	31	24	143	231	14.3
D Parnell	32	29	40	244	345	9.3
D Hogan	22	24	20	101	167	13.2
G Curran	21	20	26	149	217	9.7
K Fallon	20	12	15	123	170	11.8
P V Gilson	19	27	15	181	242	7.8

Apprentices

	1	2	3	Unpl	Total	%
K Manning	33	31	24	143	231	14.3
K Fallon	18	11	15	120	164	11.0
E Leonard	15	10	9	56	90	16.7
J P Murtagh	11	1	4	50	66	16.7
J Egan	11	24	30	242	307	3.6
W Supple	10	9	5	87	111	9.0
D V Smith	9	9	8	77	103	8.7
J Hunter	9	8	10	144	171	5.3

○ **TRAVELLER'S TALES:** Triptych collects another foreign scalp, winning the Dunnes Stores St Bernard Phoenix Champion Stakes from Entitled.

Picture: JOHN CROFTS

CHAPTER 21

Gossip and Rumour

by COLIN MACKENZIE

● **HELPING HAND: Down in the Royal Ascot car park it's time to prepare for the afternoon ahead.**
Picture: GEORGE HERRINGSHAW

○ **AWAY FROM IT ALL: A day at the races can be a tiring business, especially at Royal Ascot.**   Picture: DAVID HASTINGS

Gossip and Rumour

by COLIN MACKENZIE

PSST . . . . I GOTTA HORSE. These days you don't often get molested in the racecourse car park by a Prince Monolulu figure, desperate to earn ten bob by selling a marked racecard.

Nevertheless racecourse gossip is still the protein of the sport, the grapevine without which bookmakers and punters would be reaching for their vitamin pills, contacting their travel agents and retiring to the Costa del Wherever.

How often have you been telephoned in the morning by a friend about a horse which is not in the betting in the papers and told, "For goodness sake keep this to yourself"?

Once at the track you amble up to the bookies, looking as nonchalant and disinterested as possible, only to discover that your dark horse is 5-2 second favourite. The grapevine has delivered your deepest secrets to the world at large. What do you do? You back the horse at 5-2, watch horrified as it drifts to 4-1, and compound your feelings of unease when it finishes a promising fifth of 12.

This scenario is repeated day in and day out. I sometimes wonder if bookmakers put about the original rumours themselves, in order to create a more vibrant betting market. On second thoughts they don't really need

to indulge in this pastime these days; the odds are almost always in their favour and the results, in general, are immaterial.

The financial well-being of punters, bookmakers, trainers and owners is also fodder for the racecourse grapevine. I once heard a particularly cheeky punter being turned down by a rails bookie who was fed up with postdated and bouncing cheques. "My man," said the punter grandly, "you don't seem to understand. Credit is the lifeblood of trade!"

Racecourse gossip takes on a wider and more international flavour at the Derby and Royal Ascot. Terry Wogan once described the latter upmarket picnic as "50,000 people in search of Nigel Dempster".

Curiously enough, the doyen of gossip columnists has chosen to miss this particular nugget of the social calendar for the past five years. He was very rude about the Queen's Representative Sir Piers Bengough on his appointment in 1982. I wonder if Nigel's applications to the Royal Enclosure have met with a frosty refusal since then. He's not saying, preferring to belittle the event as a venue for publicans and second-hand car salesmen!

Certainly the Royal Enclosure takes its clientele from a far wider social mix than was the case before the last War. Marquises rub shoulders with meat porters, surgeons with secretaries. This is how it should be in 1988.

The Royals themselves are doing their bit to make Ascot and the Derby glittery, frilly, fashion-conscious events that advertise the glamour of racing and 'The Season'. Debutantes might not be presented at Court these days, but a Season undoubtedly still exists, bounded by the Chelsea Flower Show, the Derby, Royal Ascot, Wimbledon, Henley and Cowes.

The Royal Family provide their own 'Palace Dallas' at the races, with the Princess of Wales and Duchess of York giggling their way into the White's tent and causing mayhem with their umbrellas.

I'll never forget the look on the Queen's face one Derby Day when Princess Michael of Kent inadvertently got in her way as the runners were rounding Tattenham Corner. People have been sent to the Tower for less.

Prince Philip has enjoyed a love-hate relationship with racing since he married into the Royal Family in 1947. In general he likes to leave Royal Ascot after the third race, and used to slip away and play some polo chukkas. The onset of arthritis has put an end to this pursuit, but he remains indifferent to the excitement of the Turf. His eldest son, the Prince of Wales, while flirting briefly with riding and owning just before his marriage, has similar tendencies and you can always spot his azure Aston Martin being revved up

by his detective after the third race at the Royal meeting.

The Princess Royal, on the other hand, has developed a consuming passion for race riding, which is both thoroughly admirable and quite remarkable at her age (37). She is a skilled horsewoman who represented Britain in the Olympics but that was all of 12 years ago. Since then she has married and become a mother of two.

Race riding, as any jockey will tell you, requires a different kind of fitness to show jumping and Three-Day Eventing. With singular dedication she has ridden out at neighbour David Nicholson's Condicote stables whenever her busy schedule has permitted and made herself fit enough to win over fences and on the Flat at Ascot in front of the Queen and Prince Philip. Quite an achievement.

The Queen Mother's love affair with racing gained momentum after the premature death of her husband King George VI. She had already owned a chaser, Monaveen, in partnership with her daughter, then Princess Elizabeth. But when the new

Queen took over the responsibilities of the Royal Stud and the Flat horses, the Queen Mum launched her interest in National Hunt racing with a fervour and excitement of a much younger person.

She has enjoyed considerable success through her trainers, the late Peter Cazalet and now the current doyen, Fulke Walwyn. There have been almost 400 winners carrying the pale blue, black and buff colours. She had a blower commentary installed in Clarence House, her London residence, as long ago as 1967.

It is commonly believed that she has a fiver or two on her horses when they run. Certainly her charming private secretary Sir Martin Gilliat is often seen bounding around the Tattersalls' pitches trying to snaffle the best price.

What is not in doubt is that she has helped to promote the popularity of the winter sport to an enormous degree. Most Clerks of the Course estimate a Royal runner, and the likelihood that the Queen Mum will be there, adds 1,000 to the average gate. May be that's just another rumour!□

○ **STRIKE UP THE BAND: Royal Ascot takes its clientele from a wide social mix, and most of them make their way to the bandstand after racing.**

Picture: DAVID HASTINGS

194

CHAPTER 22

United States

by DAN FARLEY

○ **LEVEL BREAK: Bet Twice (fourth from right) on the way to a 14-length victory in the Belmont Stakes.**

Picture: BOB COGLIANESE

United States

by DAN FARLEY

THINGS ARE LIABLE to turn quite dull in any racing year anywhere around the world, and more often than not, they do. The United States was perhaps more fortunate than most during 1987 in that regard, though, as important races with talented runners spiced the season throughout. Moreover, purse money was on the rise everywhere and big-money races became commonplace. All this was good news, especially in light of the fact that the bloodstock side of the industry continued its decline.

THE EARLY MONTHS
The classic generation of 1986 provided the early-season fireworks, particularly in the Strub Stakes and Santa Anita Handicap at Santa Anita. The Strub, run in early-February, saw Preakness winner Snow Chief barely hold on to defeat Kentucky Derby winner Ferdinand, with Derby third Bold Brush in his Classic place once more.

Anticipation was great when the three met again in the million-dollar Santa Anita Handicap a month later. Ferdinand was favoured, but he could not resist Broad Brush's challenge at the wire and failed by the slimmest margin. Snow Chief gave way at the furlong marker and could finish only fifth.

Ferdinand's two losses were as tough as any horse ever had suffered, costing his connections well over a half-million dollars in purse money, but he was destined to become an even more important player during the long season.

THE CLASSICS
Serious Classic contenders emerged from several parts of the country during 1987, the ultimate Kentucky Derby favourite being Arkanas Derby winner Demons Begone. Unfortunately, he bled for the first time in his career and was pulled up, as Alysheba overcame a near-disastrous confrontation with Bet Twice to defeat that rival by three-quarters of a length.

The Preakness Stakes was a replay of the Derby, save for the tangle of the first Classic, and Alysheba went into the Belmont Stakes favourite to win the Triple Crown and collect millions in bonus monies in the process.

The drama of such a possibility was short-lived, however, as Bet Twice broke open the 12-furlong race with a half-mile to run and went on to record a 14-length victory.

This classic generation had several talented members, but given · the Belmont result it had no clear leader.

○ **SPLENDID ISOLATION: Bet Twice has the Belmont in the bag.**
Picture: BOB COGLIANESE

FILLIES CLASSICS

The recognized Triple Crown for fillies consists of the mile Acorn Stakes, nine-furlong Mother Goose Stakes and 12-furlong Coaching Club American Oaks, all run at Belmont Park.

Fiesta Gal, by Alleged, nearly won all three, failing only in the first when traffic problems diminished the effect of her closing punch.

She won the Mother Goose and Oaks quite handily and went into the summer months as clearly the best of her division.

DEVELOPMENTS

Among the other divisions, early results indicated that Manila and Theatrical would pick up their battle as they left it the preceding year in the Breeders' Cup Turf.

Groovy looked clearly best among the sprinters, at least among his ilk based on the East Coast.

Emerging as a factor among the three-year-olds, and ultimately among males in general was Java Gold. He had missed the Derby, his connections believing it demands too much too early, then also missed the Belmont Stakes because of a virus. But he was ready for a showdown in the Travers Stakes at Saratoga in mid-August, coming from far back over a muddy track to win handily.

Among the vanquished were Classic

winners Alysheba and Bet Twice. The off going may have compromised their chances, but leadership of the division had shifted nonetheless.

The filly and mare division was one with questionable depth and quality, but another latecomer, three-year-old Personal Ensign, maintained her unbeaten status through a brief four-race campaign impressive enough for many to call her the best around.

Manila finally met Theatrical, in the Budweiser-Arlington Million, and defeated him soundly in what sadly proved to be his final career appearance due to injury. Theatrical took over admirably in his rival's absence.

Java Gold took his top form into the early fall, defeating older horses twice

○ **GLORIOUS MUD: Conditions hold no terrors for Java Gold as he gains a handy win in the Travers Stakes.**

○ **TOP OF THE BILL: Theatrical holds off French-trained Trempolino in the Breeder's Cup Turf race.**
Picture: GEORGE SELWYN

before being sidelined by injury in early-October.

THE TWO-YEAR-OLDS

As in recent years, the two-year-old picture was dominated by trainer D. Wayne Lukas and his owners, primarily Gene Klein.

They registered victories from coast to coast and several points in between. Classic Crown among the fillies and Tejano and Success Express among the colts proved the best in the barn.

Forty Niner came along among the colts to win a pair of major races in New York then declined the issue in the Breeders' Cup Juvenile, having put away a likely championship.

Generally, though, the two-year-olds proved to be a relatively uninspiring lot, leaving us only to guess at what might happen in this year's Classics.

LATE SEASON

The Breeders' Cup races, in their brief history, have gained extraordinary influence in determining year-end

○ **DONE IT: Bill Shoemark returns after winning his first Breeders' Cup race, on Ferdinand in the Classic.** Picture: GEORGE SELWYN

○ **VICTORY RUN: Alysheba and Chris McCarron hold off Bet Twice to take the Kentucky Derby.** Picture: ASSOCIATED PRESS

champions of American racing. No fewer than 15 winners of the 21 Breeders' Cup races in the event's first three years had gone on to be voted top of the polls.

In 1987 at least four potential divisional champions did not make it to the Breeders' Cup for one reason or another. That in itself provided considerable controversy about who was best in American racing. So here are some one-sided thoughts on the subject.

Among two-year-old males the nod goes to Forty Niner. His connections passed on the Breeders' Cup in order to prepare him for the Classics, but he earned his honours in New York, racing against the best of the season.

The juvenile fillies are a tougher lot in that none of them did enough at the right time to secure a championship. Early and mid-season leaders lost late, and late winners were relative newcomers. My judgement is that Jeanne Jones probably was best, but an unlikely winner in championship polling.

Best three-year-old male during the season was Java Gold, but his season was brief. His main challenger Alysheba was around to win two Classics and was only narrowly beaten in the Breeders' Cup Classic.

In the three-year-old filly division Fiesta Gal dominated early, Personal Ensign came back from injury to keep her unbeaten record intact through another four races, and Sacahuista won big, late, and twice against her elders. Personal Ensign dodged the Breeders' Cup Distaff, which was won by Sacahuista. Still, the preference is for Personal Ensign.

The sprint title goes to Groovy for his consistency, even though once

○**NATIVE NEW YORKER: Forty Niner earns top two-year-old honours with a Travers Stakes victory over Tsarbaby (right).**   Picture: BOB COGLIANESE

more he was beaten in the Breeders' Cup.

Miesque, for her brilliance in the Breeders' Cup Mile, was best among female turf performers.

Ferdinand, ending the season with four consecutive victories, was best among older males, and Coup de Fusil dominated in Grade One races through the heart of the season to be best among older fillies and mares.

Personal philosophy dictates the choice in the two remaining

categories, champion male turf horse and Horse of the Year. With a choice between best over all or the one who had most impact on the season, my guide is the former.

For that reason Manila gets the nod for both turf champion and Horse of the Year, even with his abbreviated season. Not only was he the best horse under tack in American racing last year, he is among the best to have raced here during the last 15 years, at least.□

● **MASTER CRAFTSMAN:** Henry Cecil
points the way ahead to owner-breeder
Bob McCreery while his team move on
to the Newmarket gallops.
Picture: GERRY CRANHAM

CHAPTER 23

Henry Cecil

by SIMON CRISFORD

○ **RECORD BREAKER: Henry Cecil makes it 147 winners for the season, to beat John Day's record, as Madam Cyn and Willie Ryan land a Yarmouth seller on 15 September.**
Picture: JOHN CROFTS

Henry Cecil

by SIMON CRISFORD

HENRY CECIL lets his achievements as a trainer do most of the talking; yet his magnetism, charisma, charm and fierce ambition to be the best stand out to those who work alongside him. His success, and that of stable jockey Steve Cauthen were the highlights of the 1987 Flat season.

Among Cecil's record-breaking 180 winners were his second Epsom Derby and a first King George VI and Queen Elizabeth Diamond Stakes with Reference Point, and Cecil's handling of him was brilliant.

Because of Reference Point's relaxed nature, he worked in the style of a lazy colt and therefore needed a good deal more galloping and coaxing along than some other stable companions. It says much for Cecil that the colt remained in peak condition throughout the season until disappointing in the Arc de Triomphe because of an abcess in a foot.

One morning before the Mecca-Dante Stakes, Reference Point's owner Louis Freedman and associate Peter Willett came down to see the colt do an important piece of work on the Limekilns. At first sight Reference Point appeared to disappoint, as he failed to quicken clear of a stablemate companion. Freedman looked horrified, but it was usual for Reference Point to work like that, though at the time his owner could not be sure whether he had trained on.

Reference Point was endowed with a strong constitution as much as he was blessed with talent. Yet it can be argued that Cecil's greatest training achievement during 1987 was his handling of Indian Skimmer.

Never the best of movers in her slower paces, Indian Skimmer was prone to muscular trouble in her shoulders and back, and there was some doubt whether she would stand the pressures of training throughout the season.

Early in the spring, before she made her reappearance at Wolverhampton, she worked on Waterhall, and Cecil said then: "You know, that filly is going to be very, very good."

Before the Guineas meeting Anthony Stroud, representing owner Sheikh Mohammed, watched her work on Racecourse side with Laluche, who had been a very good, unbeaten two-year-old. Indian Skimmer went so well that I was temporarily under the impression she had galloped alone. Immediately, Cecil said she would be prepared for the Musidora Stakes at York. He was planning to run her first in the Pretty Polly Stakes, but on the Saturday before the 1,000 Guineas she appeared to go very well in a seven-furlong gallop with the Nell Gwyn Stakes winner Martha Stevens.

Cauthen rode her in the gallop, and coming from several lengths off the pace she quickened up smartly to storm in front. Cecil, cantering away on his hack, quizzed, "Was that good enough to run in the Guineas?" The obvious answer was "yes", but Cecil knew differently and she missed the Classic. Indian Skimmer might not have gone on to be the brilliant French Oaks winner she was if she had been forced into such a punishing race so early on.

In a season that will be remembered for Warren Place triumphs, Cecil also suffered a number of disappointments, which he characteristically put behind him.

One such setback was with Scimitarra, who on the Saturday before the Oaks did an outstanding right-handed piece of work on the Limekilns round gallop, suggesting she would take all the beating in the Classic. Scimitarra might not have beaten the winner Unite, but we shall never know, because she broke her off-fore cannon bone during the race.

While Group One winners El Cuite and Paean were also forced into retirement because of injury, he could not dwell on the past.

Early in the summer Cecil had pointed out a useful Topsider colt called Salse, who had done some encouraging work. He looked the sort to develop into a 2,000 Guineas prospect and I considered him the leading Warren Place two-year-old at that stage of the season. But one work morning at the beginning of July, it was a surprise to see that Cauthen was not riding Salse but the unraced Mummy's Pet colt Reprimand, whose strengths were less familiar.

The pair came up the Short gallop and Reprimand put in some high-class work with Salse. After Cecil had briefly discussed the gallop with his stable jockey, he returned to say: "Steve said he could be anything; he could be very good."

Unbeaten in three races, Reprimand missed the chance to show how good he is when the Three Chimneys Dewhurst Stakes was abandoned but he looks sure to strengthen into a high-class performer in 1988.

As well as a deep understanding of each of his 200 horses, Cecil has built a close rapport with his staff. He normally rides out on his grey Arab hack but on occasion he will instead drive out to the Heath in his grey Mercedes.

On arrival at the gallops he will often be greeted by a number of owners and agents, who generally include Charles St George, Leslie Harrison and Johnny Lewis.

By this time Cecil will have explained to each work jockey what is required in the gallop, and as they set off to the start he takes up his position near the end of the gallop.

On occasions during the summer Cecil will have three sets working at the same time, on the Long gallop, Short gallop, and Al Bahathri all-weather. From his vantage point on the Limekilns he can assess each gallop as if he was watching a single

work-out, and often he will point out individuals as they are put through their paces.

After an important gallop Cecil can be seen carefully listening as the horse blows, which provides him with a good indication of fitness before he moves on to discuss the work with his jockeys.

He puts his string back into work on Warren Hill at the end of winter, and good steady canters put condition on the horses before they move into faster work on Waterhall. By the end of March the string will be doing more work on Racecourse side where the early sorts can be sharpened up for the Craven meeting.

Given good weather the Limekilns are open by May, and on these gallops Cecil has done the important preparation for many of his stable stars.

He works his string hard, and there is none better when it comes to producing horses fit to win first time out and exposing their optimum talent.

Cecil is fiercely competitive and takes no time to rest on his laurels, yet even with the pressures of training 200 horses, he finds time to chat on the Heath, where he stands out as one of the most stylish men in Newmarket. He has an obvious passion for clothes, which are expensive, informal and fun, and it is not unusual to see him on the gallops sporting brightly-coloured suede chaps, suede jacket and navy blue cap.

He appears to be nonchalant about triumph and defeat. "That's the Derby favourite," he replied in all modesty to a group of casual onlookers, as they asked to identify the colt which was Reference Point cantering up Warren Hill in early spring.

But underneath there is a vigorous determination to be the best. And as long as he retains his dogged will to win, he will be the hardest man to beat in his profession.□

● CROWNING MOMENT: Winning owner-breeder Louis Freedman struggles through the Epsom crowd to lead in Reference Point after the Derby.
Picture: GERRY CRANHAM

● CROWNING MOMENT: Winning owner-breeder Louis Freedman struggles through the Epsom crowd to lead in Reference Point after the Derby.
Picture: GERRY CRANHAM

CHAPTER 24

Breeders

by ADRIAN COOK

○ **PURE JOY: Egon Weinfeld (right), with the Milligram team of jockey Walter Swinburn and stable girl Sira Hornsby.** Picture: ALAN JOHNSON

Breeders

by ADRIAN COOK

THE TRIUMPHS of Reference Point were the culmination of 20 years' endeavour by owner-breeder Louis Freedman, who bought the famous Cliveden Stud back in 1966.

Cliveden had been founded by Waldorf Astor 60 years earlier and became one of the most important British studs but was on the market following the death of the third Lord Astor.

Freedman acquired only the tradition of Cliveden however, as all the bloodstock had been sold by sealed bid and he had to start from scratch in building his broodmare band.

Initially his Coronation Cup winner and Derby third I Say stood at Cliveden but following his export to Brazil in 1973, the stud has concentrated on mares.

The acquisition of much of Lady Sassoon's bloodstock in 1971 greatly expanded Freedman's bloodstock interests and over half the mares on the present Cliveden strength are

derived from this source. Included in the purchase were Attica Meli, Owen Dudley and Mil's Bomb, and such good winners as Royal Hive, Mill On The Floss and the 1987 Ribblesdale Stakes winner Queen Midas come from this stock.

An early yearling purchase, Seventh Bride, became the dam of the short-lived 1,000 Guineas winner Polygamy, while the descendants of Tina II, a private purchase, include Guillotina, One Way Street and Ever Genial. Reference Point's family came into Cliveden in 1967 when his third dam Byblis was purchased for 5,700gns at the December Sales. She was sold six years later for 4,000gns at the same sale and exported to Hungary.

Her daughter Great Guns, a prolific winner at up to two miles, produced two winners for Freedman before she too was sold, for 60,000gns at Newmarket in 1981.

Easily the better of these was Home on the Range, winner of the Sun Chariot Stakes and dam of Reference

Point, who retires to Sheikh Mohammed's Dalham Hall as winner of four Group One races: the Ever Ready Derby, King George VI and Queen Elizabeth Diamond Stakes, Holsten Pils St Leger and William Hill Futurity.

Home on the Range is now the only representative of the family at Cliveden, and Reference Point's year younger sister had to be destroyed in the spring after breaking a leg.

The famous Eyrefield Lodge Stud, founded by Pretty Polly's owner Eustace Loder at the end of the last century, had two top racers in the Gold Seal Oaks and Gilltown Stud Irish Oaks winner Unite and the Guinness Peat Aviation National Stakes winner Caerwent.

Both share the same third dam, My Game, who is also third dam of the Gold Cup winner Paean, and trace back through Overture to that great mare Pretty Polly, who carried her breeder's colours to victory in the 1904 1,000 Guineas and Oaks. Eyrefield Lodge has enjoyed notable success with her descendants which include the champion sprinter Marwell, who carried Edmund Loder's silks to success in the Prix de L'Abbaye, July Cup, Cheveley Park, and King's Stand Stakes.

Marwell's son Caerwent also carries his breeder's colours as a splint prevented him from being sold as a yearling, but Unite was sold for 310,000gns at the Highflyer sales to Sheikh Mohammed.

Like Unite, Don't Forget Me completed a Classic double, winning the 2,000 Guineas at Newmarket and The Curragh and providing a real boost in the process for the small breeder.

He was bred by Liam and Frances Hutch at their Gurteenard Stud in County Cork and sold by them for 19,000gns at Tattersalls October Yearling sale.

Don't Forget Me's dam, African Doll, was also bred by Mr and Mrs Hutch, who keep about five mares. They acquired her dam Mithril for 9,600gns at the 1973 December Sales, just four lots before Reference Point's third dam Byblis went through the same ring.

Another small breeder to hit the spotlight was John Moore of the Biddlestone Stud in Wiltshire. From a mare from the same female family as Don't Forget Me, he bred the Coral-Eclipse winner Mtoto.

He bought Mtoto's dam Amazer for 5,800gns at the 1976 December Sales and her first six foals for him have all been successful, with Mtoto, whom he sold for 110,000gns as a yearling, easily the best.

The larger established studs of Lord Howard de Walden, with Paean, Wolsey, Arden and Carmelite House, and Eric Moller, with Most Welcome, Ela Romara, Pipsted and Percy's Lass, did well.

So too did the veteran American breeder Paul Mellon, who won the Goffs Irish 1,000 Guineas with Forest Flower as well as enjoying major successes in the States with Java Gold, Dance of Life and Crusader Sword.

The Budweiser Irish Derby winner Sir Harry Lewis was bred in partnership by Howard Kaskel (in whose name he races) and Joseph Allen.

Kaskel has expanded his bloodstock interests considerably since he acquired Sir Harry Lewis's grandam 10 years ago and is now involved in well over 200 horses. He owns Sugar Maple Farm in New York, where the stallions include the ex-Guy Harwood trained Raft.

Joseph Allen, breeder of Bob Back who upset Pebbles and Commanche Run at Royal Ascot in 1985, has been a partner with Kaskel in the smart US stakes winners Dr Blum and Faster Than Sound.

Other newer studs to shine were those of Egon Weinfeld, breeder of Milligram, and Khalid Abdullah, whose homebreds included Warning, Bourbon Girl, Trampship, Interval and Nashmeel.

Like Abdullah, Stavros Niarchos, breeder of the General Accident 1,000 Guineas winner Miesque as well as the leading French juvenile colt Common Grounds, operates on an international scale.

Although he has recently reduced his commitments, dissolving his partnership with Robert Sangster and offloading over 50 mares and fillies at the December Sales, Niarchos still retains a large broodmare band.

Sangster himself had numerous successes, breeding in partnership such as Acushla, Fairy Gold, Entitled and Lake Como, while his Swettenham Stud is registered as sole breeder of Blessed Event, Glacial Storm, Guest Performer and Lake Erie.

The blitz of autumn successes by the offspring of Ela-Mana-Mou provided Airlie Stud with compensation for the death of Habitat in June. His most important success came through the Airlie-bred filly Eurobird. This half-sister to Assert and Bikala developed into a high-class filly and on her final appearance ran out an eight-length winner of the Jefferson Smurfit Memorial Irish St Leger.

The history of Eurobird's dam Irish Bird is a fine example of the vicissitudes breeders have to bear.

Irish Bird was bought by Walter Haefner for a French record yearling price of 700,000 francs in 1971 but won only just over 31,000 francs on the race track and he sold her for 200,000 francs (approx £22,000) in 1979.

Her first four foals between them had recouped only about £35,000 at auction but the third and fourth, successful after Irish Bird was sold, became the Classic winners Bikala and Assert.

Airlie received IR170,000gns for the Bold Lad colt she was carrying at the time of her sale, 330,000gns for Eurobird, 330,000gns for her two-year-old Falco and IR680,000gns for her Sadlers Wells yearling this year.

However Irish Bird also had a yearling filly top the Highflyer sale in 1984 at 1,600,000gns which was returned because of a wind infirmity. But as a half-sister to three Classic winners she must be a very valuable property now.

Like Airlie, the US stud of Spendthrift had a major stake in mares plus a large stallion complex but its recent history has been much more troubled.

Financial problems led to the dispersal of its broodmare band last year but such runners, bred by the farm or in partnership, including Bint Pasha, Zaizoom, Insan, Tibullo and the good US winners Northern Aspen and Sharrood, serve as a reminder of its success.

In 1986 the dispersal sales of several leading American breeders took place, including Tartan Farms and John A. Nerud, Hermitage Farm of Warner L. Jones (breeder in partnership of Lomond, Northern Trick and Rousillon), and Paul Hexter, the breeder of Golden Fleece.

It was also announced that Nelson Bunker Hunt would be dispersing all his thoroughbred holdings, with 570 broodmares, two-year-olds and yearlings to be sold at Keeneland in January, 1988. They made $47 million.

Hunt has enjoyed tremendous success on both sides of the Atlantic, breeding such as Dahlia, Youth, Estrapade, Empery, Nobiliary, Gazala II, Super Concorde, Mississipian and Dahar.

In 1987 he figured as the breeder of Rivlia, Swink, Rosedale, Talinum and Antiqua, all major winners in the USA, the smart French three-year-old Motley and, in partnership with Ed Stephenson, of Triptych.

Hunt has received the prestigious Eclipse award for leading breeder in 1976, 1985, and 1987, and in 1986 was North America's leading breeder in races won, earnings and number of stakes winners. But times are about to change.□

○**NO JOY: Louis Freedman, after the Arc defeat of Reference Point.**
Picture: GEORGE SELWYN

● **DOUBLE VISION:** Le Glorieux flashes past the video screen showing his Japan Cup success over Southjet and Dyna Actress.

CHAPTER 25

Autumn in Japan

by GRAHAM ROCK

○ **ALL-STAR LINE UP:** Taking part in the Japanese international jockeys' challenge were, from left, Lance O'Sullivan, Yves Saint-Martin, Steve Cauthen, Cash Asmussen, Yukio Okabe, Pat Eddery, Pat Day, Laffit Pincay, Katsumi Minai and Hiroshi Kawachi.

Autumn in Japan

by GRAHAM ROCK

SHINJUKU RAILWAY STATION is the busiest in the world, handling an average of 1.7 million passengers a day. Halfway up the straight on Triptych in the 1987 Japan Cup, Tony Cruz must have felt he had been caught in its rush hour.

When the illustrious mare did find her way out of trouble, she ate up the ground, but only reached fourth place behind versatile Le Glorieux, whose exploits in the Autumn emphatically justified his name.

The running of the Japan Cup was the only disorganised event of the week. The arrival of horses and jockeys, the draw, the hype, had all gone with exemplary Japanese precision, but the race itself did not keep to the expected script.

Pat Eddery was supposed to make the running on the second favourite Moon Madness but his mount, distracted by a fractious neighbour in

the stalls, was tardily into his stride, and it was a quarter of a mile before the English challenger was in front.

Doubtless with the intent of bursting his rivals (and principally Triptych, who is best at a mile and a quarter), Eddery sent Moon Madness into an eight-length lead by the time the field was stretching down the back straight. But the effort was too much, and turning for home Le Glorieux, who had been close up throughout, was cantering in behind.

To no-one's surprise Moon Madness was eclipsed and Le Glorieux, small and lean as a greyhound, comfortably held the late challenges of Southjet and Dyna Actress. Triptych, uneasy on the hard ground, had her ears flat for take off throughout, but the traffic on Tokyo Racecourse was too crowded and her flight home too late.

The winner carried the colours of

Mrs Wolf, whose husband's first interest in racing was unexpectedly born when he won a horse at a poker table! As she collected the winner's trophy, a dozen girls in traditional geisha costume enhanced the occasion, to the accompaniment of an 80-strong band, whose triumphant fanfare was boosted by eight pristine white tubas.

It was a celebrated victory, too, for the young French trainer Robert Collet, who had landed the Washington DC International less than a month earlier with Le Glorieux, and who sent out Last Tycoon to win the Breeders' Cup Mile in 1986.

Le Glorieux's time for the 2,400 metres, 2min 24.9sec, was probably a world record for the distance, but in a country whose racing statistics are spectacular, no-one was sure.

A mere 85,062 attended the Japan

Cup, about half the record for the course, the crowd deterred mainly by unseasonably cold weather, but also able to enjoy the 21 computer-linked off-course betting centres run by the Japanese Racing Association. The largest, Korakuen in Tokyo, has nine floors and accommodates 100,000 punters a day.

Last year, the Japanese bet over £8,000,000,000 on horse racing organised by the J.R.A. There is a separate Regional Public Racing organisation which races mainly Arabian horses, and substantial betting on bicycle racing, motorcycle racing and powerboat racing.

It is not surprising that government legislation restricts opportunities to win, place and quinella (dual forecast) betting, the last-named accounting for 85 per cent of turnover.

Following previous runnings of the Japan Cup, foreign jockeys had taken part in an informal contest a week later, but in 1987 the Japan Racing Association decided to increase the prestige of this event and launched the Super Jockeys International Invitation races at Hanshin racecourse, a few miles from Osaka.

The four races, two on Saturday and two on Sunday, attracted a field worthy of the name: from the United States, Laffit Pincay and Pat Day; Americans Steve Cauthen and Cash Asmussen, now both based in Europe; Pat Eddery and Yves Saint-Martin, and the New Zealand champion Lance O'Sullivan. Australian Malcolm Johnston was absent, having fallen foul of the Stewards back home, and a local jockey Hiroshi Kawachi, joined the two Japanese representatives Yukio Okabe and Katsumi Minai to make up the numbers.

Hanshin racecourse, set against a backcloth of the dark Rokko mountains, is one of the ten tracks operated by the J.R.A. A wide sweeping course, 1,700 metres round, it encompasses a dirt track, a steeplechase course (patronised by the slowest horses) and was widely praised by the jockeys. "The home bend reminds me a bit of Longchamp," said Cauthen.

Those expecting the visiting stars to dominate were quickly put in their

○ **CASH BONUS: It's presentation time as Cash Asmussen collects his prize for victory in Japan.**

place when Kawachi and Homan Marimo proved too good for Asmussen, Cauthen and Saint-Martin in the first invitation event.

The 12-race card, which began at 10 o'clock in the morning, included races on dirt and over the steeplechase course. Saint-Martin in his last month before retiring had demonstrated all his panache in collecting an earlier dirt race on the appropriately-named Nostalgia, but he had little luck in the draw for rides in the jockeys' championship. Eddery, too, found himself demonstrating his fine talent on some particularly unappreciative horses.

Local opinion suggested the ballot had given Cauthen a chance but his first mount showed enough white in the eye to make General Wolfe trigger happy, and ran accordingly.

Pincay, a master of American courses, had ridden right-handed only twice before in his remarkable career. Leaving the hotel that morning, the swarthy Panamanian, resplendent in navy overcoat and dark glasses, looked more like the dictator of a minor republic about to address his troops than a race-hardened jockey, but on the track he was a revelation.

Riding a perfect waiting race on Shin Seikan, Pincay swept through his field to record an emphatic victory, and shared the overnight lead with Kawachi.

However, Asmussen had collected points by finishing runner-up in the

opening invitation race and won the first on Sunday, driving out Wonder Resist to defeat Shin Wind, ridden by Okabe. Asmussen clinched victory when third to Okabe and Long Sing in the final event, and received 13 million yen (£55,000) and a solid gold trophy. There were generous prizes, too, for the local runners-up Okabe and Kawachi, and all jockeys received a guaranteed one million yen (£4,300) for each ride.

The awards ceremony was preceded by a traditional dance performed by Japanese schoolgirls, and as the wind swept down seemingly straight from the Siberian wastes, those watching from the stands needed no binoculars to spot blossoming goosepimples.

At the farewell party later that evening, all the jockeys said how impressed they had been by the Japanese organisation and hospitality. At £17,000 guaranteed for four rides they could afford to be generous, but these men, who had been feted and cosseted for most of their working lives, seemed genuinely impressed.

Of course, the Japanese are protective of their racing, and the Japan Cup is the only event open to foreign horses. Their sport is exceptionally well managed, and the stallions and mares imported are of sufficient quality to produce high-class horses. It needs the razor edge of international competition to lift Japanese racing into the limelight of the world's stage.□

● **PAT EDDERY:** runner-up.

Picture: ALAN JOHNSON

CHAPTER 26

Cauthen versus Eddery

by RAY GILPIN

● **STEVE CAUTHEN: champion.**

Picture: ALAN JOHNSON

○ **ALL-OUT FINISH: Steve Cauthen, on Sanquirico in the Royal Lodge Stakes, is a narrow winner from Pat Eddery, just as he was in the jockeys' championship.** Picture: GEORGE SELWYN

Cauthen versus Eddery

by RAY GILPIN

STEVE CAUTHEN 197, Pat Eddery 195: the final statistic does no justice to the carnival atmosphere which the jockeys' championship generated in the final week of the Flat season.

The battle attracted unprecedented media hype and exerted pressure which tested the characters of both men.

It reached the far corners of the racing circuit, with Scottish racegoers enthralled by all-too-rare glimpses of world-class talent as attendances doubled at Edinburgh and Hamilton. These were occasions punters will recall and boast, "I was there."

Support for the two stars was split

50–50: they breathed life into moderate races, with even sellers counting for all – never mind the quality.

Cauthen twice delighted his fans on that Hamilton visit and wins on Master Palehouse and Cashmere N Caviar netted a modest £2,122. During the balmy days of summer, he struck gold twice when star colt Reference Point amassed £464,814 by taking Derby and King George glory, but they were no more important than any other two in championship terms as Cauthen continued his quest to keep Eddery at bay.

The American was also to emerge

as the media winner, always willing to be interviewed, until even he was forced to close the door a little. Who could blame him?

One could understand his response when approached for what must have seemed the thousandth time. "What the hell do they want me to say now?" was his desperate plea from within the Hamilton weighing-room.

What indeed? The permutations of questions – many so naive as to cause embarrassment to the profession – and answers, had run out long ago.

Eddery predicted a month before that judgement day would be November 7, not a minute sooner than the last day of the season. He was right.

His subsequent claim that there was no more to say held no water with most of the non-racing media and he came in for plenty of criticism. It was unjustified. Eddery is less at ease than Cauthen when among a sea of strange faces firing silly questions; that is the nature of the man.

Who could reasonably knock him for his 'single-minded dedication' to riding winners and doing the best job he could for those who pay his riding fees.

He turned down a request for an interview with BBC and ITV camera crews at Edinburgh, and in that, there was just a touch of poetic justice!

The TV men had gained permission to descend in numbers on the weighing-room – a facility strictly denied to the press. They took a dig at him in subsequent news clips but Eddery had lived up to his claims and upstaged them.

That determination – so vital to a winner but which left TV unimpressed – helped Eddery complete a superb double on Valtaki, and so he snatched the lead again.

Cauthen watched the race on closed-circuit TV, without any obvious emotion, then both were quickly on their way, bidding the course goodbye, with only another close title fight likely to persuade them to return in 1988.

They had come, they had seen and they had conquered Musselburgh. Now it was on to Hamilton for a repeat performance, giving Scottish racing another boost in the process.

Cauthen had stopped talking, but the championship fire was still in his belly and he swept back into the lead with the Master Palehouse–Cashmere N Caviar double.

Eddery suffered a blank day, but as the two principals made a swift exit through a rear door they were of one mind, sensing that relief was just 48 hours away.

The show moved south through the fog to Doncaster for the penultimate round. Their first four rides slipped by with not a championship blow struck in anger. But Cauthen's absent guv'nor Henry Cecil had a late ace up

his sleeve and Proud Crest came to the rescue.

Half an hour later Cauthen was beaten in a photo-finish, but he could reflect that Eddery had to strike three times against a personal whitewash to take the title outright.

D-Day dawned and two hours before racing the anticipation among racegoers flocking down Leger Way could be likened to Cup Final fever along Wembley Way.

Cauthen and Eddery decided to open up their hearts and agreed to pre-racing interviews with Brough Scott for Channel 4. Nothing startling emerged. Regulars had heard it all before, but at least it made many observers feel they were all part of the same game again.

Cauthen soon increased the pressure by winning on Vague Discretion, and those holding ante-post vouchers on him were preparing to celebrate. But Eddery was not prepared to lie down, and he raised hopes of a fairytale tie by reducing the lead to two on Night Pass. Then, just as quickly, it was over. Vilusi let down Eddery in the next and the battle was won and lost. Cauthen was champion for the third time.

Eddery beat a hasty retreat after the

last race but Cauthen stayed around to bask in the glory, making up a little more for lack of communication during the previous 48 hours.

Delaying serious celebrations as he had to go to work again in Italy the following day, he said: "We are good friends but the press tried to create the impression that we were arch enemies so we decided to say nothing.

"I always had a vague idea I was a survivor and now I know I am.

"Pat is a great champion himself so it is a good feeling to have come out on top."

Darkness had fallen as we made our way out of Town Moor but in the Members' hall the Broughton brass band was blasting away its final score.

'Down by the Riverside' was not the most appropriate farewell rendering, but as the last notes died away it was the signal that the carnival was over.

One cynic suggested we would have been spared a lot of bother if they had called a truce a week earlier; the outcome would have been the same.

Not a bit of it, most of us following the circus had loved it. Cauthen and Eddery had brought sparkle and excitement to a usually dull time for the Flat, and we would not have missed it for the world.□

○ **AT THE DOUBLE: Steve Cauthen has not one but two Edderys to beat in the Ever Ready Derby, as Reference Point wins from Most Welcome (Paul Eddery) and Belloto (Pat Eddery, left).**   Picture: GEORGE HERRINGSHAW

CHAPTER 27

Sir Noel Murless

by GEORGE ENNOR

○ **GLORIOUS FIRST: Noel Murless follows the Queen as she leads in her first Classic winner, Carrozza, after the 1957 Oaks.**
Picture: SPORT & GENERAL

Sir Noel Murless

by GEORGE ENNOR

SIR NOEL MURLESS, who died on 9 May, aged 77, was as fine a trainer as racing will ever see. There was virtually no Flat race worthy of the name which he failed to win during a career lasting more than 40 years. To list the Classic winners sets a standard which few have been or will be able to follow: three Derbys, six 1,000 Guineas, five Oaks, two 2,000 Guineas and three St Legers. The total of 19 equals the record set by Fred Darling, whom Murless succeeded at Beckhampton in 1947.

He was champion trainer nine times and by the time he retired at the end of the 1976 season had sent out the winners of 1,430 races and collected £3,650,000 in first-place money for his owners.

Those were the days before prize money was sent rocketing by sponsored Classics in England and hugely endowed prizes all over the world. The figures may not look big by modern standards but, believe me, they were.

For many of his final years as a trainer Sir Noel could have had his pick of owners and/or horse. But it was not always thus. Though his origins were by no means humble, there was never any evidence of a silver spoon and his racing career started in quiet and modest fashion.

Charles Francis Noel Murless came from a farming family in Cheshire and rode as a jump jockey, first as an amateur and then professionally, mostly for the Hampshire stable of Frank Hartigan.

Later he had five years as assistant to Hubert Hartigan in Ireland, and at the end of that time he set up as a trainer in the Yorkshire village of Hambleton in 1935.

His first winner was Rubin Wood, who won at Lanark in September

1935; by the beginning of 1939 he had 20 horses in the stable. His owners included the Marchioness of Londonderry, Sir Alfred McAlpine and Miss Gwendolen Carlow. In 1940 he and Miss Carlow were married and their only child, Julie (officially Julia), is now Mrs Henry Cecil.

It took Murless little time to make his mark after the end of the second World War, and in 1946 he was leading Northern trainer, winning 34 races worth £15,337. To put things into perspective the Derby of that year carried a first prize of £7,915.

The following year he had his first major victory when Closeburn, ridden by Gordon Richards, won the Stewards' Cup at Goodwood. He was again leading Northern trainer and finished seventh in the overall list.

During his forays South, Murless had attracted the attention of Fred Darling. "That fellow is on the job. He doesn't let his head lad carry his saddles for him," said Darling to Richards, and it was due at least in part to Darling, a little martinet of a trainer, that Murless took over at Beckhampton when he retired at the end of the 1947 season.

Richards stayed on as first jockey and the success of his relationship with Murless is vividly illustrated by this brief story.

When Sir Gordon died in November 1986, I prepared his obituary and thought that I should speak to Murless. His health had been poor for some time, and when Lady Murless answered the telephone, she was keen he should not be pressed by journalists. Sir Noel, on the other end of the phone, had different ideas. "No," he said, "I want to talk about Gordon." He did, and Lady Murless would never have been able to stop him.

In 1948 Murless had his first Classic winner (Queenpot in the 1,000 Guineas). He almost won the 2,000 with The Cobbler, and with outstanding two-year-olds in Abernant and Royal Forest he was champion trainer for the first time.

Despite his flying start at Beckhampton, Murless was not happy with the constraints imposed on him by the yard's size, and he did not

always see eye to eye with its owner John Dewar. So in 1952, by which time Ridge Wood (1949 St Leger) had provided his second Classic success, he moved to Warren Place at Newmarket.

When Gordon Richards retired in 1954, Murless retained Lester Piggott as stable jockey, and one of racing's most fruitful partnerships started.

In 1957 they won three Classics: the Derby and 2,000 Guineas with Crepello, and the Oaks with Carrozza, who gave the Queen her first Classic victory. Murless was again champion trainer, becoming the first to breach the six-figure prize-money mark, but the year was not without controversy.

Following his two Classic victories, Crepello was a hot favourite for the King George VI and Queen Elizabeth Stakes at Ascot, and, in the days before four-day forfeits, let alone overnight declarations, he was shown as a probable runner in the morning papers. But only an hour before the race Murless, who put his horses above all other considerations, decided the colt would not run.

He was bitterly criticised at the time but maybe had the last word (hardly the last laugh) as Crepello broke down the following month and never ran again.

This was a purple era for Warren Place. There were more training championships in 1959, '60 and '61, and Classic glory from Petite Etoile (Oaks and 1,000 Guineas), St Paddy (Derby and St Leger) and Aurelius (St Leger). There were also important victories from Twilight Alley (Gold Cup), Royal Avenue, and two fine fillies in The Creditor and the 1966 King George heroine Aunt Edith.

At first glance there might seem nothing unusual that Aunt Edith was ridden by Lester Piggott, but jockey and trainer had split only a few weeks before, following an acrimonious dispute.

Piggott wanted to ride Valoris for Vincent O'Brien in the Oaks, even though Murless intended to run (and did run) Varinia. Piggott got his way; Valoris won and Varinia, ridden by Stan Clayton, was third.

In 1967 the new stable jockey at Warren Place was George Moore. He

and Murless could hardly have had a happier season. Royal Palace won the Derby and 2,000 Guineas; Fleet took the 1,000; Busted won the King George and Eclipse, and the trainer's sixth championship ended four seasons of Irish domination.

Moore returned to Australia in controversial circumstances at the end of the season and was replaced by the young Scotsman "Sandy" Barclay. The advent of a new jockey had anything but an adverse effect on the stable and in 1968 Barclay rode Mrs Murless's Caergwrle to victory in the 1,000 Guineas, as well as winning the King George and Eclipse on Royal Palace.

Lupe won the 1970 Oaks, another year in which Murless topped the trainers' list but by 1971 there was another new No. 1 jockey in Geoff Lewis.

The stable won the 1,000 Guineas with the 25-1 chance Altesse Royale (ridden by Yves Saint-Martin as Lewis had chosen Magic Flute), but the stable jockey was on board when that filly took the Oaks, prefacing the double for Mysterious in 1973, the year of Murless's last Classic and final championship.

He retired in 1976, was knighted in the following summer's Birthday Honours list and elected to the Jockey Club in 1978.

For all his success Murless remained a quiet and retiring man, who always enjoyed the preparation of his horses more than the victories. He was prepared to give his horses as long as possible to prove their potential, and though (or maybe perhaps) he was seldom very publicly demonstrative, he inspired maximum respect in colleagues and others, and the greatest loyalty in those who worked for him. He was truly a giant, on and off the racecourse.□

CHAPTER 28

National Hunt Section

○ **POISED TO POUNCE: See You Then (centre) jumps the second-last flight in the Champion Hurdle behind Barnbrook Again (blinkers) and River Ceiriog.**
Picture: GEORGE SELWYN

Hurdlers

by COLIN RUSSELL

FOR THE THIRD YEAR in succession See You Then was Champion Hurdler. His defeat of the versatile American visitor Flatterer at Cheltenham in March put him on the same pedestal as those other three-time post-War champions Hatton's Grace, Sir Ken and Persian War.

But during his spell at the top, the seven-year-old has rarely captured the public imagination, and has never appeared to have supreme power over his pretenders. What See You Then lacks is the soundness to match his talent. His racecourse appearances have become increasingly restricted over the years. In 1985, the first year

he triumphed at Cheltenham, he ran only five times, the following season only three, and last season only twice.

Suspect tendons have made the task of his trainer Nick Henderson a nightmare, and it is a tribute to him and his staff that See You Then has been prepared to run for his life on the opening day of the Festival for three successive seasons.

Although Henderson is magnificently open about the gelding's progress, admitting there is only one day in his Calendar, rumours abounded about his possible absence in 1987. "See You When?" became a popular headline, as race after race

went by without him. But a troublesome corn took time to clear, and it was not until Haydock Park a mere 11 days before Cheltenham that See You Then finally came into public view.

Against three opponents, two just below top class, and the other out of her depth, See You Then put up a satisfactory performance, winning by a length and a half from Ballydurrow, with precious little in hand. He was not impressive, and the performance was well below that needed to win the Champion, but both Henderson and jockey Steve Smith Eccles expressed themselves satisfied. The object of the exercise had been achieved.

Apart from the American horse Flatterer, making his first appearance over British-type hurdles, the field for the 1987 Waterford Crystal Champion Hurdle less than a fortnight later contained nothing likely to de-throne the king at his peak. He had already proved his domination of the princes, who in their turn had quashed the upstarts.

See You Then started 11-10 favourite, with Nohalmdun, third to him in 1986, and unbeaten in the current season, second best at 11-2. Flatterer the only unknown quantity, was third best at 10-1. See You Then was not at his best this time, but he still won.

Corporal Clinger was pacemaker for the other 17 runners, but by the

○ **JACQUI'S JOY: A rare win for a woman rider at Liverpool, as Jacqui Oliver becomes the first successful female professional on Aonoch in the Sandeman Aintree Hurdle.** Picture: JOHN CROFTS

○ **NORTHERN LIGHT: Cumbrian-trained Tartan Tailor (left) jumps the last flight on his way to winning the Waterford Crystal Supreme Novices Hurdle from Hill's Pageant (No. 13).** Picture: PHIL SMITH

○ **HAT'S OFF: See You Then has the measure of Barnbrook Again as he powers towards his third triumph in the Champion Hurdle.**
Picture: GERRY CRANHAM

○ **WIDE AWAKE:** One of the best youngsters of the season, The West Awake lands the Sun Alliance Novices Hurdle.

Picture: TONY EDENDEN

You Then is no chicken-hearted Champion, and drawing on all his reserves, he prevailed by a length and a half, Flatterer finishing a gallant second with Barnbrook Again only a further length away in third.

As far as the winner was concerned that was it. The Sandeman Aintree Hurdle at Liverpool in which he was defeated by Aonoch in 1986, was ruled out and he retired for the summer to rest his suspect legs. His next battle, likely to be the toughest of the lot, will be on the same field in March.

The vanquished Flatterer, runner-up in the Grand Course de Haies the previous June, returned to the States having shared the honours but not the prize. On his first attempt at the unique English-type hurdles his performance was little short of brilliant. But sadly there will be no re-match. His legs which had carried him to 23 wins and almost $500,000 in prize money, finally gave way at Fair Hill in October and he limped into honourable retirement.

On the home scene the novice races at the Cheltenham Festival produced no obvious Champion in the hurdling field. The two-mile Waterford Crystal

third-last he had come to the end of his tether. Only then did the race develop in earnest. Barnbrook Again took over his role in front, and after jumping the penultimate flight, still in command, set sail for home with River Ceiriog close up, and See You Then going best of the trio in a perfect position.

Nohalmdun had already beaten a retreat, and Flatterer seemed tapped for speed. Over the last See You Then was in front, and needed only to produce his customary finishing speed to etch his name permanently in the hurdling Hall of Fame. But halfway up the hill, although still in front, he was struggling.

River Ceiriog fell at the last, but Barnbrook Again was sticking doggedly to his task, and Flatterer began to find his feet. In the mind of Smith Eccles there might never have been doubt, but for a fraction of a second it looked as though the American might take the title. But See

○ **MINE'S A TREBLE:** See You Then's Champion Hurdle hat-trick is on the cards as he challenges Barnbrook Again (blinkers) and River Ceiriog (almost hidden) approaching the last flight. Runner-up Flatterer is on the left.

Picture: GEORGE SELWYN

Supreme Novices event was won in workmanlike fashion by the Northern challenger Tartan Tailor, who beat the maiden Hill's Pageant by a length. The two and a half miler, the Sun Alliance, went to The West Awake, and like Tartan Tailor his future is in steeplechasing.

There was one notable absentee from the meeting. Convinced, trained by Martin Pipe, was injured whilst being loaded up to run in the Top Rank Hurdle at Chepstow the previous Saturday. He missed his intended engagement and another at Cheltenham, but returned to win the Whitbread Best Scotch Novices Hurdle at Liverpool, claiming among his victims both Hill's Pageant and Tartan Tailor. A top-class handicapper on the Flat, Convinced had won both his previous hurdle races in facile fashion and could be star material.

The Daily Express Triumph Hurdle, perhaps the most unpredictable of all Championships, was won by the See You Then stable, Alone Success getting the better of Past Glories by half a length, with Grabel from Ireland third, the trio ten lengths clear of the rest.

The winner followed the same path as his stable-companion, retiring for the season unbeaten, but the other two followed the more traditional route to Liverpool. There the form-book was turned upside down, as Aldino, only sixth at Cheltenham, came home by eight lengths, with neither Past Glories, who finished lame, nor Grabel proving a serious threat in the closing stages.

The Irish, who sell so many of their top-class horses to English stables nowadays, suffered severe losses at Cheltenham. Their team was clearly not up to scratch, and they had their worst meeting for 20 years. Their only first prize was the Waterford Crystal Stayers Hurdle, won in style by Galmoy on only his second run of the season.

One of three with a chance at the last flight, he showed a fine turn of foot for a stayer to storm clear up the hill and win by six lengths. Jacqui Oliver, who rode the runner-up Aonoch, steered an erratic course in

the closing stages and suffered the wrath of the grandstand press critics as a result. Undeterred, she took the mount on him again at Liverpool, and was rewarded with a convincing win in the Sandeman Hurdle, giving 3lb and a four-length beating to Coral Hurdle winner Taberna Lord. Aonoch subsequently went under the hammer at Doncaster Sales, and reversing the current trend, went to Irish trainer Mouse Morris for 100,000gns. Chasing will be his game.

Nowadays the Champion is not the only big prize for hurdlers, be they potential chasers or specialists in their own sphere. Valuable handicaps such as the Mecca at Sandown (won in 1986 by Aonoch) and the Swinton Insurance (in which Inlander just beat Santopadre and Janus) are part and parcel of the Calendar.

Neblin proved the top money-spinner in that division last winter, winning the Tote Gold Trophy (formerly the Schweppes) and County Hurdle. His win in the former cost bookmakers dear, for although at the time the weights were published, he

had not run in Britain, form students pounced on the 40-1 available, taking the sound view that the English Handicapper had been far more lenient than his Irish counterpart.

The other top handicap, the imaginative Ladbroke at Leopardstown, also proved costly to the sponsors and their rivals. Despite a 22-runner field, the leniently-treated Barnbrook Again started favourite at 5-2 and won like the good thing he appeared. In view of his subsequent Champion Hurdle effort he must have been the certainty of the season.

He, like so many named above, has since moved on to chasing. He leaves a void, but as the current season unwinds, names like Floyd, another to suffer from leg-trouble, Convinced and perhaps Swingit Gunner step into his place.

History will be made in March should the current champion succeed where Hatton's Grace, Sir Ken and Persian War failed, by winning four Champion Hurdles. Legs permitting, the stage will be Cheltenham, the date 15 March 1988 — See you then!□

○ **JUST WE TWO: Thirty-one set out for the Coral Golden Hurdle Final at Cheltenham but the finish concerned only Taberna Lord (left) and Sporting Mariner. Taberna Lord won by a length and a half.** Picture: TONY EDENDEN

○RACE IS ON: Grand National winner Maori Venture (No 5) is about to land safely as Lean Ar Aghaidh (nearside) and Big Brown Bear lead over Becher's on the second circuit.

Picture: JOHN CROFTS

○ **STAR PERFORMER: Desert Orchid in full flight at Kempton Park, where he returned to win the 1986 King George VI Rank Chase.**
Picture: ALAN JOHNSON

Chasers

by COLIN RUSSELL

STEEPLECHASING is the colourful side of National Hunt racing; it will be remembered in terms of black, white and grey in 1987.

Such a drab combination does not mean that the sport has lost its magic. Black was the colour of the jacket worn by jockey Steve Knight on Maori Venture, winner of the Seagram Grand National; white was the blanket of snow whose untimely arrival caused the Cheltenham Gold Cup to be postponed; and the grey was the flying Desert Orchid, who was the chaser of the season.

Although Desert Orchid had been around for several years, nipping round tight tracks such as Kempton Park and Wincanton to win valuable hurdle races over two miles, he had never given the impression he would scale the heights as a top staying

chaser. Not to the majority, that is, but his trainer David Elsworth once predicted; "I know that you'll think I'm mad, but this horse will be a top class three-mile chaser."

Prophetic words indeed, and he was right on both counts. His sanity did seem questionable and his prediction was 100 per cent correct.

Early in the season though, Desert Orchid gave no signs of what was to come. A horse much better going right-handed than left, he won handicaps at Sandown Park and Ascot over two miles and two and a half miles, in between managing only fourth to Church Warden in the H & T Goddess Chase, also at Ascot.

On Boxing Day he was only sixth-best in the betting at 16-1 for the King George VI Rank Chase at Kempton, and even stable jockey Colin Brown

deserted him, choosing the other Elsworth runner, Combs Ditch, who started second favourite to Forgive'N Forget.

Setting out in front as usual, Desert Orchid produced the performance of the season. Jumping immaculately, he was never headed. Door Latch tried hard to keep tabs on him, Forgive'N Forget was under pressure when he moved up to challenge four from home, and Bolands Cross too made a token effort. None could make the slightest impression, as the grey, an amazing chance ride for Simon Sherwood, kept on galloping. He had victory sewn up by the third-last, and came home 15 lengths ahead of Door Latch, with Bolands Cross another six lengths away in third.

The accolades flowed in. Not since the days of Arkle or Red Rum had

○ **AT THE LAST:** Cybrandian leads Wayward Lad (almost hidden) and The Thinker in the Cheltenham Gold Cup. The Thinker stayed on to win.
Picture: PHIL SMITH

one horse so captured the imagination of the public and Press. Although he won his next two races, the Gainsborough Chase at Sandown and the Jim Ford at Wincanton, a tilt at the Gold Cup was never on the cards. Cheltenham is not his track, and despite the Press pressure Elsworth resisted all temptation. Instead he ran him in the Queen Mother Champion Chase in which he finished an honourable third to Pearlyman. After a battling win under his inevitable top weight in another Ascot handicap, Desert Orchid was pulled up in the Whitbread and retired for the season.

Back on song with two easy wins in the early part of the new season, chasing's newest star burns as brightly as ever.

In his absence the 1987 Tote Gold Cup looked an open affair. Burrough Hill Lad failed to make the racecourse at all this season, so it looked another good chance for those seasoned

○ **CHAMPIONS TOGETHER:** Leading jockey Peter Scudamore and top two-miler Pearlyman lead from Very Promising at the last fence in the Queen Mother Champion Chase.
Picture: PHIL SMITH

campaigners Forgive'N Forget, who had shown his Kempton running to be all wrong with an easy win in Ireland, Wayward Lad and Combs Ditch. Pitched against them were improving types like Bolands Cross and The Thinker.

The weather played the first hand. Snow fell overnight as close as Birmingham in the north and Bristol in the south, but Prestbury Park, Cheltenham escaped . . . temporarily. Shortly after Observe had taken the Christies Foxhunters Chase, the skies opened.

The runners paraded, and were despatched to the post. Inevitably, though, racing had to give way. The fences looked like well-proportioned snow drifts, and only a few blades of grass could be seen poking through

○ **CIRCLE OF FRIENDS: The Thinker and Ridley Lamb return to the winner's enclosure after the Cheltenham Gold Cup.**　　　Picture: GERRY CRANHAM

○ **TWO OF THE BEST: Kildimo (left) on his way to beating another smart novice Playschool at Cheltenham on New Year's Eve 1986.**
Picture: ALAN JOHNSON

the white desert. To their credit the stewards showed great patience, and armed with local forecasts, postponed the race, first for half an hour, then for an hour. Finally, 80 minutes late, the race got under way.

After the waiting it was no anti-climax. The unconsidered Cybrandian, ridden by the iron man of the north Chris Grant in place of the injured Lorcan Wyer, set them a merry dance. Jumping with precision he led virtually all the way. In his wake, challengers fell by the wayside. Charter Party was an early casualty, Earls Brig was pulled up and Bolands

Cross unseated Peter Scudamore when prominent at the 15th.

Rounding the last bend with two to jump, there were still five with a chance. At the last there were three, Cybrandian showing with a two-length lead from the old man Wayward Lad and The Thinker, who had recovered well from an almighty mistake at the third-last. Once again the Cheltenham hill found out Wayward Lad, but The Thinker, winner of the Midlands National the previous season, has stamina in abundance. Staying on strongly, he caught the luckless Cybrandian halfway up the hill, going

on to win by a length and a half, with Door Latch an honourable third and West Tip, running one of the best races of his life over conventional fences a creditable fourth.

For jockey Ridley Lamb, who eight months later retired from the saddle, victory was the climax of a 15-year career. It was also the pinnacle for trainer Arthur Stephenson, who typically chose to go to Hexham instead of Cheltenham.

Originally The Thinker had been programmed to appear in the Seagram Grand National at Aintree, but easy wins in the Rowland Meyrick Chase at

○ **SUPER SUB: Simon Sherwood makes the most of his unexpected ride on Desert Orchid in the 1986 King George VI Rank Chase.**
Picture: GERRY CRANHAM

○ **GREY FOR GLORY: The winning combination of Desert Orchid and Colin Brown.**
Picture: ALAN JOHNSON

Wetherby and the Peter Marsh Chase had persuaded Stephenson to alter course. The big Liverpool chase, though, was still on the agenda; he was not a horse who could stand many hard races, but would never be so well handicapped again.

Stephenson, although fully open about his plans, kept supporters in suspense until the last moment. The well-being of his horse was his only consideration, and at the last hour he pulled him out.

The Thinker's presence would have added extra class to the spectacle, but there may be other years. In his absence the 1986 winner West Tip was 5-1 favourite, with Dark Ivy, attempting to give trainer Gordon Richards his third win in the race, 11-2 second best. Neither featured in the finish.

The almost unpronounceable Lean

○ **ACTION STUDY: Forgive'N Forget takes**

an open ditch in his stride at Haydock Park.   Picture: ALAN JOHNSON

○ **THRILLS GALORE:** There's no more exciting course in Britain than Liverpool. Above: The Grand National field takes the Chair, with the winner Maori Venture jumping on the left, and previous winner West Tip (sash) clearing towards the right. Below: Becher's for the first time in the REA Bott Foxhunters Chase, and the winner Border Burg (white cap) is in midair towards the left as Clonncormick (No 11) has a slight lead.

Pictures: KICKSPORT/GEORGE SELWYN

Ar Aghaidh looked like stealing the show, making most of the running, and appearing to enjoy every moment of it. Still in front at the last, he seemed as if he might succeed for young rider Guy Landau and experienced trainer Stan Mellor. But on the run-in he was passed by Maori Venture and then by The Tsarevich.

Maori Venture, ridden by Steve Knight and trained by Andy Turnell, proved the stronger, running on to take the honours by five lengths, The Tsarevich finishing second and Lean Ar Aghaidh third. Although not one of the more fancied contenders, Maori Venture gained a universally popular win, for he is owned by that great enthusiast Jim Joel, who sadly was not there to see it. A staunch supporter of both codes of racing for almost half a century, Joel has had his colours of black, red cap carried into the winner's enclosures on almost every racecourse in the country. But Maori Venture will not sport them again. Within hours of his win it was announced that the 11-year-old, who slightly surprised both Turnell and Knight with the way he tackled the fences, would be retired.

Black spot of the race was the death of Dark Ivy at Becher's. Jockey Niall Madden, riding Attitude Adjuster, unfairly shouldered most of the blame. At a point where the course bears left, his mount went left, whereas the horse on the inside kept straight on. Dark Ivy, between the pair, was left with no room. His death became a public debate, so much so that Madden was summoned before the Jockey Club, who bowed to pressure and instigated an inquiry. Madden was absolved of blame. It was the correct decision, but his use of the whip on Attitude Adjuster, who finished eighth, was more than unsightly, and he was fortunate to be cleared of improper riding on this point.

Not surprisingly, Attitude Adjuster ran poorly in the Jameson Irish National next time, the race going to Brittany Boy, who had previously finished third to Kildimo in the Sun Alliance Novices Chase at Cheltenham.

That result suggested the novices

○ **TRAGEDY STRIKES: The grey Dark Ivy, second favourite for the Seagram Grand National, takes a fatal fall at Becher's on the first circuit. Top: Dark Ivy (centre) crashes; below: the field thunders on as he and jockey Phil Tuck are down on the ground.** Pictures: PRESS ASSOCIATION

were well up to scratch, particularly among the stayers. Kildimo, apart from one lapse in a slowly-run and controversial race at Ascot, won on all his outings over fences. In fact, the Sun Alliance began to look more and more a hotly contested contest, for besides Brittany Boy, and Kildimo, who landed the odds at Ayr, Against the Grain (fourth), Mr Frisk (fifth), Midnight Madness (eighth) and Dixton House (last of 11 finishers) all won their next races.

Mr Frisk, who had entered novice chasing from point-to-points failed his big Cheltenham test but had proved a rare money-spinner, winning seven of his nine races. Another from the same sphere was J-J-Henry, who also made his mark novice chasing, but at around two or two and a half miles. J-J-Henry was not entered for the Arkle Chase, which was a pity, for it appeared a sub-standard affair, with the 25-1 shot Gala's Image, who had not previously won a chase, getting the better of

○ **SOARAWAY SUCCESS: Lean Ar Aghaidh, followed by Desert Orchid, puts in a great leap at the 12th fence in the Whitbread Gold Cup.**

Picture: ALAN JOHNSON

Northern challenger Allten Glazed.

Other notable wins during the year were by Forgive'N Forget in the Vincent O'Brien Irish Gold Cup, a IR£50,000 event which added a new dimension to steeplechasing, and by Lean Ar Aghaidh, who came back from his Aintree exploits to make virtually every yard in the Whitbread Gold Cup. The Queen Mother Champion Two Mile Chase also provided stirring sport, the second-season novice Pearlyman holding on by a neck from Very Promising. With Desert Orchid leading the way, the

scene at the top of the steeplechasing tree seems as strong as ever — if, and what a big if it is, injuries can be avoided.

However, 1987, marked the end of an era, with the win of Wayward Lad in the Whitbread Gold Label Cup at Liverpool. Just when everyone seemed to have written him off — even Graham Bradley gave up the ride to partner Stearsby — the old horse produced one last, memorable performance. That he had to be the victim of an ownership dispute was sad, but thankfully his original part-

owner Mrs Shirley Thewlis and trainers Monica and Tony Dickinson, won the day at an emotional Doncaster Sales ring in May. His career, guided by all three members of the Dickinson family, spanned eight years. During that time he set prize money records, and won three King George VI Chases and a million admirers. Thanks to those who contributed towards the 42,000gns needed to buy him back, he is now enjoying retirement as a hack and hunter with Michael Dickinson in Fair Hill, Maryland. Long may he live.□

○ **FOOT PERFECT: Forgive'N Forget jumps the last fence to win the inaugural Vincent O'Brien Gold Cup at Leopardstown.**
Picture: CAROLINE NORRIS

Irish National Hunt

by TONY O'HEHIR

RESULTS at the 1987 Cheltenham Festival clearly identified the dilemma in which Irish jump racing finds itself. Over the three days, 13 of the 18 winners were Irish bred, but only Galmoy was Irish trained, by John Mulhern.

In Britain the demand for young Irish-bred National Hunt horses remains strong and most Irish breeders and owners cannot afford to ignore those agents and U.K. trainers flashing cheque books at them. But the prize-money situation in Ireland has improved considerably and long-term possibilities for keeping some of the better jumping stock are good.

The '87–88 season opened with Weather The Storm striking an early blow for Ireland's younger chasers when he won the H&T Walker Gold

Cup at Ascot in November. And, in Abbey Glen, Pat Hughes has a worthy successor to Barrow Line, the champion Irish novice of last season.

Barrow Line is a credit to Hughes' ability and patience. Now an 11-year-old, he broke down three times before he first raced in December 1985. Unbeaten in novice events, and a game third in the Vincent O'Brien Gold Cup on his only other start, Barrow Line gained his most important success in the Arkle Trophy at Leopardstown in February. Victory there earned owner Michael Foley a bonus of IR£24,000 as Barrow Line, who missed the Cheltenham Festival because of recurring corn problems, had won two qualifiers and the final of that novice chase series.

With the exception of eight-year-old

Super Furrow, a much-improved horse in 1987, most of Ireland's established chasers are entitled to be termed Dad's Army.

Bobsline, Excursion (who suffered a stroke in 1986) and the general himself, Royal Bond, now 15, continued to give good service, with the last-named jumping better in '87 than at any stage of his career.

Champion trainer Paddy Mullins mainly relied on young horses, with Grabel, Cloughtaney, Tradehimin and Innocent Choice among the pick. Darkorjon's win in the Tattersalls Gold Cup at Punchestown in April was Mullins' only significant chase success.

Cork trainer Kelvin Hitchmough achieved national prominence when his Brittany Boy landed the first

○ **HOME OF JUMPING: Over the last flight of hurdles at Dundalk.**

Picture: GERRY CRANHAM

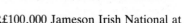

○ **HELP YOURSELF: Barnbrook Again has the lead at the last flight before landing a gamble in The Ladbroke at Leopardstown. Chrysaor (left) was fourth.**

Picture: CAROLINE NORRIS

IR£100,000 Jameson Irish National at Fairyhouse in April. But some of the money would have been better spent improving facilities at the track, which increasingly resembles a crumbling ruin.

With no funds made available by the Racing Board, the plight of Fairyhouse is serious. In the circumstances falling attendances of recent months are hardly surprising. Unless there is a major re-development of the stands, one of which is already condemned, people will lose the habit of racing.

The decision to move this year's National from its traditional Easter Monday date to the third Saturday in April is unlikely to make it a better race. Instead of coming five days before the Aintree National, it will be run a week after it and a week before the Whitbread at Sandown.

Brittany Boy, a big strong gelding with no stamina limitations, won by six lengths from Bankers Benefit and gave Tom Taaffe, whose father Pat was a six-times winner of the race, his most important success to date.

Castle Warden, in fourth, fared best of the six English challengers. But the visitors, tempted by the improved prize money, lifted four important events during the year.

○ **NUMBER ONE: Randoss gave Anne Collen the glory as the first woman to train a Galway Plate winner.** Picture: CAROLINE NORRIS

Pride of place must go to Forgive 'N Forget, who slammed Very Promising by eight lengths in the inaugural Vincent O'Brien Gold Cup at Leopardstown in February. Though technically an English victory, the result was a splendid advertisement for Irish breeding – owner Tom Kilroe, trainer Jimmy FitzGerald and jockey Mark Dwyer are all Irish-born, and Forgive 'N Forget was a Leopardstown bumper winner in 1982 before joining the trail to England.

At Leopardstown in January the old Sweeps Hurdle became The Ladbroke and the new sponsors were among those stung when Barnbrook Again, backed from 5-1 to 5-2, became trainer David Elsworth's first winner in Ireland when he beat Feroda by five lengths. Winning jockey Colin Brown was among those of the opinion the race distance was short of the advertised two miles. Leopardstown manager Tony Corcoran hit back, re-measured the track and invited any doubting Thomases to measure it for themselves.

FitzGerald and Dwyer scored again at Fairyhouse in April, when Tickite Boo won the Power Gold Cup by five lengths from Super Furrow, and then survived a Stewards' inquiry into an incident at the last fence, where he appeared to hamper the runner-up.

Later that month High Plains, who ended the year in the United States, won Ireland's most valuable novice hurdle for David Nicholson and Richard Dunwoody when he beat Wolf Of Badenoch by eight lengths in the B.M.W. Champion Novice Hurdle.

Few jockeys can have had a more embarrassing experience in '87 than British champion Peter Scudamore, who found himself badly in need of a map and compass in the Harold Clarke Leopardstown Chase. Scudamore rode Lastofthebrownies, trained by Mouse Morris for Racing Board Chairman Michael Smurfit, and after two out the seven-year-old was travelling like a winner, until he ran the wrong side of a marker flag on the final bend.

Lastofthebrownies cruised home 15 lengths clear of The Ellier, but was disqualified and Scudamore received a four-day suspension and a fine of IR£200.

Galmoy's win in the Waterford Crystal Stayers Hurdle at Cheltenham continued trainer John Mulhern's love affair with the track, where he was previously successful as an owner with Friendly Alliance and Mack's Friendly.

For jockey Tommy Carmody it was another successful return to the meeting which in 1978 launched his career over fences with a Festival double on Mr Kildare and Hilly Way.

In a year when he was twice suspended for alleged lack of effort in races and was later lucky to escape serious injury in a car accident, Carmody kept his name in lights with Galmoy's win. And there were other

○ **JUST CHAMPION: Deep Idol and Brendan Sheridan clear the last flight in the Wessel Cable Champion Hurdle.** Picture: CAROLINE NORRIS

examples of his shining, yet underused talent. Most notable was in Australia in August, when he was the star of the Irish jockeys' team which on their first trip Down Under beat the locals in the eight-race Mark Sensing Series.

Carmody's performance on Cooa Prince in the first race of the competition in Victoria Park, Adelaide, almost defies description. Virtually shot out of the saddle when his mount blundered at halfway, he recovered and though hard at work from four out, rode one of his strongest finishes to beat Australia's best, Nick Harnett, in a photo-finish.

Carmody won three races and the individual award, and with teammates Frank Berry, Joe Byrne and Tony Mullins received Akulra hats from Australian Prime Minister Bob Hawke. The presentation was made on the final day of the competition at Moonee Valley racecourse, which as part of the mammoth promotion of

○ **NATIONAL HERO: Brittany Boy has the race sewn up as he jumps the last fence in the Jameson Irish Grand National** Picture: PRESS ASSOCIATION

○ **NOT THIS TIME: Barrow Line (right), one of Ireland's brightest stars, has to give best to Brittany Boy at Fairyhouse.** Picture: CAROLINE NORRIS

○ **TOP LINE: A good jump by Barrow Line at the last fence gives him the edge over the grey Weather The Storm in the Dennys Gold Medal Chase at Leopardstown.**
Picture: CAROLINE NORRIS

the Ireland-Australia series was renamed Mooney O'Valley for the day.

The Australians had their revenge in Ireland in November – with the assistance of Tony Mullins, whose mount Erins Invader ran inside a marker before the last, an error which cost the home team a draw.

Carmody was never in the national championship race with a chance as Frank Berry, who shared the '86 title with Tom Morgan, narrowly beat Brendan Sheridan for the honour.

Morgan landed a job with John Edwards in England towards the end of the summer, and Sheridan has emerged as the new pretender to Berry's crown. Sheridan's most important win in '87 was aboard Deep Idol in the Wessel Cable Champion Hurdle at Leopardstown in February. But Barney Burnett's failure to adapt to fences put a slight damper on an otherwise splendid year for this talented rider.

Ken Morgan, elder brother of Tom, Charlie Swan, for whom the transition from the Flat was successfully achieved, and leading claiming rider Ultan Smyth also ended the year with enhanced reputations.

And the Collen sisters, Ann and Sarah, can be proud of their achievements. In July, Anne became the first woman to train a Galway Plate winner when Randoss, owned by her father and ridden by Ken Morgan, landed the highlight of Ireland's biggest racing carnival. And in December, Sarah achieved another first when she won the Conyngham Cup, regarded as Ireland's Grand National for amateur riders, on Feltrim Hill Lad, trained by Paddy Griffin and jointly owned by her father Standish Collen and Mrs Patricia Leeman.□

○ **NONE KEENER: Whatever the weather, the Queen Mother will be out to watch her jumpers. At Ascot she joins trainer's wife Cath Walwyn and stud manager Michael Oswald to hear what Keven Mooney has to say about his win on Sun Rising.**
Picture: GERRY CRANHAM

Owners

by NEIL MORRICE

MAORI VENTURE'S fairytale Seagram Grand National triumph provided 92-year-old Jim Joel, one of National Hunt's best-loved patrons, with the realisation of a long-held dream.

It was the most memorable highlight of the 1986-87 season and said virtually everything there is to say about the sport of jumping.

For 30 years Joel had tried to add the world's greatest chase to his catalogue of Classic successes on the Flat.

Those who had carried his famous black and red colours over the towering Aintree fences included Glorious Twelfth (fourth to Sundew in 1957), Beau Normand, Bowgeeno, The Laird and Door Latch.

But where that quintet failed, the Andy Turnell-trained Maori Venture gloriously triumphed as Steve Knight brought him from third to first on the run-in, overhauling first Lean Ar Aghaidh and then The Tsarevich.

The only disappointment was that Joel, sitting in an aircraft on the

Johannesburg runway, missed seeing the historic triumph.

He wasted no time in returning home, however, announcing the retirement of his 11-year-old as he arrived for the traditional post-National celebrations at Turnell's East Hendred stables in Oxfordshire.

His summing up of what the win meant to him encapsulated the unique nature of National Hunt steeplechasing.

Joel said: "It was an amazing achievement by horse, jockey and trainer, and even though I have won more than 1,000 races, including a Derby with Royal Palace, there is nothing quite like the National. There are so many very steep obstacles to overcome."

The tributes to Joel, remarkably spry for a man of his years, came flooding in to the picturesque village.

Turnell, who won 98 races for Joel in his riding days, said: "He is the most marvellous man you could wish to meet and I could not have managed without his support over the difficult times.

"I am glad Mr Joel has decided to retire Maori Venture because the old horse would have had a lot more weight next year and it would have been a crying shame to see him have a hard race and, in all probability, get beaten."

Joel's decision to give Maori Venture to Steve Knight touched the 32-year-old jockey, who said: "It is a fabulous gesture and I will keep the horse on my father's farm."

Joel became the first owner to complete the Derby-Grand National double since Raymond Guest, who won the Derby with Larkspur in 1962 and Sir Ivor in 1968, and the Grand National with L'Escargot in 1975.

Maori Venture's victory carried Joel well clear at the top of the owners' table with £115,556 prize money won from nine horses in training.

He won 13 races in the season, including Newbury's Bradstone Mandarin Chase with Maori Venture and the SGB Chase at Ascot with Door Latch.

The Thinker's Tote Gold Cup triumph, in which Door Latch was a gallant third, put Irishman Tommy McDonagh next in the list.

Desert Orchid's owners, the Burridge family scooped third place with the six chases won by this spectacular-jumping grey.

These included the King George VI

○ **TOP OF THE LIST: Jim Joel, the season's leading owner, greets Ballyhane after his win at Sandown Park.** Picture: GERRY CRANHAM

Top Rank Chase at Kempton Park on Boxing Day. They earned Desert Orchid the 'Horse of the Season' award, but it was another one-horse race for the owners' title.□

○ **CHELTENHAM CHEER: Nick Henderson stands between his Festival hurdle heroes, Alone Success (left, with Taffy Davies), winner of the Daily Express Triumph Hurdle, and See You Then (with Glyn Foster), Champion Hurdler for the third time.**
Picture: PADDOCK STUDIOS

Trainers

by NEIL MORRICE

NICKY HENDERSON won the National Hunt trainers' title for the second season running with prize money of £222,638 from 67 successes. And it was See You Then's marvellous Champion Hurdle hat-trick triumph that enabled the master of Windsor House to resist stiff opposition from Toby Balding, Josh Gifford, John Edwards, Martin Pipe and David Elsworth.

That success alone was worth more than £43,000 and virtually clinched the title for Henderson, though after The Thinker's Tote Gold Cup success, he had to fend off a late challenge from Arthur Stephenson to remain top dog by a margin of £20,000.

The fact that six of the top seven trainers were separated by about £40,000 shows what kind of

○ **BIG WINNER: Martin Pipe collected more first prizes than any other jump trainer.**
Picture: ALAN JOHNSON

the top trainers' slot for the Festival meeting by winning the Daily Express Triumph Hurdle, and with it more than £25,000.

Before the Festival, the destination of the title looked wide open, the initiative swinging from one trainer to the other.

Toby Balding had staked his claim by winning Newbury's Tote Gold Trophy with Neblin, who added the County Hurdle to his tally at Cheltenham. Kildimo was also successful for Fyfield here, in the Sun Alliance Chase.

But once Henderson had his head in front, no-one was going to stop him and Balding ended in third place with £195,828, his horses winning 57 races.

Josh Gifford's total of 60 winners, which put him fourth on £183,421, was highlighted by Door Latch's second SGB Handicap Chase at Ascot in December.

Pearlyman's Queen Mother Champion Chase triumph helped John Edwards toward a best-ever £171,364 and fifth place.

Spare a thought for Martin Pipe, trainer of no fewer than 106 winners and £166,926 prize money.

If the title had been decided on winners rather than stakes earned, the Somerset trainer would have been clear by a street. And who is to say it does not take as much ability to land dozens of selling hurdles and chases as better class contests.

Pipe almost cleaned up at the West Country meetings which traditionally open and close the season, and but for the lack of half a dozen top-flight jumpers would have been very hard to beat in the title race.

That theory has been endorsed during the first half of the current season after Beau Ranger, Positive and Sabin du Loir found their way to Pipe's Wellington stables.

Finally, a mention for David Elsworth, whose Whitsbury yard is full of top flight jumpers from season to season.

Once again it was Desert Orchid who went down in the record books as the stable's top money-earner, his six wins netting around £72,000. Little wonder the flying grey was nominated 'Horse Of The Season.' □

horsepower the Henderson stable had to repel. But thanks mainly to See You Then and a splendid piece of training by Henderson to have the gelding spot-on when it mattered, they did. The seven-year-old has been plagued with leg problems since joining Henderson four seasons ago, and it was not until 11 days before Cheltenham that he tuned up for the hurdling crown by beating Ballydurrow at Haydock Park.

Henderson reflected that he had been farther behind with See You Then than he would have liked through January and February, pinpointing Haydock as the turning point.

He said: "I had virtually given up the ghost when I went on holiday at the end of January – we were so far behind. See You Then was getting too lazy and it was my head lad, Corky Browne, who talked me into running him at Haydock. Without that run he would not have won." At the Festival, See You Then joined the elite trio of Hatton's Grace, Sir Ken and Persian War by beating the American horse Flatterer by a length and a half.

Just as he had done the previous two seasons, Henderson's stable star rose to the occasion at Cheltenham. And Alone Success guaranteed him

○ **THANKS A MILLION: Steve Knight leaped into the limelight on Maori Venture, winner of the Grand National.**
Picture: ALAN JOHNSON

Jockeys

by NEIL MORRICE

PETER SCUDAMORE retained his jump jockeys' title with a total 50 per cent greater than his closest pursuer, Mark Dwyer.

In achieving 123 successes from 578 mounts, Scudamore was simply the busiest and best rider of the 1986/87 season.

It was his highest score, three more than in 1981–82, when he shared the honours with John Francome. But to single out Scudamore as being in a different league from his pursuers – as the statistics suggest – would be a

gross injustice to the likes of Mark Dwyer, Richard Dunwoody, Simon Sherwood, Chris Grant and Phil Tuck.

Scudamore had the title under wraps – barring accidents – before the horses he partnered at the Cheltenham Festival had reappeared. Courtesy of Martin Pipe's ability to churn out winners from August through to June, Scudamore soon established a clear lead over the rest.

The studious, poker-faced Scudamore is a hard man to beat at the best of times. His determination

and unquenchable appetite for success lends comparison to former champions such as Stan Mellor and Graham Thorner.

It is hardly surprising that Scudamore was one of the two men responsible for the most enthralling race of the season. And how appropriate it should be at Cheltenham, home of steeplechasing, in a race run in honour of its best-loved patron, the Queen Mother.

The Queen Mother Champion Chase lived up to its billing as the race

○ **SEE YOU AGAIN: Steve Smith Eccles returns after winning his third Champion Hurdle on See You Then.**
                                                                    Picture: TONY EDENDEN

winner's circle at Cheltenham. But in doing so he paid a price which, ultimately, signalled the end of his career.

Riding Gala's Image for Mercy Rimell in the Arkle Trophy, Linley dislocated his right collarbone as the gelding made a mistake while challenging at the last fence. Remarkably, Linley kept his mount balanced on the run-in, and they led 50 yards out to score by threequarters of a length from Allten Glazed.

The whys and wherefores of Graham Bradley's exaggerated waiting tactics on top staying novice chaser Kildimo at Ascot in February was a talking point for the remainder of the season.

Bradley came in for criticism from Toby Balding, among others, after he had been beaten a total of 19 lengths into fourth by Tawridge in the Reynoldstown Chase.

Kildimo started well behind the others and jumped moderately early on. Though making some ground up on the second circuit, mistakes at the

of the Festival, with Pearlyman and Very Promising, Scudamore and Dunwoody, making the ingredients for a battle which, with Desert Orchid thrown in for good measure, would decide the two-mile championship.

Desert Orchid was the first to crack two out, and Pearlyman raced to the last with a half-length lead over Very Promising. A better jump put Very Promising back in contention, and only through persistent driving was Scudamore able to force Pearlyman a neck in front at the post. The same riders, up the same Cheltenham hill, had fought out a similar epic struggle four months earlier in the Mackeson Gold Cup. But this time the boot was on the other foot, Dunwoody and Very Promising staying on too strongly for the Scudamore-ridden Half Free.

The thrills of the Festival cannot go by without a word about Richard Linley.

Barely two months after his return to the saddle, following the death of his wife Beverley in a car crash, Linley was back where he belonged – in the

○ **HEADING FOR A FALL: Cnoc Na Cuille and the Princess Royal (still Princess Anne) before they parted company at the last fence at Towcester in May 1987.**
                                                                    Picture: ALAN JOHNSON

○ **DOWN TO BUSINESS: Gee Armytage and Gee-A, a powerful combination.**

Picture: ALAN JOHNSON

○ **GOOD GUY: One of the new stars of the season, Guy Landau, goes for home on Lean Ar Aghaidh in the Whitbread Gold Cup.**
Picture: GEORGE SELWYN

fourth and third last fences put paid to his chances.

How reassuring for Bradley that, despite a rollicking from Balding, he was still in the hot seat on the day of the Sun Alliance Chase. This had been Kildimo's target all season and, as cool as a cucumber, Bradley delivered the goods in his own inimitable manner.

Hunting Kildimo round on the first circuit, the Yorkshireman asked his mount to improve at the top of the hill and the response was immediate.

Kildimo ranged up to his old rival Playschool before the second last and, being sent on before the final obstacle, went seven lengths clear up the hill.

Gee Armytage made Festival history at the meeting by becoming the first woman rider to beat male professionals on 33–1 outsider Gee-A in the Mildmay of Flete Challenge Cup. The previous day she won the Kim Muir Memorial Challenge Cup against fellow amateurs on The Ellier.

Miss Armytage, Scudamore and Steve Smith Eccles were the leading

riders at Cheltenham with two winners each. But Scudamore snatched the Ritz Club Trophy because he rode more placed horses. Steve Knight wrote himself into the history books with an unforgettable Grand National triumph on Maori Venture. The combination were not given a bright chance of completing the course, as 'Maori' had had his jumping problems in the past, but the testing track proved the making of both horse and rider.□

○ **HAT'S OFF: Irish trainer Arthur Moore relishes the success of Weather The Storm in Ascot's H&T Walker Gold Cup.**
Picture: GERRY CRANHAM

National Hunt Update

by COLIN RUSSELL

FOR MORE THAN 900 years the English Channel has remained an inpenetrable barrier to foreign invaders. Yet it seems no more than a mountain stream for modern-day thoroughbreds, who criss-cross almost every week in the summer, often returning home the same night.

Possibly because of the differences in the make and shape of the obstacles, steeplechasers and hurdlers rarely foray across the Channel. The French go south, and the British travel west to Ireland.

So when Lamorlaye trainer Francois Doumen decided on the ambitious plan to challenge the cream of British chasers in the King George

VI Rank Chase with Nupsala, it looked a highly-optimistic plan. Although a proven performer in his native land, few had even heard of him on this side of the water. The bookmakers dismissed him as a 50-1 chance, and interest in the race centred on the flying grey Desert Orchid, the in-form Beau Ranger and the late change of plan by Jimmy FitzGerald to run the 1986 Gold Cup winner Forgive'N Forget.

But after Nupsala's schooling session and work-out at Lambourn three days before the race, under the careful eye of Oliver Sherwood who was providing temporary accommodation, the 50-1 on offer about the French raider gradually dried up.

Nupsala was no mug, no rank outsider. By the time the nine runners were sent on their way his odds had tumbled to 25-1. Even so it was a lot to ask for him to threaten Desert Orchid on his own patch, and even if he failed there were always the other two.

A break-neck pace was assured with three front runners – Cybrandian, Beau Ranger and Desert Orchid – going at it hammer and tongs from the outset.

○ **BACK ON TOP: No danger to Beau Ranger as he takes the last fence in the Mackeson Gold Cup.**　　　　　　　　　Picture: ALAN JOHNSON

○ **STILL ON TOP: Pearlyman leads from Karenomore at Cheltenham in November to confirm his star status.**
Picture: EDWARD WHITAKER

By the time Cybrandian, runner-up in the 1987 Gold Cup, fell at the 14th fence, he was already a spent force, but the other two were still there, plus Forgive'N Forget, with Nupsala running remarkably well in fifth place.

Only turning for home did the truth begin to dawn. Beau Ranger was struggling, Desert Orchid, although in front, was being driven hard, and Forgive'N Forget was beginning to feel the pace.

Nupsala, though, was cruising, and approaching the third last, his rider Andre Pommier had the audacity to take a pull. Setting sail for home jumping the next, he had the race won when Forgive'N Forget fell heavily at the last, and galloped home by 15 lengths from Desert Orchid, with Golden Friend running on to finish an honourable third.

Like the flying grey's the year before, it was a staggering performance, but whether Nupsala is truly a new-born star, or just a star for a day remains to be seen.

Not since Burrough Hill Lad in 1984 has one horse won more than one of the top chasing prizes. Dawn Run was tragically killed; Forgive'N Forget, at times so brilliant, seems to need everything in his favour; Desert Orchid is best right-handed, Wayward Lad has retired, and The Thinker had not reappeared by Christmas.

Other possible stars did emerge in the early months of the new season. Kildimo looked an heir apparent after an impressive win at Cheltenham in November, but below-par efforts in the Hennessy and Corals Welsh National quickly knocked him off his pedestal. His conqueror on both occasions was the game Playschool, whom he had beaten in the Sun Alliance Chase in March.

With two big handicap wins to his credit, Playschool followed the path trodden by so many recent Cheltenham Gold Cup winners. A tough, game performer, he gained his Chepstow win, which saved the bookmakers a fortune, the hard-fought way from a rejuvenated Rhyme 'N' Reason, backed from 25-1 ante-post to 4-1.

See You Then was, as usual, absent early season, and the picture for the Waterford Crystal Champion Hurdle remained murky. Star novice of '86–87 Convinced, second favourite at start of play, failed to live up to expectations, but bursting on the scene in his place came Osric, who stormed home from Aldino in Kempton Park's Christmas Hurdle, and Pat's Jester, who underlined his improvement by taking the Glen International Bula Hurdle.

Cynics could say their prominence was due to the mediocrity of the rest but at least it meant supporters of the three-times Champion could spend the deep winter dreaming of an unprecedented fourth.□

○ **GOING DOWN: Andre Pommier, on French-trained Nupsala, looks back to find Forgive'N Forget (Mark Dwyer) capsizing at the last fence in the 1987 King George VI Rank Chase.**
Picture: GERRY CRANHAM

10 January – Sandown Park
GOOD   3m 5f 18y

Anthony Mildmay, Peter Cazalet Memorial Handicap Chase

1st £10,870

1		STEARSBY 8 11-5	G McCourt	**11-8F**
2	3	CATCH PHRASE 9 10-1	R Rowe	**10-1**
3	2	SACRED PATH 7 10-0	C Cox	**9-2**
4	12	WEST TIP 10 11-7	R Dunwoody	**11-2**
5	8	RHYME 'N' REASON 8 10-6	P Scudamore	**14-1**
6	20	LUCKY VANE 12 10-5	J Frost	**6-1**
7	30	YOU'RE WELCOME 11 10-0	E Murphy	**16-1**

7 ran
TIME 7m 47.1s
1st OWNER: T Ramsden TRAINER: Mrs J Pitman

24 January – Haydock Park
GOOD TO SOFT   3m

Peter Marsh Chase (Limited Handicap)

1st £11,222

1		THE THINKER 9 11-10	R Lamb	**9-2**
2	3	GOLDEN FRIEND 9 11-0	H Davies	**4-1**
3	2½	WEST TIP 10 11-9	R Dunwoody	**11-1**
4	20	TOWNLEY STONE 8 11-9	S Smith Eccles	**4-1**
Fell		CYBRANDIAN 9 11-10	L Wyer	**7-2JF**
Fell		MAORI VENTURE 11 11-7	S Knight	**7-2JF**

6 ran
TIME 6m 26.1s
1st OWNER: T P McDonagh Ltd TRAINER: W A Stephenson

7 February – Sandown Park
GOOD TO FIRM   3m 118y

FU's Jeans Gainsborough Handicap Chase

1st £15,666

1		DESERT ORCHID 8 11-10	C Brown	**11-4**
2	10	STEARSBY 8 11-4	G McCourt	**3-1**
3	3	BOLANDS CROSS 8 11-0	P Scudamore	**9-4F**
4	12	CATCH PHRASE 9 10-7	R Rowe	**12-1**
5	dist	MACOLIVER 9 10-7	M Perrett	**50-1**
Fell		CHARTER PARTY 9 10-13	R Dunwoody	**13-2**

6 ran
TIME 6m 12.2s
1st OWNER: R Burridge TRAINER: D Elsworth

11 February – Ascot
GOOD TO FIRM   3m

Charterhouse Handicap Chase

1st £15,322

1		CASTLE WARDEN 10 9-12	Mr M Richards	**10-1**
2	4	SIMON LEGREE 10 11-3	P Hobbs	**5-1**
3	2	THE LANGHOLM DYER 8 10-4	P Tuck	**11-2**
4	4	OREGON TRAIL 7 11-7	R Beggan	**9-2F**
5	4	CHURCH WARDEN 8 10-4	B de Haan	**8-1**
6	30	MAORI VENTURE 11 1-7	S Knight	**7-1**
Fell		HOMESON 10 10-0	E Murphy	**50-1**
Fell		SIGN AGAIN 9 10-5	K Mooney	**7-1**
PUp		BEAU RANGER 9 11-1	C Brown	**12-1**
PUp		RAINBOW WARRIOR 10 11-6	S Sherwood	**12-1**

10 ran
TIME 6m 10.2s
1st OWNER: M Shone TRAINER: J Edwards

11 February – Ascot
GOOD TO FIRM   3m

Reynoldstown Novices Chase

1st £10,092

1		**TAWRIDGE** 7 11-12	S Knight **2-1**
2	3	**AGAINST THE GRAIN** 6 11-8	S Sherwood **8-1**
3	1	**CAVVIES CLOWN** 7 11-12	R Arnott **8-1**
4	15	**KILDIMO** 7 11-8	G Bradley **6-5F**
Fell		**CRAMMER** 7 11-8	C Brown **12-1**

5 ran
TIME 6m 13.8s
1st OWNER: L Ames Ltd TRAINER: A Turnell

14 February – Newbury
SOFT   2m 100y

Tote Gold Trophy (Handicap Hurdle)

1st £21,053

1		**NEBLIN** 8 10-0	S Moore **10-1**
2	2½	**MRS MUCK** 6 10-10	P Scudamore **5-1F**
3	2	**SAFFRON LORD** 5 10-7	B Powell **14-1**
4	2	**YABIS** 6 10-8	T Morgan **14-1**
5	3	**HELYNSAR** 6 10-1	J R Quinn **33-1**
6	5	**PREDOMINATE** 6 10-1	S Sherwood **14-1**
7		**RUSTSTONE** 7 10-1	J H Brown **33-1**
8		**JIM THORPE** 6 10-5	P Tuck **25-1**
9		**SPROWSTON BOY** 4 10-5	R Rowe **12-1**
10		**JIMSINTIME** 6 10-12	K Mooney **16-1**
11		**RECORD HARVEST** 6 10-0	L Wyer **25-1**
12		**JAMESMEAD** 6 10-1	C Brown **12-1**
13		**FREEMASON** 6 10-0	C Cox **33-1**
14		**ORYX MINOR** 7 9-11	G Landau **33-1**
0		**HUMBERSIDE LADY** 6 11-7	G McCourt **14-1**
0		**RA NOVA** 8 11-4	M Perrett **12-1**
0		**ROBIN WONDER** 9 11-2	R Arnott **14-1**
0		**SOUTHERNAIR** 7 11-3	A Webb **16-1**
0		**TANGOGNAT** 5 9-7	D Gallagher **20-1**
0		**TIMELY STAR** 6 10-9	B de Haan **33-1**

21 ran
TIME 4m 6.1s
1st OWNER: A Leather TRAINER: G Balding

14 March – Sandown Park
GOOD TO FIRM   2m

William Hill Imperial Cup (Handicap Hurdle)

1st £11,756

1		**INLANDER** 6 10-3	S Smith Eccles **10-1**
2	1	**KESCAST** 7 10-6	P Scudamore **11-1**
3	5	**TIMELY STAR** 6 11-0	M Pitman **25-1**
4	1½	**TAELOS** 6 10-0	J R Quinn **11-1**
5	½	**HOW NOW** 6 10-0	M Perrett **22-1**
6	1½	**TERRYASH** 8 9-11	I Shoemark **11-1**
7	shd	**MENINGI** 6 9-10	L Harvey **66-1**
8	2	**BALLYDURROW** 10 11-13	M Hammond **6-1F**
9	8	**WHITHER GOEST THOU** 5 10-0	D Murphy **16-1**
10	1	**YABIS** 6 11-8	T Morgan **8-1**
11		**TACHEO** 6 10-0	R Rowell **33-1**
12		**EASTER LEE** 7 10-1	R Arnott **12-1**
13		**JAMESMEAD** 6 10-11	C Brown **16-1**
14		**SNOWBALL DANNY** 7 9-7	K Caplen **33-1**
15		**NEBLIN** 8 11-6	R Guest **11-1**
16		**POLAR BEAR** 7 10-11	S Sherwood **14-1**
17		**MUSICAL MYSTERY** 5 10-1	R Rowe **20-1**
18		**STRAY SHOT** 9 9-13	Miss G Armytage **25-1**
19		**AVERON** 7 10-0	M Brennan **100-1**
20		**OWEN'S PRIDE** 5 10-0	S Keightley **40-1**
21		**AMRULLAH** 7 10-1	G Moore **100-1**
Fell		**FUEGO BOY** 7 10-1	K Mooney **20-1**
BrtDn		**TACHADOR** 6 9-7	W Irvine **33-1**

23 ran
TIME 3m 50.1s
1st OWNER: J Daniels TRAINER: R Akehurst

17 March – Cheltenham
GOOD   2m

Waterford Crystal Supreme Novices Hurdle

1st £23,190

1		TARTAN TAILOR 6 11-8	P Tuck	**14-1**
2	1	HILL'S PAGEANT 8 11-8	K Mooney	**50-1**
3	2½	OUTRIDER 5 11-8	N Madden	**28-1**
4	3	HIGH PLAINS 5 11-8	R Dunwoody	**20-1**
5	nk	HAVE FAITH 6 11-8	M Richards	**16-1**
6	nk	BILOXI BLUES 5 11-8	F Berry	**66-1**
7	nk	WELCOME PIN 6 11-8	T Carmody	**5-1**
8	2½	PROTECTION 5 11-8	S Knight	**7-2JF**
9	½	CHRISTIAN SCHAD 5 11-8	A Webb	**20-1**
10	½	OFFICER'S MESS 5 11-8	B Sheridan	**100-1**
11	4	TELETRADER 6 11-8	B Powell	**12-1**
12	shd	FOURTH TUDOR 5 11-8	G McCourt	**50-1**
13	½	SPECIAL VINTAGE 7 11-8	M Dwyer	**9-1**
14	½	KISSANE 6 11-8	J Shortt	**7-2JF**
15	4	BLACK SAND 5 11-8	N Byrne	**66-1**
16		SMITH'S GAMBLE 5 11-8	P Scudamore	**33-1**
Fell		CELTIC SHOT 5 11-8	J Duggan	**20-1**
BrtDn		AU-REVOIR JOAN 5 11-3	Mr M Wellings	**500-1**
RnOut		CUDDY DALE 4 11-0	Miss G Armytage	**500-1**
PUp		MR PARKER 5 11-8	R Rowe	**100-1**

20 ran
TIME 4m 2.1s
1st OWNER: Edinburgh Woollen Mill Ltd TRAINER: G W Richards

17 March – Cheltenham
GOOD   2m

Arkle Challenge Trophy Chase

1st £21,965

1		GALA'S IMAGE 7 11-8	R Linley	**25-1**
2	¾	ALLTEN GLAZED 10 11-8	C Grant	**16-1**
3	2	FIRST BOUT 6 11-8	S Smith Eccles	**11-4F**
4	4	HILLS GUARD 8 11-8	A Stringer	**25-1**
5	15	DAN THE MILLAR 8 11-8	G Bradley	**11-2**
6	shd	DALBURY 9 11-8	G Moore	**20-1**
7	1	EVENING SONG 8 11-3	Mr P Townsley	**100-1**
8	7	RIBOBELLE 6 11-3	M Perrett	**20-1**
9	8	COTTAGE RUN 7 11-8	R Dunwoody	**14-1**
10		PATRICK'S FAIR 11 11-8	R Beggan	**100-1**
Fell		BLEUCHER 6 11-8	R Goldstein	**50-1**
Fell		KOUROS 8 11-8	M Brennan	**12-1**
Fell		PENNY'S DREAM 8 11-8	J Shortt	**300-1**
Fell		SOUND ARGUMENT 8 11-8	P Scudamore	**11-1**
Fell		TICKITE BOO 7 11-8	M Dwyer	**9-2**
BrtDn		RAISE AN ARGUMENT 8 11-8	S Sherwood	**14-1**
BrtDn		STRATHLINE 7 11-8	E Buckley	**100-1**
BrtDn		WILLIAM CRUMP 6 11-8	T Morgan	**20-1**
PUp		GENERAL CHANDOS 6 11-8	Mr J Bradburne	**66-1**

19 ran
TIME 3m 58.6s
1st OWNER: Sheikh Ali Abu Khamsin TRAINER: Mrs M Rimell

CAVALRY CHARGE: Alone Success has a narrow lead over Past Glories (left) in the Daily Express Triumph Hurdle.
Picture: GEORGE SELWYN

17 March – Cheltenham
GOOD   2m

Waterford Crystal Champion Hurdle

1st £43,205

1		SEE YOU THEN 7 12-0	S Smith Eccles	**11-10F**
2	1½	FLATTERER 8 12-0	J Fishback	**10-1**
3	1	BARNBROOK AGAIN 6 12-0	S Sherwood	**14-1**
4	6	DEEP IDOL 7 12-0	N Madden	**14-1**
5	hd	STEPASIDE LORD 5 12-0	R Dunwoody	**50-1**
6	1½	PRIDEAUX BOY 9 12-0	M Bowlby	**28-1**
7	4	HERBERT UNITED 8 12-0	H Rogers	**100-1**
8	½	NOHALMDUN 6 12-0	L Wyer	**11-2**
9	2½	JIMSINTIME 6 12-0	R Beggan	**300-1**
10	1½	MRS MUCK 6 11-9	S Morshead	**66-1**
11		CORPORAL CLINGER 8 12-0	P Scudamore	**12-1**
12		BONALMA 7 12-0	T Taaffe	**50-1**
13		RA NOVA 8 12-0	M Perrett	**66-1**
14		BRUNICO 5 12-0	G McCourt	**33-1**
Fell		RIVER CEIRIOG 6 12-0	D Browne	**14-1**
Fell		SAFFRON LORD 5 12-0	B Powell	**100-1**
PUp		COMANDANTE 5 12-0	E Murphy	**80-1**
PUp		I BIN ZAIDOON 6 12-0	G Bradley	**100-1**

18 ran
TIME 3m 57.6s
1st OWNER: Stype Wood Stud Ltd TRAINER: N Henderson

○ **IN THE PINK: Pearlyman and Peter Scudamore after winning the Queen Mother Champion Chase.**
Picture: TONY EDENDEN

17 March – Cheltenham
GOOD   3m 1f

Waterford Crystal Stayers Hurdle

1st £21,710

1		GALMOY 8 11-10	T Carmody	**9-2**
2	6	AONOCH 8 11-10	Miss J Oliver	**2-1F**
3	4	MODEL PUPIL 7 11-10	S J O'Neill	**6-1**
4	3	ATRABATES 7 11-5	S Sherwood	**14-1**
5	1	CRIMSON EMBERS 12 11-10	S Shilston	**9-1**
6	4	CIMA 9 11-10	R Dunwoody	**25-1**
7	4	DAD'S GAMBLE 6 11-10	R Rowe	**50-1**
8	1½	MALFORD LAD 9 11-10	E Waite	**300-1**
9	¾	SINGLECOTE 7 11-10	M Bastard	**33-1**
10	1½	ROBIN WONDER 9 11-10	G Bradley	**12-1**
11	1½	SPIDER'S WELL 11 11-10	Miss T Davis	**33-1**
12		OUT OF THE GLOOM 6 11-10	P Scudamore	**7-1**
13		ACE OF SPIES 6 11-10	J Bryan	**100-1**
PUp		SHEPHERD'S HYMN 6 11-10	R Beggan	**300-1**

14 ran
TIME 6m 39s
1st OWNER: Miss D Threadwell TRAINER: J Mulhern, Ireland

18 March – Cheltenham
GOOD   2m

Queen Mother Champion Chase

1st £25,775

1		PEARLYMAN 8 12-0	P Scudamore	**13-8F**
2	nk	VERY PROMISING 9 12-0	R Dunwoody	**3-1**
3	3	DESERT ORCHID 8 12-0	C Brown	**9-4**
4	25	TOWNLEY STONE 8 12-0	S Smith Eccles	**10-1**
5	3	CHARCOAL WALLY 8 12-0	S Morshead	**33-1**
6	20	MILESIAN DANCER 7 12-0	J Hansen	**1,000-1**
7	nk	CAPTAIN DAWN 11 12-0	R Rowe	**200-1**
Fell		LITTLE BAY 12 12-0	P Tuck	**16-1**

8 ran
TIME 3m 58.3s
1st OWNER: Mrs P Shaw TRAINER: J Edwards

18 March – Cheltenham
GOOD   2m 4f

Sun Alliance Novices Hurdle

1st £24,570

1		**THE WEST AWAKE** 6 11-7	S Sherwood	**16-1**
2	4	**CITY ENTERTAINER** 6 11-7	M Dwyer	**13-2**
3	¾	**FLYING TROVE** 6 11-7	T Taaffe	**16-1**
4	¾	**L'ANE ROUGE** 6 11-7	L Wyer	**20-1**
5	2½	**WOLF OF BADENOCH** 6 11-7	T Carmody	**9-1**
6	hd	**MIDSUMMER GAMBLE** 6 11-7	P Scudamore	**4-1JF**
7	3	**ABU KADRA** 6 11-7	S Smith Eccles	**25-1**
8	2½	**RANDOLPH PLACE** 6 11-7	P Tuck	**20-1**
9	hd	**BONANZA BOY** 6 11-7	P Hobbs	**4-1JF**
10	2½	**LODDON LAD** 5 11-7	R Dunwoody	**33-1**
11	1½	**WILD FLYER** 6 11-7	B Dowling	**66-1**
12	1	**LACIDAR** 7 11-7	G Landau	**100-1**
13	1	**CINDIE GIRL** 5 11-2	M Harrington	**33-1**
14	2	**MODTECH** 6 11-7	T G Dun	**100-1**
15	½	**KYLEMAKILL** 6 11-7	J Duggan	**66-1**
16	hd	**LONGGHURST** 4 10-12	P Leach	**25-1**
17	½	**HARRY'S BAR** 5 11-7	B de Haan	**66-1**
18	2½	**CREDIT CUT** 5 11-7	C Cox	**100-1**
19	1½	**HASSLE MONEY** 5 11-7	M Meagher	**33-1**
20	hd	**TIVIAN** 7 11-7	M Perrett	**66-1**
0		**EROSTIN RULER** 6 11-7	E Buckley	**66-1**
0		**HIGHWAY EXPRESS** 6 11-7	G McCourt	**100-1**
0		**MONRITA** 5 11-7	S Morshead	**100-1**
0		**OLAN LAD** 7 11-7	J Shortt	**16-1**
0		**SPARK OF PEACE** 5 11-7	R Beggan	**100-1**
0		**SURPASS** 7 11-7	Mr R Tate	**100-1**
URdr		**SCARLET RUNNER** 5 11-7	S Shilston	**33-1**
PUp		**CLOUGHTANEY** 6 11-7	A Mullins	**33-1**

28 ran
TIME 5m 15s
1st OWNER: Mrs C Heath TRAINER: O Sherwood

18 March – Cheltenham
GOOD   3m

Sun Alliance Chase

1st £27,740

1		**KILDIMO** 7 11-4	G Bradley	**13-2**
2	7	**PLAYSCHOOL** 9 11-4	P Nicholls	**6-1**
3	4	**BRITTANY BOY** 8 11-4	T Taaffe	**20-1**
4	4	**AGAINST THE GRAIN** 6 11-4	R Dunwoody	**16-1**
5	4	**MR FRISK** 8 11-4	A Jones	**11-2**
6	20	**THE HACIENDEROS** 8 11-4	D Murphy	**50-1**
7	hd	**LASTOFTHEBROWNIES** 7 11-4	N Madden	**10-1**
8	4	**MIDNIGHT MADNESS** 9 11-4	B Wright	**100-1**
9		**CHEEKY RUPERT** 7 11-4	R Crank	**100-1**
10		**REGULAR TIME** 6 11-4	M Flynn	**8-1**
11		**DIXTON HOUSE** 8 11-4	T Morgan	**100-1**
Fell		**ALKEPA** 7 11-4	M Hammond	**11-1**
Fell		**CAVVIE'S CLOWN** 7 11-4	R Arnott	**16-1**
Fell		**TAWRIDGE** 7 11-4	S Knight	**9-2F**
URdr		**FRIENDLY HENRY** 7 11-4	S Moore	**100-1**
PUp		**GRAGARA PRIDE** 10 11-4	J R Quinn	**100-1**
PUp		**MASTERPLAN** 10 11-4	S Morshead	**20-1**

18 ran
TIME 6m 15.9s
1st OWNER: Lady Harris TRAINER: G Balding

○ **SOMETHING TO LEARN: Sun Alliance Chase winner Kildimo shows another side of his jumping character.**
Picture: ALAN JOHNSON

19 March – Cheltenham
GOOD   2m

Daily Express Triumph Hurdle (4yo)

1st £25,895

1		ALONE SUCCESS 11-0	S Smith Eccles **11-1**
2	½	PAST GLORIES 11-0	P Farrell **20-1**
3	1½	GRABEL 11-0	A Mullins **20-1**
4	10	HIGH KNOWL 11-0	P Scudamore **4-1F**
5	5	OSRIC 11-0	H Davies **25-1**
6	3	ALDINO 11-0	S Sherwood **12-1**
7	1	FINGEST 11-0	A Webb **100-1**
8	6	ANYTHING BETTER 11-0	G Bradley **33-1**
9	1	TURN'EM BACK JACK 11-0	A Carroll **100-1**
10	hd	AGATHIST 11-0	R Dunwoody **20-1**
11	2	CAPULET 11-0	D Browne **100-1**
12		MASNOON 11-0	C Grant **50-1**
0		ALBERT HALL 11-0	J White **25-1**
0		CAROUSEL ROCKET 11-0	M Dwyer **50-1**
0		CASHEW KING 11-0	T Wall **8-1**
0		LLANARMON 11-0	B de Haan **100-1**
0		MASTER DON 11-0	T Morgan **66-1**
0		PRAIRIE OYSTER 11-0	C Cox **50-1**
0		PRINCE BOLD 11-0	J Duggan **100-1**
0		RAYON VERT 11-0	G McCourt **40-1**
0		SPRING PALM 11-0	K Ryan **100-1**
0		SPROWSTON BOY 11-0	R Rowe **6-1**
Fell		DAWN PRINCE 11-0	P Hobbs **100-1**
Fell		DHONI 11-0	M Hammond **20-1**
Fell		MIAMI IN SPRING 11-0	D Wilkinson **100-1**
Fell		NOS NA GAOITHE 11-0	L Wyer **20-1**
URdr		WINDBOUND LASS 10-9	N Coleman **100-1**
BrtDn		FULL FLOW 11-0	T Carmody **33-1**
BrtDn		IRISH DREAM 10-9	C Swan **66-1**

29 ran
TIME 4m 3.6s
1st OWNER: Sheikh Amin Dahlawi TRAINER: N Henderson

19 March – Cheltenham
GOOD TO SOFT   3m 2f

Tote Cheltenham Gold Cup Chase

1st £55,500

1		THE THINKER 9 12-0	R Lamb **13-2**
2	1½	CYBRANDIAN 9 12-0	C Grant **25-1**
3	2½	DOOR LATCH 9 12-0	R Rowe **9-1**
4	hd	WEST TIP 10 12-0	P Hobbs **50-1**
5	2½	WAYWARD LAD 12 12-0	G Bradley **11-1**
6	5	GOLDEN FRIEND 9 12-0	D Browne **16-1**
7	7	FORGIVE'N FORGET 10 12-0	M Dwyer **5-4F**
8	15	MR MOONRAKER 10 12-0	B Powell **50-1**
Fell		CHARTER PARTY 9 12-0	R Dunwoody **25-1**
URdr		BOLANDS CROSS 8 12-0	P Scudamore **8-1**
PUp		COMBS DITCH 11 12-0	C Brown **9-1**
PUp		EARLS BRIG 12 12-0	P Tuck **25-1**

12 ran
TIME 6m 56s
1st OWNER: T P McDonagh Ltd TRAINER: W A Stephenson

2 April – Liverpool
GOOD   3m 1f

Whitbread Gold Label Cup Chase

1st £10,762

1		WAYWARD LAD 12 11-5	G McCourt **7-1**
2	7	SIMON LEGREE 10 11-5	R Rowe **11-1**
3	5	CYBRANDIAN 9 11-5	C Grant **4-1**
4	10	BOLANDS CROSS 8 11-5	P Scudamore **3-1**
5	5	STEARSBY 8 11-5	G Bradley **5-2F**
PUp		GALWAY BLAZE 11 11-5	S Smith Eccles **8-1**

6 ran
TIME 6m 6s
1st OWNER: Mrs S Thewlis TRAINER: Mrs M Dickinson

3 April – Liverpool
GOOD   2m

Glenlivet Hurdle (4yo)

1st £19,223

1		**ALDINO** 11-0	S Sherwood	**11-1**
2	8	**HIGH KNOWL** 11-0	P Scudamore	**9-4F**
3	2½	**SPROWSTON BOY** 11-0	R Dunwoody	**10-1**
4	2	**PAST GLORIES** 11-0	P Farrell	**4-1**
5	1	**GRABEL** 10-9	A Mullins	**6-1**
6	20	**CAROUSEL ROCKET** 11-0	G Bradley	**33-1**
7		**DEVIL'S RUN** 11-0	B de Haan	**33-1**
8		**TAMATOUR** 11-0	G McCourt	**12-1**
9		**MASNOON** 11-0	C Grant	**33-1**
10		**CASHEW KING** 11-0	T Wall	**11-1**
11		**HURRICANE HENRY** 11-0	R Beggan	**33-1**
PUp		**FINAL TRY** 11-0	E Murphy	**33-1**
PUp		**FINGEST** 11-0	A Webb	**33-1**

13 ran
TIME 3m 51.7s
1st OWNER: A Boyd-Rochfort TRAINER: O Sherwood

4 April – Liverpool
GOOD   2m 5f 110y

Sandeman Aintree Hurdle

1st £14,960

1		**AONOCH** 8 11-9	Miss J Oliver	**5-2F**
2	4	**TABERNA LORD** 6 11-6	L Harvey	**6-1**
3	1½	**FLYING TROVE** 6 11-6	T Taaffe	**14-1**
4	6	**IBN MAJED** 5 11-9	J McLaughlin	**3-1**
5	hd	**MODEL PUPIL** 7 11-6	G Bradley	**7-1**
6	2	**RIVER CEIRIOG** 6 11-11	S Smith Eccles	**4-1**
7		**BARWAR** 9 11-6	R Lamb	**200-1**

7 ran
TIME 5m 14.5s
1st OWNER: H Oliver TRAINER: Mrs S Oliver

4 April – Liverpool
GOOD   4m 4f

Seagram Grand National Chase (Handicap)

1st £64,710

1		**MAORI VENTURE** 11 10-13	S Knight	**28-1**
2	5	**THE TSAREVICH** 11 10-5	J White	**20-1**
3	4	**LEAN AR AGHAIDH** 10 10-0	G Landau	**14-1**
4	4	**WEST TIP** 10 11-7	R Dunwoody	**5-1F**
5	1½	**YOU'RE WELCOME** 11 10-2	P Hobbs	**50-1**
6	1½	**TRACYS SPECIAL** 10 10-0	S J McNeill	**50-1**
7	4	**THE ELLIER** 11 10-0	F Berry	**18-1**
8	½	**ATTITUDE ADJUSTER** 7 10-6	N Madden	**25-1**
9	½	**NORTHERN BAY** 11 10-1	R Crank	**50-1**
10	shd	**MONANORE** 10 10-3	T Morgan	**20-1**
11	shd	**SMITH'S MAN** 9 10-0	M Perrett	**14-1**
12		**CORBIERE** 12 10-10	B de Haan	**12-1**
13		**BIG BROWN BEAR** 10 10-2	R Stronge	**200-1**
14		**CRANLOME** 9 10-0	M Richards	**500-1**
15		**COLONEL CHRISTY** 12 10-0	S Moore	**300-1**
16		**PLUNDERING** 10 10-11	P Scudamore	**16-1**
17		**PREBEN FUR** 10 10-0	A Stringer	**66-1**
18		**BRIGHT DREAM** 11 10-2	R Rowe	**50-1**
19		**WHY FORGET** 11 10-0	C Grant	**40-1**
20		**GALA PRINCE** 10 10-0	T Jarvis	**500-1**
21		**BRIT** 8 10-1	A Jones	**500-1**
22		**INSURE** 9 10-10	Mr C Brooks	**45-1**
Fell		**DARK IVY** 11 10-2	P Tuck	**11-2**
Fell		**GLENRUE** 10 10-3	B Powell	**33-1**
Fell		**VALENCIO** 10 12-0	R Rowell	**500-1**
Fell		**LUCKY REW** 12 10-0	C Mann	**500-1**
Fell		**SMARTSIDE** 12 10-0	P Gill	**100-1**
URdr		**BROWN TRIX** 9 10-8	Mr D Pitcher	**100-1**
URdr		**CLASSIFIED** 11 10-3	S Smith Eccles	**9-1**
URdr		**EAMONS OWEN** 10 10-0	Miss J Oliver	**200-1**
URdr		**LITTLE POLVEIR** 10 10-2	C Brown	**33-1**
URdr		**MARCOLO** 10 10-0	P Leech	**66-1**
URdr		**SPARTAN ORIENT** 11 10-0	L Harvey	**500-1**
BtDn		**BEWLEY'S HILL** 10 12-0	Mr W Dixon Stroud	**100-1**
Ref		**BROWN VEIL** 12 10-1	Mr M Armytage	**200-1**
Ref		**HI HARRY** 9 10-0	M Flynn	**100-1**
PUp		**DALTMORE** 9 10-0	A Mullins	**100-1**
PUp		**DRUMLARGAN** 13 11-2	Mr G Wragg	**66-1**
PUp		**LE BAMBINO** 10 10-2	C Warren	**500-1**
PUp		**RUN TO ME** 12 10-2	Mr N Mitchell	**150-1**

40 ran
TIME 9m 19.3s
1st OWNER: H J Joel TRAINER: A Turnell

11 April – Ayr
HEAVY   4m 120y

William Hill Scottish National (Handicap Chase)

1st £23,618

1		LITTLE POLVEIR 10 10-0	P Scudamore **12-1**
2	10	JIMBROOK 10 10-1	L Wyer **6-1**
3	8	BURANNPOUR 7 10-1	S Sherwood **7-1**
4	12	HARDY LAD 10 10-3	M Hammond **4-1**
Fell		KNOCK HILL 11 10-0	G Mernagh **12-1**
PUp		DROPS O'BRANDY 12 10-2	P Warner **33-1**
PUp		HOMESON 10 10-2	R Rowe **20-1**
PUp		SOLARES 7 10-0	N Doughty **10-1**
PUp		STEARSBY 8 11-7	G Bradley **3-1F**
PUp		SUCCEEDED 10 10-0	C Grant **9-1**
PUp		WHY FORGET 11 9-7	T White **25-1**

11 ran
TIME 9m 9.6s
1st OWNER: M Shone TRAINER: J Edwards

25 April – Sandown Park
FIRM   4m 5f 18y

Whitbread Gold Cup (Handicap Chase)

1st £32,250

1		LEAN AR AGHAIDH 10 9-10	G Landau **6-1**
2	5	CONTRADEAL 10 10-0	K Mooney **5-1**
3	7	BROADHEATH 10 10-6	P Nicholls **14-1**
4	6	I HAVENTALIGHT 8 10-2	P Scudamore **14-1**
5	2	DOOR LATCH 9 11-1	R Rowe **3-1F**
6	15	PLUNDERING 10 10-3	S Sherwood **12-1**
7		TORSIDE 8 10-0	M Perrett **20-1**
PUp		DESERT ORCHID 8 12-0	C Brown **7-2**
PUp		THE LANGHOLM DYER 8 10-0	P Tuck **17-2**

9 ran
TIME 7m 11.5s
1st OWNER: Mrs W Tulloch TRAINER: S Mellor

○ **JOHN EDWARDS: Trainer of Little Polveir.**
Picture: GEORGE SELWYN

○ **STAN MELLOR: Trainer of Lean Ar Aghaidh.**
Picture: GEORGE HERRINGSHAW

News Diary

by PAUL HAYWARD

January

5: Edinburgh's first NH meeting.

6: De Rigueur disqualified from Ascot's Balmoral Handicap (Sept. '86) in "Mars Bar" case; costs connections over £10,000.

9: Schweppes announce Gold Trophy sponsorship to end.

11: Trainer Syd Woodman (67) and owner Sir David Robinson (82) die.

14: John Smith to succeed John Sanderson as Clerk of the Course at York.

16: William Hill abandon Dewhurst Stakes sponsorship. John Dunlop and Michael Wyatt appointed to Pattern Race Committee.

17: Badsworth Boy's lad, Graham Burrows, killed in car crash.

20: Jockey Club launches campaign for Sunday Racing.

30: Shelbourne gives Jonjo O'Neill first win as a trainer.

February

5: Schweppes announce sponsorship of new handicap, the Golden Mile, at Goodwood.

9: Walter Swinburn appeals against two-year driving ban. Reduced to six months ten days later.

10: United Racecourses announce that Epsom Derby will carry £450,000 purse. Frank Jordan loses four of his 12 winners after positive samples.

12: Kevin Darley suspended until 31 Jan. 1988 by Stewards in Bombay; sentence reduced to three months on appeal.

17: Dancing Brave sustains minor injuries when hit by car in Newmarket.

○ **DISTINGUISHED VISITOR: Aldaniti, ridden by the Princess Royal, turns up at Cheltenham on his charity walk from London to Liverpool.** Picture: TONY EDENDEN

21: Michael Dickinson flies out to establish new career in Maryland with "no plans to train again in England".

23: F1-11 bomber crashes near stables on the Bury Road, Newmarket.

28: Princess Anne last of four on NH debut at Kempton.

March

1: Aldaniti and Jonjo O'Neill begin London to Liverpool walk, raising £820,000 for Bob Champion Cancer Trust. Former jockey Bill Rickaby (69) dies.

5: Summons taken out against Lester Piggott by Customs and Excise alleging tax and VAT evasion.

17: See You Then joins Hatton's Grace, Sir Ken and Persian War as triple Champion Hurdle winner. Chancellor Nigel Lawson abolishes on-course betting duty.

19: Trainer Arthur Stephenson watches on T.V. from Hexham as The Thinker wins Gold Cup.

23: Reference Point undergoes sinus operation.

April

1: Josh Gifford's travelling head lad, Mike Palmer, mugged and stabbed outside Aintree.

3: Accompanist is Barry Hills' first winner from Manton.

4: Maori Venture wins Grand National for nonagenarian owner Jim Joel; Dark Ivy is killed at Becher's Brook.

7: Three Chimneys Farms to sponsor Dewhurst.

14: Jockey Club instigates inquiry into Niall Madden's riding of Attitude Adjuster in Grand National.

24: Barney Curley disqualified for two years for making "threatening" phone calls to Monica Dickinson and Graham Bradley.

25: Lean Ar Aghaidh and Guy Landau win the Whitbread.

30: Miesque sprints away from Milligram and Interval to win 1,000 Guineas. Barney Curley wins temporary injunction against Jockey Club.

May

2: Don't Forget Me wins 2,000 Guineas.

5: Satellite racing goes live in Bristol and Colchester.

7: Lester Piggott committed for trial at the Old Bailey.

9: Sir Noel Murless (77) dies.

21: Wayward Lad goes through the ring at Doncaster to join Michael Dickinson in America.

25: Martin Pipe passes the 100-winner mark for NH season; Peter Scudamore beats his previous best of 120.

30: Les Kennard retires from training with double at Stratford.

○ **BATTLING BARNEY: Newmarket trainer Barney Curley made news throughout the year.**   Picture: TONY EDENDEN

June

3: Reference Point wins Derby in fastest time since Mahmoud.

4: Triptych wins Coronation Cup.

6: Unite wins Oaks for Sheikh Mohammed, but his Scimitarra breaks down.

10: Declan Murphy banned until 1 Oct. for his riding of Barney Curley-trained Solvent at Sedgefield.

14: Indian Skimmer beats Miesque in Prix de Diane Hermes.

16: Royal Ascot: Largest ever crowd (205,574) for the week; Henry Cecil trains post-war record seven winners.

22: Graham Bradley banned until 1 Nov. for failing to gain best placing on Deadly Going at Market Rasen in April.

23: Habitat dies at Grangewilliam Stud.

24: Gold Cup winner Paean forced to retire through injury.

25: Lester Piggott's trial switched to Ipswich Crown Court.

27: Bombscare delays start of Irish Derby by 49 minutes; Sir Harry Lewis gives Ulsterman John Reid first Irish Classic victory.

31: Michael Dickinson's first runner in America wins by 13 lengths.·

○ **WELL DONE, MA'AM: David Nicholson is first to congratulate the Princess Royal after her win on Ten No Trumps at Ascot in July.**

Picture: TONY EDENDEN

July

3: Credit bookmakers Heronglade collapse, owing £½m.

4: Mtoto beats Reference Point in the Coral Eclipse.

7: Ahonoora sold to Coolmore Stud.

9: Ajdal reverts to sprinting and wins July Cup.

11: Unite completes English-Irish Oaks double.

13: Reference Point to join Dancing Brave at Dalham Hall Stud.

15: Natroun to stand at National Stud. Jockey Club issues new set of guidelines on racecourse hooliganism.

19: Philip Robinson accepts 10-month contract to ride in Hong Kong.

22: Pat Eddery and Steve Cauthen both pass 100 winners.

25: Reference Point wins King George VI and Queen Elizabeth Diamond Stakes.

August

2: Yves Saint-Martin to retire at the end of the season. Consortium headed by Ian and Toby Balding buys Windsor racecourse.

3: Jockey Club quashes ban on Barney Curley.

○ **HIGHEST HONOUR: Ridley Lamb returns on The Thinker after winning the Cheltenham Gold Cup; eight months later he hung up his saddle.**
Picture: KICKSPORTS

5: Steve Cauthen records 1,000th winner in Britain. RCA to restrict use of cellular telephones on British racecourses after 1 Sept.

10: Terry Ramsden's appearance before Tattersalls Committee ends in scuffles with pressmen.

20: Trusthouse Forte abandon sponsorship of the "Arc". Cigahotels takes over.

September

2: Alan Jarvis to relinquish trainer's licence.

3: Princess Royal rides first NH winner, on Cnoc Na Cuille at Worcester.

4: Stock Hill Lass collects £50,000 bonus for winning third race in season at Kempton. Ladbrokes buy Hilton International hotel chain.

5: Dominique Boeuf to replace Yves Saint-Martin as first jockey to Aga Khan. Fred Winter fractures skull in fall at home.

12: Reference Point wins St Leger. Henry Cecil provisionally breaks John Day's record of 146 winners in season.

20: Daniel Wildenstein and Patrick Biancome to part company.

21: Brent Thomson to return to Australia.

22: Quexioss disqualified (positive sample); Henry Cecil fined £500, and Madam Cyn (Yarmouth seller, 15 Sept.) becomes 147th winner.

24: Nelson Bunker Hunt abandons racing and bloodstock interests.

26: Festival of British Racing Day at Ascot; Milligram upsets Miesque in featured race, the Queen Elizabeth II Stakes.

29: Geoff Huffer and Gary Carter part company.

30: American jockey Gary Stevens makes English debut. Ravinella wins the Cheveley Park.

October

3: Balthus (50-1) wins Cambridge-shire.

4: Trempolino wins Arc in record time to give Pat Eddery third successive victory.

5: Richard Linley retires.

13: Trempolino to stand at Gainesway Farm.

15: New threshold levels for prohibited substances come into force.

16: Near-hurricane sweeps across southern England; Dewhurst abandoned and not re-scheduled.

17: Triptych wins Champion Stakes; Private Audition (50-1) completes long-shot Autumn double.

21: Sam Morshead retires.

23: Lester Piggott sentenced to three years' imprisonment.

27: Alan Clore to liquidate his bloodstock interests; Triptych goes on the market.

28: Lester Piggott moved to High Point jail (low-security).

31: Iran Scam gives Jeremy Hindley winner on last day as trainer.

November

2: Englishman John Hammond to train 45 horses for Daniel Wildenstein; rest to join Andre Fabre.

5: Of 23 Jockey Club peers eligible to vote only four attend crucial debate on Lord Wyatt's Sunday Sports Bill; vote on betting shops lost by three votes.

6: Walter Swinburn arrested for drunkeness in London's West End but not charged.

7: Flat Season ends: Cauthen beats Eddery by 197 to 195; Henry Cecil has 180 domestic winners.

9: Epsom Derby entry fee to rise 31% to £3,500.

10: Dancing Brave suffering from Marie's Disease. Walter Swinburn loses ride on Sonic Lady in Breeders Cup Mile to Laffit Pincay.

14: Beau Ranger (Mark Perrett) wins Mackeson.

20: Robert Earnshaw's first training success (Happy Voyage).

21: Breeders' Cup Day: Miesque wins Mile in record time; Trempolino pipped by Theatrical in Turf in joint record time.

22: Phoenix Park grandstand destroyed by fire.

27: Ridley Lamb retires.

28: Playschool (Paul Nicholls) wins Hennessy.

29: Le Glorieux wins Japan Cup.

30: SIS Chief Executive John Beard resigns. Master Willie to return from USA.

December

2: All-weather track trials over jumps at Newmarket.

○ **IN THE MONEY:** Gerald Cottrell trained Stock Hill Lass to pick up a £50,000 bonus by winning three races at Kempton Park.　　　Picture: DAVID HASTINGS

3: Epsom to receive £8m facelift in 1989.

5: Chase at Chepstow declared void as runners collide with running rail after being directed on to wrong course.

7: All-weather racing put back at least 12 months. Vernons Sprint Cup to carry Group One status; King's Stand Stakes demoted to Group Two.

9: City Entertainer backed to win £250,000 for 1989 Cheltenham Gold Cup.

11: Robert Sangster plans to sell Vernons Pools.

16: Lord Wyatt's Sunday Sports Bill passes Report Stage in House of Lords.

22: Barney Curley collects £250,000 in bets by saddling his tenth jump winner before 1 January. Chepstow Clerk of the Course John Hughes fined £500 over 'wrong-course' incident.

26: Nupsala (first French-trained NH winner in Britain since 1963) lands King George VI Rank Chase.

28: Playschool becomes first horse to complete Hennessy-Welsh National double in same year.

1987 Flat Statistics

Owners

	Win stakes £	Horses	Races
Sheikh Mohammed	1,232,287	76	126
Louis Freedman	741,044	4	13
Robert Sangster	468,289	47	73
Khalid Abdullah	348,573	33	51
Alan Clore	334,632	8	18
Hamdan Al-Maktoum	302,620	58	73
Ahmed Al-Maktoum	256,741	6	10
Helena Springfield Ltd	229,333	2	4
Fahd Salman	225,523	24	35
Aga Khan	191,985	24	37
Stavros Niarchos	184,332	11	19
Charles St George	179,800	17	34

Apprentices

	1	2	3	Unpl	Total	%	£ level stake
G Bardwell	27	28	34	214	303	8.9	−£17.90
A Culhane	24	42	36	315	417	5.8	−£160.50
J Carroll	23	28	26	185	262	8.8	−£24.87
J Quinn	14	15	22	287	338	4.1	−£195.25
R Lappin	13	5	4	66	88	14.8	+£4.50
Dale Gibson	13	11	10	123	157	8.3	−£66.00
P Barnard	12	16	16	175	219	5.5	−£130.87
A Shoults	11	22	14	177	224	4.9	−£155.77
K Bradshaw	10	7	9	69	95	10.5	−£0.17
R Morse	10	6	12	92	120	8.3	−£11.50
Dana Mellor	9	5	13	95	122	7.4	−£48.42
S Wood	9	5	10	99	123	7.3	−£40.00

Trainers

	Win stakes £	Wins	Runners	%	£ level stake
H Cecil	1,896,689	180	446	40	+£79.29
M Stoute	1,069,761	105	409	26	−£7.02
L Cumani	530,250	83	295	28	+£12.95
B Hills	509,881	96	548	18	−£19.61
J Dunlop	401,205	61	500	12	−£167.26
A Stewart	397,663	37	181	20	+£59.47
G Harwood	343,545	67	350	19	−£98.40
P Biancone	293,748	4	11	36	+£4.62
P Cole	269,873	55	452	12	−£175.63
J Tree	227,402	32	174	18	−£42.81
W Hern	208,765	37	247	15	−£58.44
M H Easterby	205,997	68	432	16	−£80.83

Sires

(Stakes won in Britain and Ireland)

	Winners	Races	Win stakes £	Places	Place stakes £	Total £
Mill Reef (1968, Never Bend)	12	19	963,136	44	280,861	1,243,997
Riverman (1969, Never Bend)	11	21	674,205	26	72,326	746,531
Nureyev (1977, Northern Dancer)	18	25	378,024	52	192,248	570,272
Alleged (1974, Hoist the Flag)	11	17	397,476	44	142,796	540,272
Ahonoora (1975, Lorenzaccio)	17	40	374,820	73	77,033	451,853
Be My Guest (1974, Northern Dancer)	16	29	233,208	51	212,725	445,933
Kris (1976, Sharpen Up)	17	27	337,102	54	46,652	383,754
Busted (1963, Crepello)	13	25	313,805	35	60,572	374,377
Ela-Mana-Mou (1976, Pitcairn)	11	19	259,627	42	99,370	358,997
Blushing Groom (1974, Red God)	10	17	283,048	21	44,081	327,129
Northern Dancer (1961, Nearctic)	10	15	235,469	22	87,591	323,060
Known Fact (1977, In Reality)	26	41	241,080	61	53,426	294,506
Mummy's Pet (1968, Sing Sing)	24	44	229,611	66	52,421	282,032
Danzig (1977, Northern Dancer)	12	18	144,180	32	136,495	280,675
Dominion (1972, Derring-Do)	24	46	175,587	75	98,165	273,752
Kings Lake (1978, Nijinsky)	21	33	148,485	65	121,178	269,663
Try My Best (1975, Northern Dancer)	15	30	203,934	48	61,465	265,399
Ile De Bourbon (1975, Nijinsky)	19	29	90,469	67	141,023	231,492

Jockeys

	1	2	3	Unpl	Total	%	£ level stake
S Cauthen	197	119	103	423	842	23.4	−£114.12
Pat Eddery	195	153	126	522	996	19.6	−£140.54
R Cochrane	111	88	76	462	737	15.1	−£138.96
W Carson	100	130	85	467	782	12.8	−£225.31
W Swinburn	92	77	67	342	578	15.9	−£171.17
M Birch	92	72	58	366	588	15.6	−£30.12
J Reid	81	77	64	438	660	12.3	−£114.32
M Hills	75	55	57	304	491	15.3	+£35.54
M Roberts	74	66	70	344	554	13.4	−£9.79
T Ives	70	76	70	407	623	11.2	−£51.11
W Ryan	69	52	33	218	372	18.5	−£58.59
G Duffield	64	67	60	461	652	9.8	−£296.81

Amateur Riders

	1	2	3	Unpl	Total	%	£ level stake
T Easterby	5	2	0	4	11	45.5	+£12.75
T Thomson Jones	5	2	3	7	17	29.4	−£3.87
Jenny Goulding	3	1	4	9	17	17.6	+£1.33

National Hunt Statistics 1986–87

Owners

	Win stakes £	Horses	Races
H J Joel	115,556	9	13
T McDonagh Ltd	83,087	2	7
R Burridge	72,577	1	6
Sheikh Ali Abu Khamsin	62,847	4	8
G Hubbard	56,008	6	17
T Ramsden	52,993	13	15
Lady Harris	51,770	2	10
Stype Wood Stud Ltd	46,821	1	2
M Shone	45,588	3	5
H Oliver	45,282	1	6
Mrs P Shaw	43,726	2	6
Mrs C Heath	42,236	4	6

Trainers

	Win stakes £	Wins	Runners	%	£ level stake
N Henderson	222,638	67	297	23	+£89.84
W A Stephenson	202,776	65	480	14	−£154.33
G Balding	195,828	57	249	23	+£78.74
J Gifford	183,421	60	343	17	−£13.71
J Edwards	171,364	54	244	22	+£77.85
M Pipe	166,926	106	460	23	−£65.85
D Elsworth	162.242	34	191	18	+£32.05
G Richards	145,795	59	325	18	−£34.28
J FitzGerald	132,354	73	248	29	−£24.60
Mrs J Pitman	129,810	39	265	15	+£25.65
F Winter	128,632	51	281	18	−£60.79
D Nicholson	126,863	42	299	14	−£54.75

Jockeys

	1	2	3	Unpl	Total	%	£ level stake
P Scudamore	123	87	66	302	578	21.3	−£131.41
M Dwyer	81	54	35	167	337	24.0	−£36.05
R Dunwoody	70	70	74	344	558	12.5	−£177.86
S Sherwood	64	45	37	140	286	22.4	+£49.67
C Grant	63	75	72	259	469	13.4	−£191.38
P Tuck	59	50	42	187	338	17.5	−£85.32
S Smith Eccles	56	33	35	135	259	21.6	+£31.84
G Bradley	53	32	21	126	232	22.8	−£31.52
R Rowe	50	46	34	182	312	16.0	−£36.88
R Lamb	48	35	23	173	279	17.2	−£50.00
B Powell	48	52	46	295	441	10.9	−£136.95
S Morshead	41	39	30	201	311	13.2	+£34.01

Amateur Riders

	1	2	3	Unpl	Total	%	£ level stake
T Thomson Jones	19	13	12	71	115	16.5	−£47.52
Miss G Armytage	18	16	23	95	152	11.8	+£43.50
Miss T Davis	16	9	3	32	60	26.7	+£67.85
J Osborne	13	12	8	82	115	11.3	−£53.86
Miss A Beaumont	11	1	3	52	67	16.4	+£57.92
T Grantham	10	5	11	70	96	10.4	+£1.25
M Armytage	9	9	14	65	97	9.3	−£43.58
M Richards	9	6	4	65	84	10.7	−£15.83

Sires

	Winners	Races	Win stakes £
Deep Run (1966, by Pampered King)	41	76	216,457
Cantab (1957, by Cantaber)	7	12	126,707
Grey Mirage (1969, by Double-U-Jay)	4	12	89,572
St Columbus (1967, by Saint Crespin III)	5	9	82,173
Proverb (1970, by Reliance II)	12	22	81,601
Idiot's Delight (1970, by Silly Season)	12	24	80,194
Menelek (1957, by Tulyar)	18	31	79,012
The Parson (1968, by Aureole)	13	21	74,321
Royal Palace (1964, by Ballymoss)	5	8	60,785
Master Owen (1956, by Owen Tudor)	9	18	57,089
Little Buskins (1957, by Solar Slipper)	11	22	55,214
Precipice Wood (1966, by Lauso)	8	16	51,495

○ **IT'S OVER: Maori Venture (Steve Knight) gives Jim Joel his first Grand National success.** Picture: KICKSPORTS

○ **ONE WAY DOWN: Irish amateur John Queally finds thirteen his unlucky number as Nether Wallop crashes out of a race at Ascot in November. Miraculously, horse and rider walked away unhurt.** Pictures: MARK CRANHAM

Quiz Answers

1. He was disqualified after a positive post-race test brought about by eating a Mars bar.
2. He took the wrong course, going inside a marker doll, on Lastofthebrownies.
3. The Tote.
4. Peter Scot, in 1979.
5. Ghazal, trained as a two-year-old by Jack Hardy.
6. Maryland.
7. Satellite Information Services.
8. Steve Woodman.
9. Tartan Tailor, in the Waterford Crystal Supreme Novices Hurdle.
10. Luke Harvey.
11. At Hexham, saddling runners.
12. One; Galmoy, trained by John Mulhern, in the Waterford Crystal Stayers Hurdle.
13. First Bout, third in the Arkle Challenge Trophy.
14. See You Then, Pearlyman, Observe and Half Free.
15. Jack Berry, with Great Chaddington in the Philip Cornes Brocklesby Stakes at Doncaster.
16. Gold Prospect.
17. West Tip, at 5-1.
18. Jacqui Oliver, who rode Eamons Owen and was unseated at the 15th fence.
19. Raymond Guest, with Derby winners Larkspur (1962) and Sir Ivor (1968) and Grand National winner L'Escargot (1975).
20. Tracys Special, who finished sixth.
21. Cranlome, fifth in the Whitbread and 14th in the National.
22. Willie Haggas.
23. Kelvin Hitchmough.
24. The Westbury Stakes.
25. 4lb.
26. John Hills.
27. A length and a half.
28. Fair Salinia (1978), Our Home (1980), Royal Heroine (1983, disqualified), and Maysoon (1986).
29. Midyan.
30. High Top (1972) and Known Fact (1980).
31. Christian Wall.
32. Legal Bid and Sadjiyd.
33. Khalid Abdullah, with Bourbon Girl.
34. Then Again (Queen Anne Stakes) and Half A Year (St James's Palace Stakes).
35. Richard Casey, at Dullingham.
36. Colmore Row, in the Norfolk Stakes.
37. Valuable Witness, fourth at 100-30.
38. Richard Quinn, on Bel Byou.
39. Ray Cochrane, Willie Ryan and Walter Swinburn, with two apiece.
40. None; he had eight place-money earners: All Haste, Sadeem, Sher Shah, Soviet Star, Kribensis, Port Helene, Sonic Lady and Nom de Plume.
41. Ron Quinton, on holiday from Australia.
42. David Smaga (1984), David O'Brien (1985) and Patrick Biancone.
43. Prix Jean Prat and Grand Prix de Paris.
44. The Ulster Harp Derby at Down Royal in Northern Ireland.
45. Wolverhampton.
46. Ten No Trumps, in the Dresden Diamond Stakes on 25 July.
47. Andre Fabre (Soviet Star), Henry Cecil (Star Cutter) and Vincent O'Brien (Fair Judgment).
48. Rod Fabricius.
49. John Dunlop, after winning the Goodwood Cup with Sergeyevich.
50. Racing manager to Maktoum Al-Maktoum.
51. Yarmouth, on Red Guitars for Henry Cecil.
52. Ascot Knight.
53. Precocious, in 1983.
54. Paul Eddery, who won on Ela Romara, and Pat Eddery, second on Madam de Seul.
55. Ayr.
56. £50,000, given by the track for the first horse to win three races there in 1987.
57. Their 25th.
58. In 1984, at the age of six.
59. Warning, the winner, and runner-up Always Fair, at evens.
60. Tony Cruz.
61. Nijinsky, in 1970.
62. Peter Walwyn and Geoff Murphy (Australia).
63. Three Chimneys Farm, the US stud.
64. Jeremy Glover (Balthus, Cambridgeshire); Mark Tompkins (Private Audition, Cesarewitch).
65. Eddie Leonard, representing Ireland.
66. One; with Protection Racket in the Irish St Leger.
67. Jeremy Tree (Rainbow Quest, 1985), Guy Harwood (Dancing Brave, 1986), Andre Fabre (Trempolino, 1987).
68. Steve Cauthen, with 191 winners to Pat Eddery's 188.
69. Ray Cochrane, on Media Starguest in the Cenotaph Stakes at Doncaster.
70. Four: Steve Cauthen (197), Pat Eddery (195), Ray Cochrane (111) and Willie Carson (100).
71. Barry Hills, behind Henry Cecil, Michael Stoute and Luca Cumani.
72. Perion and Not So Silly, with seven apiece.
73. Maries Disease.
74. John Hammond.
75. Miesque (winner), Sonic Lady (third), Deputy Governor (fourth), and Short Sleeves (sixth).

Ascot Flat

Course Characteristics
Right-handed triangle, galloping and stiff, with few undulations. Just over 1m 6f round, with 2½f run-in. Straight mile and round mile. All races up to 7f on straight course.

Draw: When stalls on stands side on straight course, low numbers slightly favoured; on round course, high numbers slightly favoured.

How to get there
Road: W of town on A329 Bracknell road. M4(Jctn6); M3(Jctn3). **Rail:** 500 yds, Ascot Stn (from London Waterloo). **Air:** 15m, London (Heathrow); 12m, White Waltham Airfield.

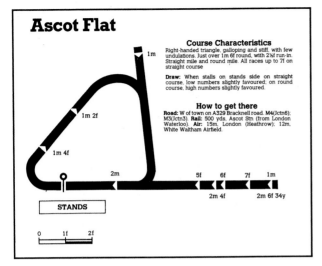

Ayr Jumps

How to get there
Road: E of city on A758 Mauchline road. **Rail:** ½m, Ayr Stn (from Glasgow). **Air:** 3m, Prestwick Airport; 40m, Glasgow Airport.

Course Characteristics
Left-handed, mainly flat. Circuit 1m 4f.

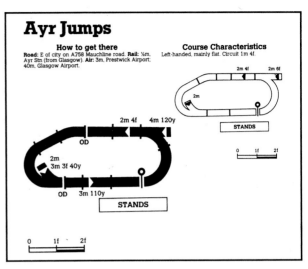

Ascot Jumps

Course Characteristics
Right-handed, galloping, with stiff fences. Circuit 1m 5f.

How to get there
Road: W of town on A329 Bracknell road. M4(Jctn6); M3(Jctn3). **Rail:** 500 yds, Ascot Stn (from London Waterloo). **Air:** 15m, London (Heathrow); 12m, White Waltham Airfield.

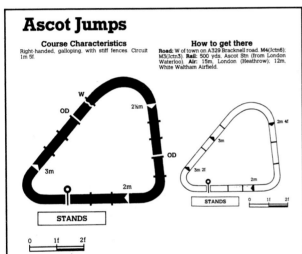

Bangor

How to get there
Road: 5m SE of Wrexham off B5069 Bangor-Oswestry road. **Rail:** 5m, Wrexham Stn. Bus to Bangor.

Course Characteristics
Left-handed, sharp and flat with a long run-in. Circuit 1m 4f.

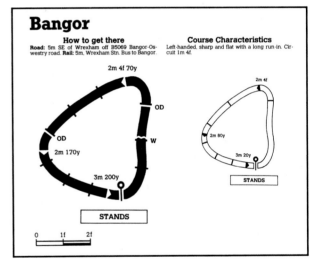

Ayr Flat

Course Characteristics
Left-handed oval, galloping with minor undulations. About 1m 4f round.

Draw: When stalls on stands side on straight course, high numbers favoured; on soft going, low numbers slightly favoured.

How to get there
Road: E of city on A758 Mauchline road. **Rail:** ½m, Ayr Stn (from Glasgow). **Air:** 3m, Prestwick Airport; 40m, Glasgow Airport.

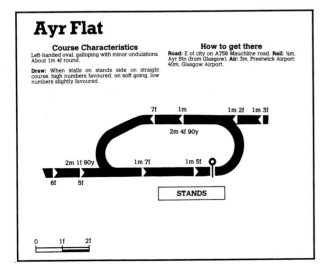

Bath

How to get there
Road: 2m NW of city at Lansdown (access A431 Bristol road). M4(Jctn18). **Rail:** 2m, Bath Stn (access London Paddington, or Bristol Temple Meads from N).

Course Characteristics
Left-handed oval, galloping, just over 1m 4f round. 4f run-in, bending to left, against collar throughout. Ground seldom testing.

Draw: Up to 1m, low numbers slightly favoured.

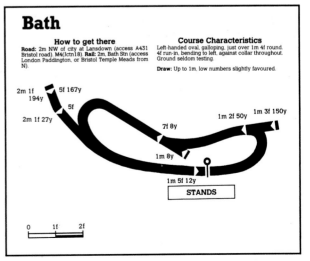

Beverley

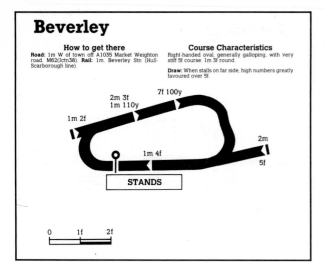

How to get there
Road: 1m W of town off A1035 Market Weighton road. M62(Jctn38). **Rail:** 1m, Beverley Stn (Hull-Scarborough line).

Course Characteristics
Right-handed oval, generally galloping, with very stiff 5f course. 1m 3f round.

Draw: When stalls on far side, high numbers greatly favoured over 5f.

Carlisle Jumps

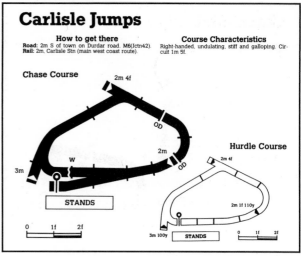

How to get there
Road: 2m S of town on Durdar road. M6(Jctn42). **Rail:** 2m, Carlisle Stn (main west coast route).

Course Characteristics
Right-handed, undulating, stiff and galloping. Circuit 1m 5f.

Brighton

Course Characteristics
Left-handed, U-shaped, markedly undulating and sharp. Suits handy types. 1m 4f in length.

Draw: Low numbers generally favoured.

How to get there
Road: E of town off A27 Lewes road. **Rail:** 1m, Brighton Stn (from London Victoria).

Cartmel

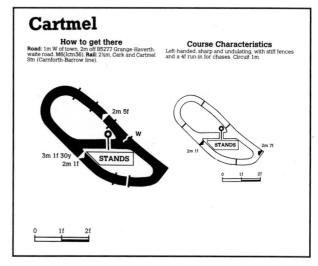

How to get there
Road: 1m W of town, 2m off B5277 Grange-Haverthwaite road. M6(Jctn36). **Rail:** 2¼m, Cark and Cartmel Stn (Carnforth-Barrow line).

Course Characteristics
Left-handed, sharp and undulating, with stiff fences and a 4f run-in for chases. Circuit 1m.

Carlisle Flat

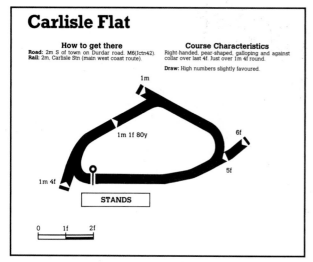

How to get there
Road: 2m S of town on Durdar road. M6(Jctn42). **Rail:** 2m, Carlisle Stn (main west coast route).

Course Characteristics
Right-handed, pear-shaped, galloping and against collar over last 4f. Just over 1m 4f round.

Draw: High numbers slightly favoured.

Catterick Bridge Flat

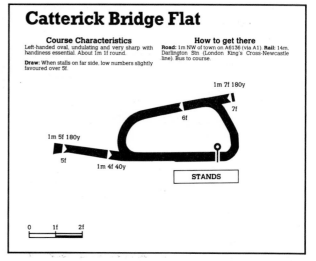

Course Characteristics
Left-handed oval, undulating and very sharp with handiness essential. About 1m 1f round.

Draw: When stalls on far side, low numbers slightly favoured over 5f.

How to get there
Road: 1m NW of town on A6136 (via A1). **Rail:** 14m, Darlington Stn (London King's Cross-Newcastle line). Bus to course.

Catterick Bridge Jumps

How to get there
Road: 1m NW of town on A6136 (via A1). **Rail:** 14m, Darlington Stn (London King's Cross-Newcastle line). Bus to course.

Course Characteristics
Left-handed, sharp and undulating, suiting handy types. Circuit 1m 3f.

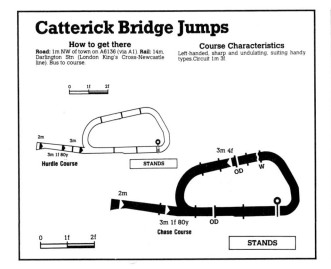

Chepstow Flat

How to get there
Road: 1m NW of town on A466 Monmouth road. M4(Jctn22). **Rail:** 1m, Chepstow Stn (from Newport).

Course Characteristics
Left-handed oval, undulating, 1m 7f round with 4½f run-in. Races up to 1m on straight course. Tends to have extremes of going.

Draw: Up to 1m on good or fast going, high numbers slightly favoured; on soft going, low numbers slightly favoured.

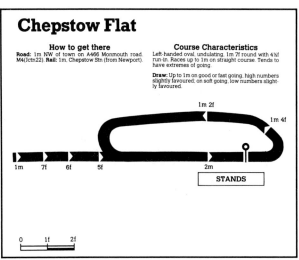

Cheltenham Old

How to get there
Road: 1½m N of town off A435 Evesham road. M5(Jctn10 or 11). **Rail:** 2m, Cheltenham Spa Stn (from London Paddington, Bristol or Birmingham). **Air:** 6m, Staverton Airport.

Course Characteristics
Left-handed, galloping, with stiff fences. Old Course circuit 1m 4f. New Course slightly longer.

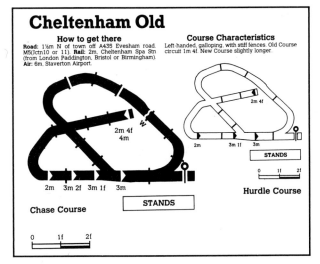

Chepstow Jumps

Course Characteristics
Left-handed, undulating oval course of almost 2m. Tends to have extremes of going.

How to get there
Road: 1m NW of town on A466 Monmouth road. M4(Jctn22). **Rail:** 1m, Chepstow Stn (from Newport).

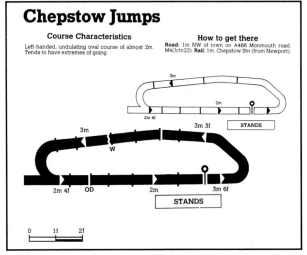

Cheltenham New

How to get there
Road: 1½m N of town off A435 Evesham road. M5(Jctn10 or 11). **Rail:** 2m, Cheltenham Spa Stn (from London Paddington, Bristol or Birmingham). **Air:** 6m, Staverton Airport.

Course Characteristics
Left-handed, galloping, with stiff fences. Old Course circuit 1m 4f. New Course slightly longer.

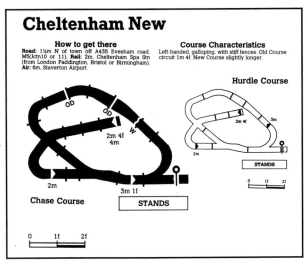

Chester

Course Characteristics
Left-handed, flat, just over 1m round with short run-in. Very sharp, not favouring long-striding horses.

Draw: Up to 7f 122yds, low numbers slightly favoured.

How to get there
Road: In SW of city on A548 Queensferry road. Junction of M56 with M53. **Rail:** 1m, Chester General (from London Euston). **Bus:** ¾m, Crosville Stn. **Air:** 2m, Hawarden Airport.

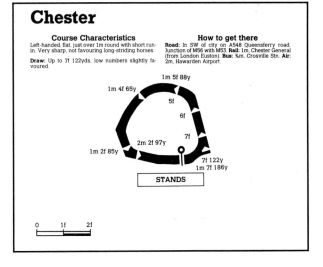

Devon & Exeter, Summer

How to get there
Road: 5m SW of Exeter on A38 Plymouth road. **Rail:** 5m, three stations in Exeter (St David's on main London Paddington-Cornwall route). Bus to course.

Course Characteristics
Right-handed and undulating.Stiff test of stamina. Circuit 2m.

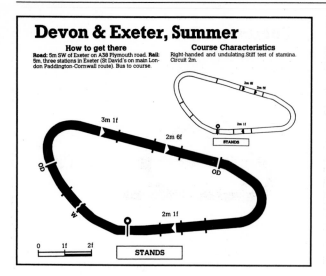

Doncaster Jumps

Course Characteristics
Left-handed, galloping, generally flat. Heavy ground rare. Circuit 2m.

How to get there
Road: E of town off A638 Bawtry road. M18(Jctn3 cr 4). **Rail:** 1½m, Doncaster Stn (London King's Cross-NE line). **Air:** Airport nearby.

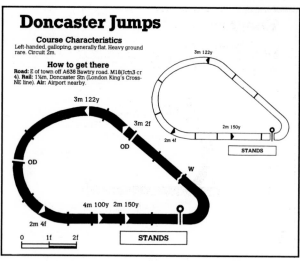

Devon & Exeter, Winter

How to get there
Road: 5m SW of Exeter on A38 Plymouth road. **Rail:** 5m, three stations in Exeter (St David's on main London Paddington-Cornwall route). Bus to course.

Course Characteristics
Right-handed and undulating.Stiff test of stamina. Circuit 2m.

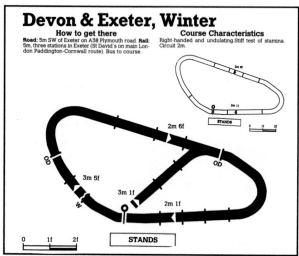

Edinburgh Flat

How to get there
Road: 5m E of city on A1 in Musselburgh. **Rail:** 5m, Edinburgh Stn. Bus to course.

Course Characteristics
Right-handed oval of 1m 2f with tight turns. 4f run-in. Going rarely testing.

Draw: When stalls on stands side on straight course, low numbers greatly favoured; on round course, high numbers favoured.

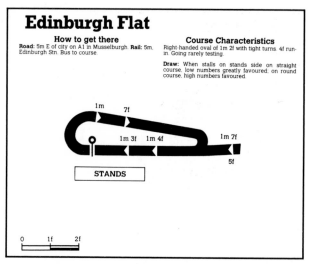

Doncaster Flat

How to get there
Road: E of town off A638 Bawtry road. M18(Jctn3 or 4). **Rail:** 1½m, Doncaster Stn (London King's Cross-NE line). **Air:** Airport nearby.

Course Characteristics
Left-handed, pear-shaped, galloping. Almost 2m round with 4½f run-in. Round and straight miles. Mainly flat, providing fair test.

Draw: When stalls on stands side on straight course and going is soft, high numbers slightly favoured; on round course, low numbers slightly favoured

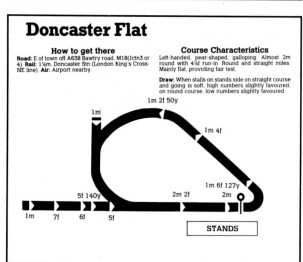

Edinburgh Jumps

How to get there
Road: 5m E of city on A1 in Musselburgh. **Rail:** 5m, Edinburgh Stn. Bus to course.

Course Characteristics
Level, right-handed oval of 1m 3f with tight turns.

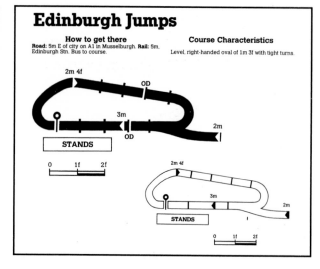

Epsom

How to get there

Road: 2m S of town on B290 Tadworth road. M25(Jctn8 or 9). **Rail:** ½m., Tattenham Corner Stn (from London Bridge, Charing Cross, Victoria or Waterloo, change at Purley). **Air:** 20m, London (Heathrow) and London (Gatwick).

Course Characteristics

Left-handed, U-shaped course of 1m 4f noted for steep undulations. 3½f run-in with pronounced camber, initially downhill, rising in final furlong. Races up to 8½f essentially sharp, particularly on 5f track, which is fastest in world.

Draw: Over 5f, high numbers favoured; 1m 110yds to 1m 2f, low numbers greatly favoured.

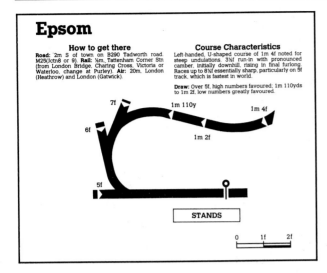

Folkestone Jumps

How to get there

Road: 6m W of town at Westenhanger, off A20 Ashford road. M20(Jctn11). **Rail:** Adjoining course. Westenhanger Stn (London Charing Cross-Ramsgate line).

Course Characteristics

Right-handed, undulating. Circuit 1m 2f.

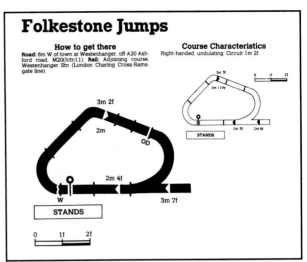

Fakenham

How to get there

Road: 1m S of town off B1146 East Dereham road. **Rail:** 26m, Norwich Stn (from London Liverpool Street). Bus to Fakenham.

Course Characteristics

Left-handed, sharp and undulating, suiting nippy types. Circuit 1m.

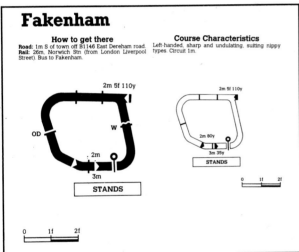

Fontwell Park

How to get there

Road: S of village at junction of A29 Bognor road with A27 Brighton-Chichester road. **Rail:** 2m, Barnham Stn (Brighton-Portsmouth line, access London Victoria).

Course Characteristics

Left-handed hurdle course. Figure-of-eight chase course does not suit long-striding gallopers. Ground can be very testing. Circuit 1m.

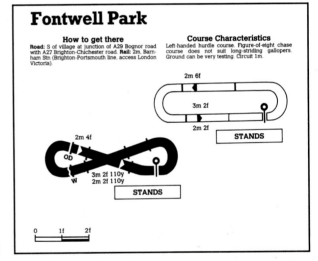

Folkestone Flat

How to get there

Road: 6m W of town at Westenhanger, off A20 Ashford road. M20(Jctn11). **Rail:** Adjoining course, Westenhanger Stn (London Charing Cross-Ramsgate line).

Course Characteristics

Right-handed, undulating oval of 1m 2f with 2f run-in.

Draw: On straight course on soft going, low numbers slightly favoured; on round course, high numbers favoured.

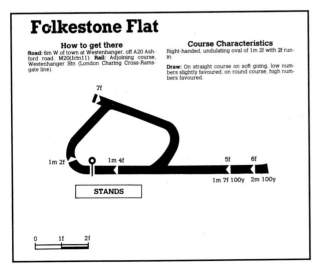

Goodwood

Course Characteristics

Right-handed with a loop for longer races. Long run-in, but primarily sharp, particularly on downhill sprint course.

Draw: When stalls on stands side, low numbers slightly favoured over 5 and 6f; 7f to 1m 4f, high numbers favoured.

How to get there

Road: 6m N of Chichester between A286 Midhurst road and A285 Petworth road. **Rail:** 6m, Chichester Stn (Brighton-Portsmouth line, access London Victoria). Bus to course. **Air:** 2m, Goodwood Airfield; 25m, Shoreham Airport.

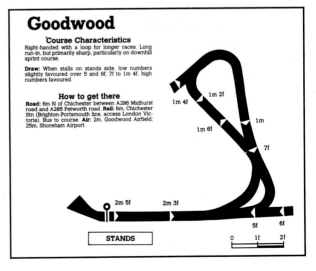

Hamilton Park

How to get there

Road: N of town off A74 close to Junction 5 of M74. **Rail:** 1m, Hamilton West Stn (from Glasgow). **Air:** 20m, Glasgow Airport.

Course Characteristics

Right-handed, loop course with 5f run-in part of straight 6f. Undulating, with pronounced finishing climb. Can become very testing.

Draw: High numbers slightly favoured.

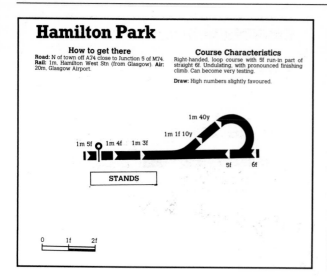

Hereford

How to get there

Road: 1m NW of city off A49 Leominster road. **Rail:** 1m, Hereford station (access Oxford, Birmingham, S.Wales.

Course Characteristics

Right-handed, sharpish and generally flat. Suits nippy types. Circuit 1m 4f.

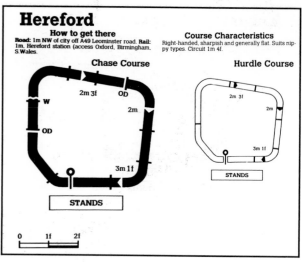

Haydock Park Flat

Course Characteristics

Left-handed oval, galloping. 1m 5f round, with 4½f run-in and 6f straight.

Draw: When stalls on stands side, high numbers slightly favoured over 5f.

How to get there

Road: On A49 Wigan road. M6(Jctn23). **Rail:** 2m, Newton-le-Willows Stn (Manchester-Liverpool line). Warrington Bank Quay or Wigan Stns better from London Euston. **Air:** 20m, Manchester International and Liverpool Speke Airports. Light aircraft on course.

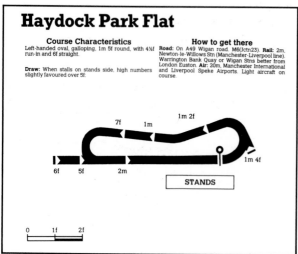

Hexham

How to get there

Road: 2m SW of town off B6305 Allendale road. **Rail:** 2m, Hexham Stn (Newcastle-Carlisle line).

Course Characteristics

Left-handed, severe and undulating, placing emphasis on stamina. Circuit 1m 4f.

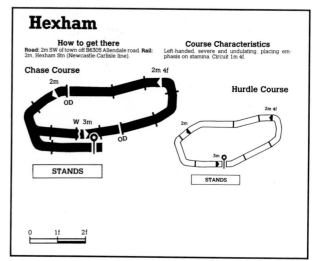

Haydock Park Jumps

How to get there

Road: On A49 Wigan road. M6(Jctn23). **Rail:** 2m, Newton-le-Willows Stn (Manchester-Liverpool line). Warrington Bank Quay or Wigan Stns better from London Euston. **Air:** 20m, Manchester International and Liverpool Speke Airports. Light aircraft on course.

Course Characteristics

Left-handed, flat and galloping. Drop fences and long run-in on chase course. Old hurdle course suits gallopers; New Course much sharper. Circuit 1m 5f.

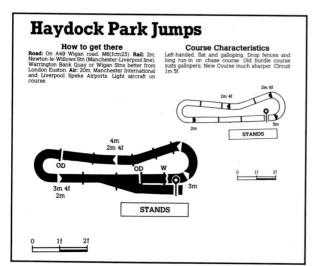

Huntingdon

How to get there

Road: 2m W of town off A604 Kettering road. **Rail:** 2m, Huntingdon Stn (London King's Cross-Peterborough line).

Course Characteristics

Right-handed and galloping. Circuit 1m 4f.

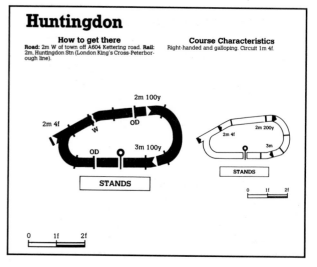

Kelso

How to get there
Road: 1m N of town off B6461 Berwick road. **Rail:** 23m, Berwick-on-Tweed Stn. Bus to Kelso.

Course Characteristics
Left-handed and undulating. Hurdles course of 1m 1f is sharp, more so than chase track of 1m 3f, which has 2f run-in.

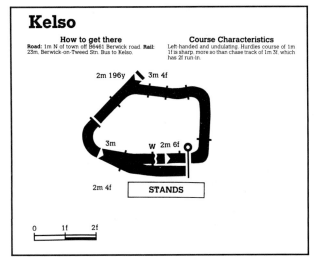

Leicester Flat

How to get there
Road: 2½m SE of city (signs to Oadby) off A6 Market Harborough Road. M1(Jctn21, with M69). **Rail:** 2½m, Leicester Stn (London St Pancras-Sheffield line).

Course Characteristics
Right-handed, undulating oval, about 1m 6f round with 5f run-in. Straight mile.

Draw: When stalls on far side, low numbers favoured up to 1m, especially on soft.

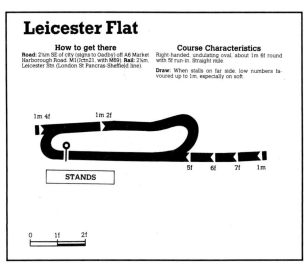

Kempton Park Flat

How to get there
Road: On A308 Kingston road, close to Junction 1 of M3. **Rail:** Adjoining course, Kempton Park Stn (from London Waterloo). **Air:** 6m, London (Heathrow).

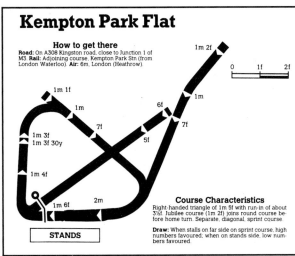

Course Characteristics
Right-handed triangle of 1m 5f with run-in of about 3½f. Jubilee course (1m 2f) joins round course before home turn. Separate, diagonal, sprint course.

Draw: When stalls on far side on sprint course, high numbers favoured; when on stands side, low numbers favoured.

Leicester Jumps

Course Characteristics
Right-handed and undulating, placing emphasis on stamina. Circuit 1m 6f.

How to get there
Road: 2½m SE of city (signs to Oadby) off A6 Market Harborough Road. M1(Jctn21, with M69). **Rail:** 2½m, Leicester Stn (London St Pancras-Sheffield line).

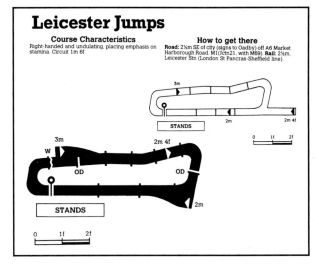

Kempton Park Jumps

How to get there
Road: On A308 Kingston road, close to Junction 1 of M3. **Rail:** Adjoining course, Kempton Park Stn (from London Waterloo). **Air:** 6m, London (Heathrow).

Course Characteristics
Right-handed, flat and fair. Circuit 1m 5f.

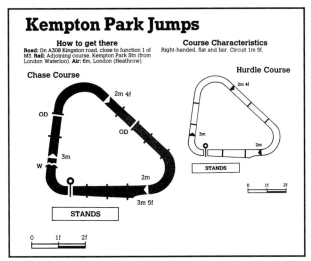

Lingfield Park Flat

Course Characteristics
Left-handed, undulating triangle of 1m 2f with 3½f run-in. Straight 7f 140yds.

Draw: When stalls on stands side on straight course, high numbers favoured; when on far side, low numbers favoured.

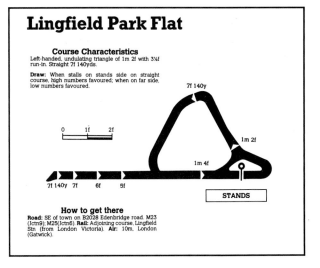

How to get there
Road: SE of town on B2028 Edenbridge road. M23 (Jctn9); M25(Jctn6). **Rail:** Adjoining course, Lingfield Stn (from London Victoria). **Air:** 10m, London (Gatwick).

Lingfield Park Jumps

Course Characteristics

Left-handed, undulating and sharp. Chase circuit 1m 5f, hurdles shorter.

How to get there

Road: SE of town on B2028 Edenbridge road. M23 (Jctn9); M25(Jctn6). **Rail:** Adjoining course, Lingfield Stn (from London Victoria). **Air:** 10m, London (Gatwick).

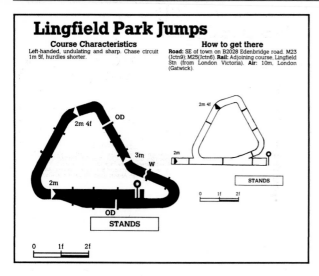

Ludlow

Course Characteristics

Right-handed. Chase course flat with sharp bends, circuit 1m 4f. Hurdles track, 150 yds longer, slightly undulating, with easier bends.

How to get there

Road: 2m NW of town off A49 Shrewsbury road. **Rail:** 2m, Ludlow Stn (Hereford-Shrewsbury line).

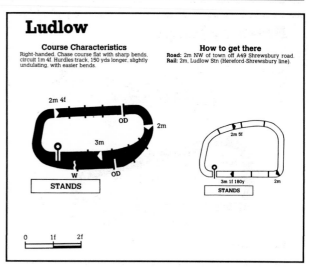

Liverpool Grand National

Course Characteristics

Two left-handed courses. Grand National circuit, 2m 2f, is flat and has big fences with drop on landing side. Long run-in. Mildmay Course of 1m 3f, flat with conventional fences, is sharper than hurdles course.

How to get there

Road: N of city, 1m S of junction of M57 and M58 with A59 Preston road. M6(Jctn21a). **Rail:** Adjoining course, Aintree Stn (London Euston-Liverpool Lime Street then local service). **Air:** 10m, Liverpool Speke Airport.

Market Rasen

How to get there

Road: 1m E of town on A631 Louth road. **Rail:** 1m, Market Rasen Stn (Lincoln-Grimsby line). **Air:** Light aircraft on course.

Course Characteristics

Right-handed oval, sharp and somewhat undulating. Circuit 1m 2f.

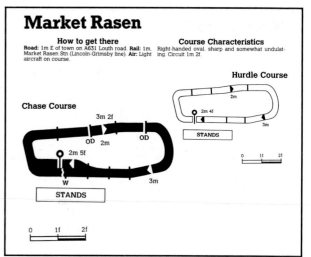

Liverpool Mildmay

How to get there

Road: N of city, 1m S of junction of M57 and M58 with A59 Preston road. M6(Jctn21a). **Rail:** Adjoining course, Aintree Stn (London Euston-Liverpool Lime Street then local service). **Air:** 10m, Liverpool Speke Airport.

Course Characteristics

Two left-handed courses. Grand National circuit, 2m 2f, is flat and has big fences with drop on landing side. Long run-in. Mildmay Course of 1m 3f, flat with conventional fences, is sharper than hurdles course.

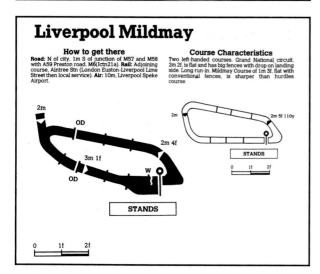

Newbury Flat

How to get there

Road: E of town off A34 Winchester road. M4(Jctn12) from E; M4(Jctn13) from W. **Rail:** Adjoining course, Newbury Racecourse Stn (from London Paddington). **Bus:** 1m, Newbury Bus Stn. **Air:** Light aircraft on course.

Course Characteristics

Left-handed, almost flat, roughly 1m 7f with 4½f run-in. Races on round mile and and over 7f 60yds start on chute. Straight mile has minor undulations.

Draw: When stalls on stands side on straight course, high numbers slightly favoured, especially on soft going; up to 1m on round course, low numbers favoured.

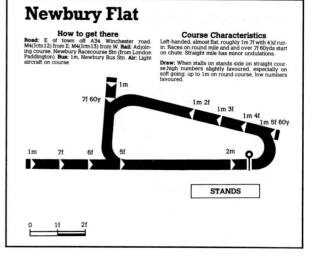

Newbury Jumps

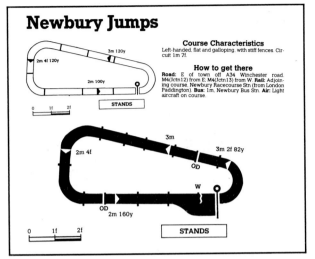

Course Characteristics
Left-handed, flat and galloping, with stiff fences. Circuit 1m 7f.

How to get there
Road: E. of town off A34 Winchester road. M4(Jctn12) from E; M4(Jctn13) from W. **Rail:** Adjoining course, Newbury Racecourse Stn (from London Paddington). **Bus:** 1m, Newbury Bus Stn. **Air:** Light aircraft on course.

Newmarket July

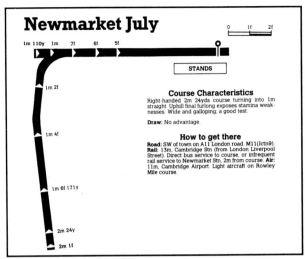

Course Characteristics
Right-handed 2m 24yds course turning into 1m straight. Uphill final furlong exposes stamina weaknesses. Wide and galloping; a good test.

Draw: No advantage.

How to get there
Road: SW of town on A11 London road. M11(Jctn9). **Rail:** 13m, Cambridge Stn (from London Liverpool Street). Direct bus service to course, or infrequent rail service to Newmarket Stn, 2m from course. **Air:** 11m, Cambridge Airport. Light aircraft on Rowley Mile course.

Newcastle Flat

How to get there
Road: 4m N of city off A6125. From S use Tyne Tunnel (A19/A1) then B1318 Killingworth road. **Rail:** 4m, Newcastle Stn (London King's Cross-Scotland line). Metro to Four Lane Ends then bus. **Air:** 6m, Newcastle Airport.

Course Characteristics
Left-handed oval of 1m 6f with easy bends. Uphill 4f run-in places emphasis on stamina. Straight 7f. Can become very testing.

Draw: Low numbers generally favoured, especially on soft.

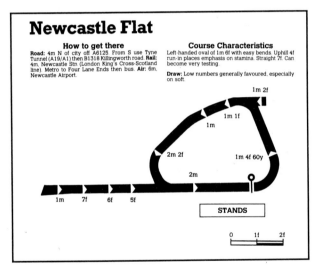

Newmarket Rowley Mile

Course Characteristics
Right-handed 2m 4f Cesarewitch Course turning into undulating 1m 2f straight. Uphill final furlong exposes stamina weaknesses. Wide and galloping, a good test.

Draw: Up to 1m, high numbers slightly favoured.

How to get there
Road: SW of town on A11 London road. M11(Jctn9). **Rail:** 13m, Cambridge Stn (from London Liverpool Street). Direct bus service to course, or infrequent rail service to Newmarket Stn, 2m from course. **Air:** 11m, Cambridge Airport. Light aircraft on Rowley Mile course.

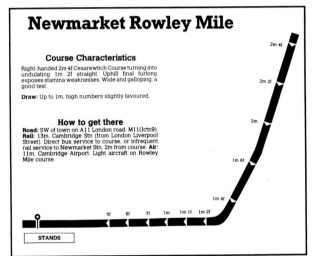

Newcastle Jumps

How to get there
Road: 4m N of city off A6125. From S use Tyne Tunnel (A19/A1) then B1318 Killingworth road. **Rail:** 4m, Newcastle Stn (London King's Cross-Scotland line). Metro to Four Lane Ends then bus. **Air:** 6m, Newcastle Airport.

Course Characteristics
Left-handed, with uphill finish. Going can be very testing. Circuit 1m 6f.

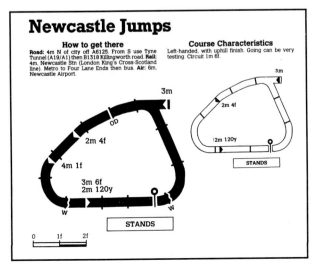

Newton Abbot

How to get there
Road: N of town on A380 Exeter road. **Rail:** ¾m, Newton Abbot Stn (on main line from London Paddington). **Air:** 20m, Exeter Airport.

Course Characteristics
Left-handed oval, sharp, with short run-in. Circuit 1m 2f.

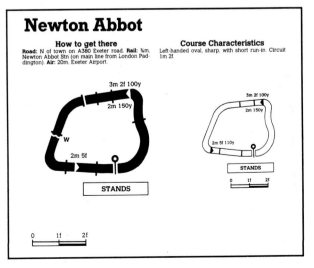

Nottingham Flat

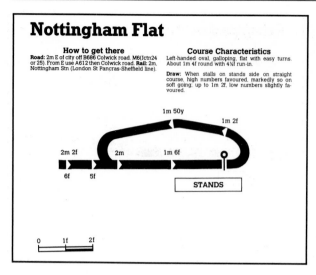

How to get there
Road: 2m E of city off B686 Colwick road. M6(Jctn24 or 25). From E use A612 then Colwick road. **Rail:** 2m, Nottingham Stn (London St Pancras-Sheffield line).

Course Characteristics
Left-handed oval, galloping, flat with easy turns. About 1m 4f round with 4½f run-in.

Draw: When stalls on stands side on straight course, high numbers favoured, markedly so on soft going; up to 1m 2f, low numbers slightly favoured.

Plumpton

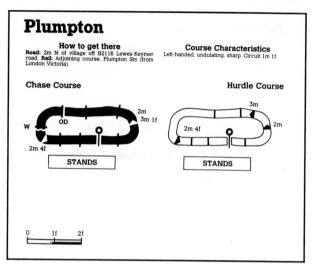

How to get there
Road: 2m N of village off B2116 Lewes-Keymer road. **Rail:** Adjoining course, Plumpton Stn (from London Victoria).

Course Characteristics
Left-handed, undulating, sharp. Circuit 1m 1f.

Nottingham Jumps

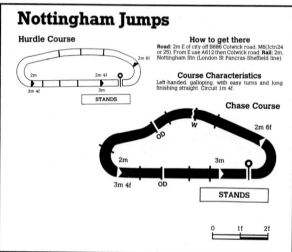

How to get there
Road: 2m E of city off B686 Colwick road. M6(Jctn24 or 25). From E use A612 then Colwick road. **Rail:** 2m, Nottingham Stn (London St Pancras-Sheffield line).

Course Characteristics
Left-handed, galloping, with easy turns and long finishing straight. Circuit 1m 4f.

Pontefract

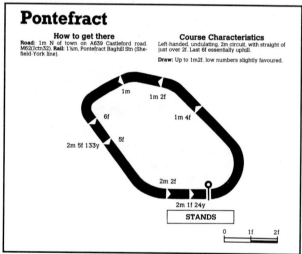

How to get there
Road: 1m N of town on A639 Castleford road. M62(Jctn32). **Rail:** 1½m, Pontefract Baghill Stn (Sheffield-York line).

Course Characteristics
Left-handed, undulating, 2m circuit, with straight of just over 2f. Last 6f essentially uphill.

Draw: Up to 1m2f, low numbers slightly favoured.

Perth

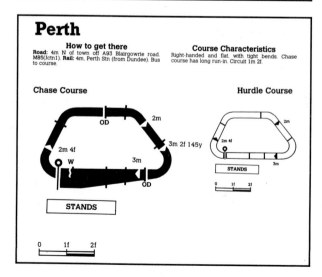

How to get there
Road: 4m N of town off A93 Blairgowrie road. M85(Jctn1). **Rail:** 4m, Perth Stn (from Dundee). Bus to course.

Course Characteristics
Right-handed and flat, with tight bends. Chase course has long run-in. Circuit 1m 2f.

Redcar

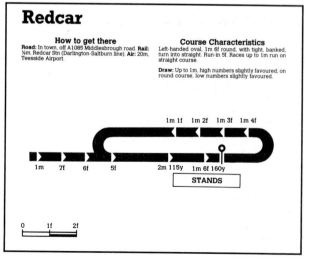

How to get there
Road: In town, off A1085 Middlesbrough road. **Rail:** ½m, Redcar Stn (Darlington-Saltburn line). **Air:** 20m, Teesside Airport.

Course Characteristics
Left-handed oval, 1m 6f round, with tight, banked, turn into straight. Run-in 5f. Races up to 1m run on straight course.

Draw: Up to 1m, high numbers slightly favoured; on round course, low numbers slightly favoured.

Ripon

Course Characteristics
Right-handed, 1m 5f oval with slight undulations and sharp bend before 5f run-in.

Draw: When stalls on stands side, low numbers slightly favoured; on round course, high numbers favoured.

How to get there
Road: 2m SE of town on B6265 Boroughbridge road. **Rail:** 11m, Harrogate Stn (Leeds-York line) and Thirsk Stn (York-Darlington line). Bus to Ripon.

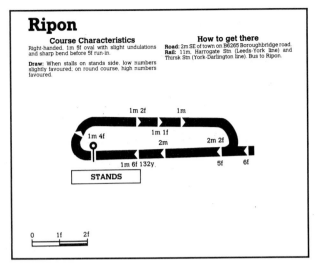

Salisbury

How to get there
Road: 3m SW of city off A3094 at Netherhampton. **Rail:** 3m, Salisbury Stn (London Waterloo-Exeter line). Bus to course.

Course Characteristics
Right-handed and galloping. Loop course for races of 1m 2f plus. 7f run-in (part of a nearly-straight mile) is mainly uphill and makes for a stiff test.

Draw: When stalls on stands side on straight course, low numbers markedly favoured up to 1m.

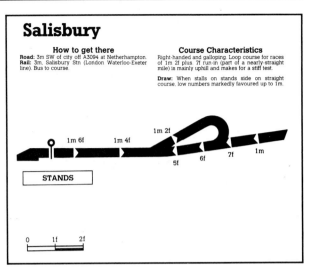

Sandown Park Flat

How to get there
Road: 4m SW of Kingston on A307 Esher road. M25(Jctn10). **Rail:** Adjoining course, Esher Stn (from London Waterloo). **Bus:** 4m, Kingston Bus Stn, direct to course. **Air:** 12m, London (Heathrow).

Course Characteristics
Right-handed oval of 1m 5f with 4f uphill run-in. Essentially galloping. Separate diagonal 5f also uphill.

Draw: When stalls on far side on sprint course, a high draw is vital, particularly on soft ground; when on stands side, low numbers favoured.

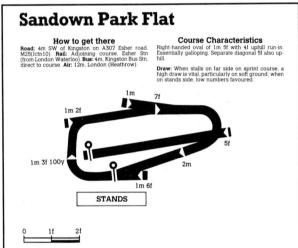

Sedgefield

Course Characteristics
Left-handed, undulating oval. Sharp bends. Chase course has easy fences and particularly long run-in. Circuit 1m 2f.

How to get there
Road: ¾m SW of town near junction of A689 Bishop Auckland road with A177 Durham road. **Rail:** 9m, Stockton-on-Tees Stn, or 12m, Durham Stn. Bus to Sedgefield.

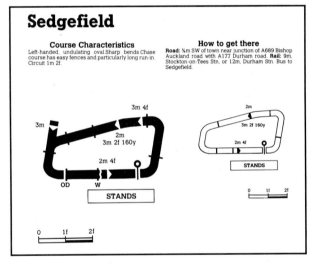

Sandown Park Jumps

How to get there
Road: 4m SW of Kingston on A307 Esher road. M25(Jctn10). **Rail:** Adjoining course, Esher Stn (from London Waterloo). **Bus:** 4m, Kingston Bus Stn, direct to course. **Air:** 12m, London (Heathrow).

Course Characteristics
Right-handed with stiff uphill finish. Chase course tricky, especially for novices. Hurdles run on Flat course. Circuit 1m 5f.

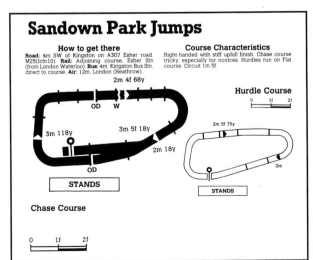

Southwell

How to get there
Road: 3m SE of town at Rolleston. **Rail:** Adjoining course. Rolleston Stn (Nottingham-Newark line).

Course Characteristics
Left-handed, sharp, flat triangle. Circuit 1m 2f.

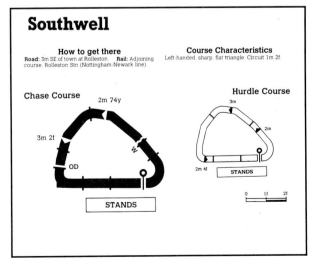

Stratford

How to get there
Road: 1m SW of town off A439 Evesham road. **Rail:** 1m, Stratford Stn (from Birmingham Moor Street or Leamington).

Course Characteristics
Left-handed, flat and sharp, with short finishing straight. Circuit 1m 2f.

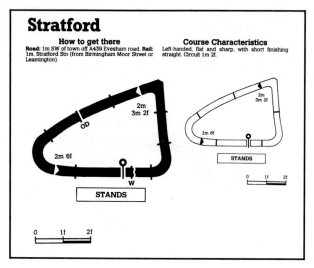

Towcester

Course Characteristics
Right-handed, with last mile uphill. Very testing. Circuit 1m 6f.

How to get there
Road: 1m SE of town on A5 Milton Keynes road. M1(Jctn16) from N; M1(Jctn15) from S.

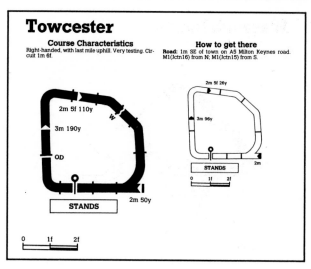

Taunton

How to get there
Road: 2m S of town on B3170 Honiton road. M5(Jctn25). **Rail:** 2½m, Taunton Stn (access London Paddington, Bristol Temple Meads, Exeter St David's).

Course Characteristics
Right-handed oval, on sharp side with short run-in. Circuit 1m 2f.

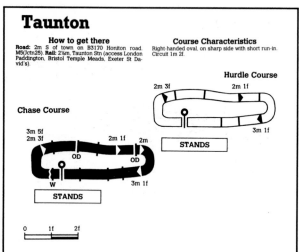

Uttoxeter

How to get there
Road: SE of town off B5017 Marchington road. **Rail:** Adjoining course, Uttoxeter Stn (Derby-Crewe line)

Course Characteristics
Left-handed with some undulations. Circuit 1m 3f.

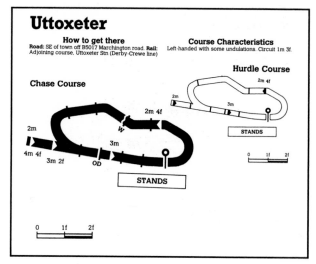

Thirsk

How to get there
Road: W of town on A61 Ripon road. **Rail:** 1m, Thirsk Stn (York-Newcastle line).

Course Characteristics
Left-handed oval of about 1m 2f with 4f run-in. Sharp and almost level.

Draw: When stalls on stands side on straight course, high numbers favoured on good or fast going; low numbers slightly favoured on soft.

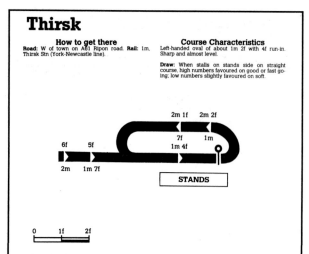

Warwick Flat

Course Characteristics
Left-handed, sharp, about 1m 6f. Dog-leg 5f course.

Draw: When stalls on far side and going not soft, high numbers slightly favoured over 5f.

How to get there
Road: W of town on A41 Birmingham road. **Rail:** 1m, Warwick Stn. Difficult from London.

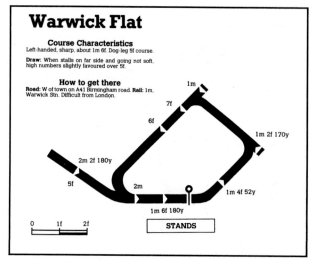

Warwick Jumps

How to get there
Road: W of town on A41 Birmingham road. **Rail:** 1m, Warwick Stn. Difficult from London.

Course Characteristics
Left-handed with tight turns and short run-in. Circuit 1m 5f.

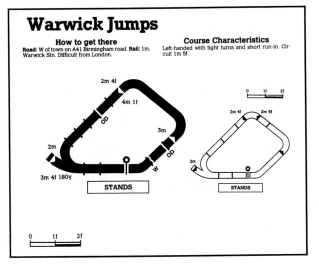

Windsor Flat

How to get there
Road: On A308 Maidenhead road N of town. M4(Jctn6). **Rail:** 2m, Windsor and Eton Riverside Stn (from London Waterloo) or Windsor and Eton Central Stn (from London Paddington). **Bus:** 1m, Greenline stop. **Riverbus:** Direct to course from near Riverside Stn (summer only).

Course Characteristics
Figure-of-eight course of 1m 4f, flat and, up to 1m 70yds, on sharp side.

Draw: In 1m 70yds races, high numbers slightly favoured.

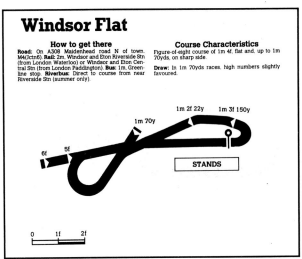

Wetherby

How to get there
Road: E of town, off B1224 York road. **Rail:** 12m, Leeds City Stn. Bus to Wetherby.

Course Characteristics
Left-handed oval, with easy bends. Circuit 1m 4f. Old hurdles course (used occasionally) much sharper.

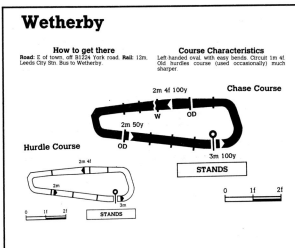

Windsor Jumps

Course Characteristics
Figure-of-eight shape, sharp and flat. Circuit 1m 4f.

How to get there
Road: On A308 Maidenhead road N of town. M4(Jctn6). **Rail:** 2m, Windsor and Eton Riverside Stn (from London Waterloo) or Windsor and Eton Central Stn (from London Paddington). **Bus:** 1m, Greenline stop. **Riverbus:** Direct to course from near Riverside Stn (summer only).

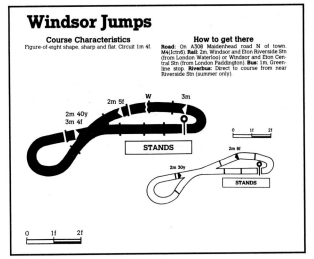

Wincanton

How to get there
Road: 1m N of town on B3081 Shepton Mallet road. **Rail:** 8m, Gillingham Stn (London Waterloo-Exeter line).

Course Characteristics
Right-handed, mainly flat. A fair test. Circuit 1m 3f.

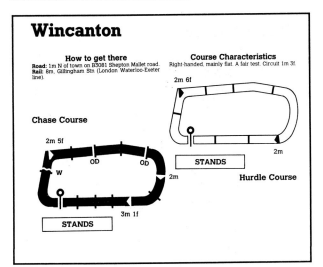

Wolverhampton Flat

How to get there
Road: 1m N of town off A449 Stafford road. M54(Jctn2) best from S. M6(Jctn12), A5, A449 best from N. **Rail:** 1m, Wolverhampton Stn (from London Euston).

Course Characteristics
Left-handed triangle, flat, about 1m 4f round with 5f run-in. 5f course easy.

Draw: When stalls on stands side on straight course, low numbers greatly favoured over 5f on soft going; up to 1m 1f, low numbers slightly favoured.

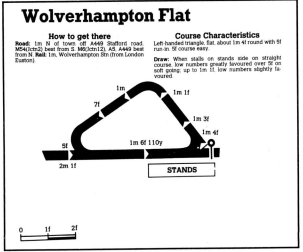

Wolverhampton Jumps

Course Characteristics
Left-handed triangle, essentially galloping. Circuit 1m 4f.

How to get there
Road: 1m N of town off A449 Stafford road. M54(Jctn2) best from S. M6(Jctn12), A5, A449 best from N. **Rail:** 1m, Wolverhampton Stn (from London Euston).

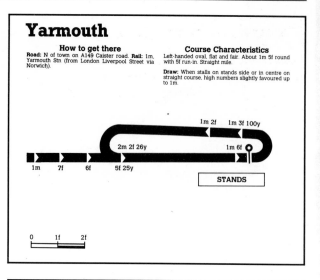

Yarmouth

How to get there
Road: N of town on A149 Caister road. **Rail:** 1m, Yarmouth Stn (from London Liverpool Street via Norwich).

Course Characteristics
Left-handed oval, flat and fair. About 1m 5f round with 5f run-in. Straight mile.

Draw: When stalls on stands side or in centre on straight course, high numbers slightly favoured up to 1m.

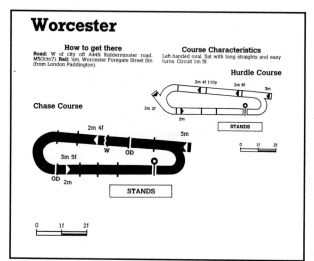

Worcester

How to get there
Road: W of city off A449 Kidderminster road. M5(Jctn7). **Rail:** ½m, Worcester Foregate Street Stn (from London Paddington).

Course Characteristics
Left-handed oval, flat with long straights and easy turns. Circuit 1m 5f.

Hurdle Course

Chase Course

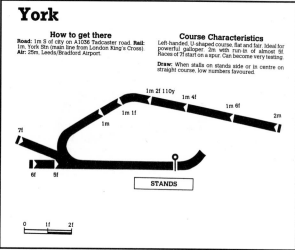

York

How to get there
Road: 1m S of city on A1036 Tadcaster road. **Rail:** 1m, York Stn (main line from London King's Cross). **Air:** 25m, Leeds/Bradford Airport.

Course Characteristics
Left-handed, U-shaped course, flat and fair. Ideal for powerful galloper. 2m with run-in of almost 5f. Races of 7f start on a spur. Can become very testing.

Draw: When stalls on stands side or in centre on straight course, low numbers favoured.